soda bread.
ème brûlée
y poly

2 yolk.
2 tbsp Sugar
200 d. cream.
30 b currant.
150°C bag
25-35 mins

soda bread

330 flour.
1 bicarb
1/2 salt.
2 dbs.
300 buttermlk.

Introducing Ruby Tandoh — *Great British Bake Off* finalist, *Guardian* columnist and a major new talent in food writing

Crumb is about flavour, first and foremost — a celebration of the simple joy of baking. Ruby's recipes delight in new tastes and combinations, as well as the rediscovery of old favourites, to create food that is exciting without ceremony or pretence.

In a delicious blend of practicality and creativity, Ruby encourages novices and seasoned bakers alike to roll up their sleeves and bake — even if they don't have the proper equipment or know-how. From Lemon & Marzipan Cupcakes and Rye Caraway Bagels, Rose & Burnt Honey Florentines, Croissants and Custard Doughnuts, to Butternut Squash & Mozzarella Tartlets and Sticky Toffee Pudding, these are recipes that will quickly become some of your best loved. With writing to be savoured as much as the recipes, tips and techniques to guide you and plenty of ideas for variations, this is a baking book to be inspired by, to read and cherish.

CRUMB

In Memory of Renee Eder

Died 14th April 2022

Renee loved to cook and would love
to think of you enjoying this
book in your kitchen

CRUMB

THE BAKING BOOK

Ruby Tandoh

Photographs by Nato Welton

Chatto & Windus
London

Published by Chatto & Windus 2014

2 4 6 8 10 9 7 5 3 1

Epigraph taken from *The Journals of Sylvia Plath* by Sylvia Plath
© 1982, Faber & Faber Ltd

Extract on page 54 from *Matilda* by Roald Dahl, published by
Jonathan Cape Ltd & Penguin Books Ltd. Reprinted by kind
permission of David Higham Associates

First published in Great Britain in 2014 by Chatto & Windus
Random House, 20 Vauxhall Bridge Road, London SW1V 2SA
www.randomhouse.co.uk

Addresses for companies within The Random House Group Limited
can be found at: www.randomhouse.co.uk/offices.htm

The Random House Group Limited Reg. No. 954009

A CIP catalogue record for this book is available from the
British Library

ISBN 9780701189310

Design & Art Direction: Hyperkit
Photography: Nato Welton
Index: Ben Murphy

The Random House Group Limited supports the Forest Stewardship
Council® (FSC®), the leading international forest-certification
organisation. Our books carrying the FSC label are printed on
FSC®-certified paper. FSC is the only forest-certification scheme
supported by the leading environmental organisations, including
Greenpeace. Our paper procurement policy can be found at:
www.randomhouse.co.uk/environment

Printed and bound by FIRMENGRUPPE APPL,
aprinta druck, Wemding, Germany

" Instead of studying Locke, for instance,
or writing – I go make an apple pie."
Sylvia Plath

There's a lot more to baking than meets the eye. Millions of air bubbles suspended in a bowl of beaten egg whites can make a meringue melt on the tongue. There's science behind the deep brown crust of a brioche loaf and the tenderness of a pastry shell. Just a few degrees can nudge a pot of boiling sugar from sweet syrup to caramel (or to bitter cinder, if you're unlucky). I've taken great care here to explain the whys and hows of baking, in the hope that this will give you the confidence to get started and adapt recipes to suit your tastes and preferences.

But science alone won't bake a cake. It can't replicate the feeling of cool pastry under your fingertips or completely describe the consistency of the perfect custard. Something happens between the numbered steps of a recipe and the end result that can't be predicted or prepared for. This is where baking soars clear of plain chemistry. It's not the kind of thing that can be dissected under bullet-pointed headings or jargon — it has to be witnessed first-hand. For that reason I urge you to get stuck in, make a mess and don't be squeamish about getting your hands dirty. Enjoy the sensory pleasures that baking has to offer, from the exertion of a long knead to the crackle of a cob loaf cooling on the countertop. You'll soon find that the processes of baking are every bit as exciting as tucking in to the finished product.

This sensuous side of baking is about more than just hedonism. A finger gently pressed into a rising loaf can tell you whether it's ready for baking; a piece of dough is well kneaded if you can stretch it so thinly that, when it's held up to the sun, you can almost see straight through it. Baking isn't just about the tasting: prod, sniff, listen to and squeeze your food. This is not baking by rote.

The recipes in this book aren't grand or highly decorated: their roots lie in the thrill of a new ingredient, or the comfort of a familiar food. They aim to please, rather than to impress. I hope that they'll make it to your table over and over again. I may digress at points, singing the praises of blackcurrants or writing an ode to doughnuts. I make no apologies for this: I bake for the love of it, and I hope that you will, too.

INTRODUCTION

Crumb started long, long before it was bound into the book you hold now. Perhaps the story begins with childhood birthday cakes, or at three years old — felt-tip pen clutched between my stubby fingers as I circled each and every dessert in my parents' illustrated cookbook. Maybe it was *The Very Hungry Caterpillar* — so well-thumbed that its pages wore thin at the edges — or Bruce Bogtrotter's chocolate cake in *Matilda*. Later there were food supplements torn out of newspapers and messily archived, lunchtime feasts in the school canteen, homemade bundles of fudge and a whole summer spent rereading the Great Hall feast scenes in *Harry Potter*. Teenage romances played out against a backdrop of cake: to charm, to celebrate, to appease, and to soothe the hurt of the break-up.

It could be that this book started while I was at university, at the Christmas market baking stall that I spent three months preparing for and made £30 from. Or maybe it was in a Lisbon backpackers' hostel, where a cheesecake landed me a kitchen job and where, from that point onwards, I spent every second of each day jotting down recipes, writing shopping lists and planning menus in what felt like a dream come true. Then again, it could've been in the park at Belém, eating the fabled *pasteis de nata* that the penny finally dropped.

I was living in a dank London flat when I saw a TV baking show and wondered whether it was something I could do. Perhaps the book really began to take shape there: in the pages of scrawled notes on baking theory and chemistry that I made in a bid to learn all that I needed to know to survive in the competition. Before long, I was spending my weekends filming, during which some of the recipes in these pages began to crystallise. Notes still stored on my phone ('try coffee & blackcurrant. do washing. make croissants') are the reminders of this baking storm.

By the time that *The Great British Bake Off* began to air, I had dozens of books of notes: paeans to profiteroles, half-finished recipes, flavour combinations, diary entries fondly recounting good meals, sketches of cakes, breads and biscuits, and scores of shopping lists. This book is built from those musings, experiments and memories. It's the distillation of my obsession with food. It's been a pleasure.

GETTING STARTED

There's a misconception that baking is different from cooking. I hear friends sincerely proclaim that they can cook but not bake, or bake but not cook, as though it makes any sense to abstract one from the other. Baking *is* cooking. If you enjoy food — if you can operate an oven and follow a recipe — you're most of the way there already. Don't overthink it, and don't assume the worst before you've even got started.

That said, I'll admit that the equipment, methods and vocabulary of baking can be daunting if you're new to it. To take out the guesswork, I've made a note of some of the baking-specific terms used in this book, below, along with a few words on ingredients and kit. If you're a seasoned baker, just head straight to the recipes — you'll find that there's a mix of easier and more involved recipes in each chapter, and a progression through the book from familiar cakes to meringues, tarts and pastries.

EQUIPMENT

As someone who has always baked in tiny kitchens and student flats, I have little tolerance for unnecessary culinary clutter. You'll find no heart-shaped cupcake moulds or cake turntables in this book, and where a recipe calls for an unusual shape or size of tin (such as the madeleines on page 29), I've given advice and baking times for those who don't have that piece of specialist equipment. There are some pieces of (cheap, easy to source) equipment that I would recommend, though.

Electronic kitchen scales
I can't overstate just how important these are. I've used various mechanical scales for baking in the past and suffered a string of disappointments: they're not sensitive enough for small measurements, they distort when too heavily loaded, there's the worry of manually resetting to zero. Most irritatingly of all, there's the agonising over the needle on the dial as it flickers between one number and another, depending on which eye you squint through. Unless you have saint-like patience and the Rolls-Royce of mechanical scales, you really should go electronic. There's no need to break the bank, though: a set of £10 electronic scales will do just fine.

Teaspoon and tablespoon measures
A teaspoon is 5ml, a tablespoon is 15ml. Don't use your normal cutlery to approximate these, as the quantity measured by the sort of teaspoon you use to stir your tea can range between 2 and 10ml. This might not sound like much, but a cake can stand or fall on as little as a few grams too much or too little of baking powder. Measuring spoons are inexpensive and if you plan to do much baking, they'll prove invaluable.

A measuring jug or cup measures
These are useful for measuring liquids, but if you don't have them, it's not a disaster. You can weigh liquids, too — actually a great deal more accurately than the average measuring jug will allow: 1ml of water or milk weighs 1g.

Oven thermometer
Do your cakes often emerge from the oven either burnt or raw, despite having followed the recipe to the letter? Your oven might not be operating at the correct temperatures. Oven thermostats are notoriously unreliable — they may cook 20°C warmer or cooler than the temperature shown on the dial, and for foods as temperamental as cakes and meringues, this can spell disaster. Luckily, there's no need to invest in a new oven. An oven thermometer costs just £5 and will sit happily on your oven shelf, giving you peace of mind. (Whether you have a fan, gas or conventional oven, an oven thermometer should read the temperature that you've set your oven to. If a recipe specifies 180°C/fan 160°C/gas mark 4, your thermometer should display 180°C in a gas or conventional oven, or 160°C in a fan oven.)

Coffee grinder
This isn't essential but I find it useful for grinding nuts, seeds and spices. A food processor is an alternative. If you have neither, use a pestle and mortar instead for spices and small seeds, and buy ready-ground nuts.

And the rest
Flat baking trays
Roasting dish or deep baking tray, around 20x30cm
20cm round loose-bottomed or spring-form cake tin
900g loaf tin, approximately 20x9cm at its base
0.8–1.2 litre pudding basin
Large pie dish
12-bun muffin tin
Hand-held blender
Grater
Wire whisk
Wooden spoons
Rolling pin
Spatula
Heavy-bottomed saucepan
Large mixing bowls
Baking parchment
Cling film
Dried pulses or rice (for blind baking)
Ruler
Pastry brush
Sieve
Disposable piping bags

Useful but inessential extras
Electric hand-held whisk
Fluted flan or tart tin
Sugar thermometer
Individual pudding moulds
Round pastry cutters, in different sizes
Madeleine tin
Bundt tin
Dough scraper
Palette knife
Piping nozzles

INGREDIENTS

I've included nothing in these recipes that you shouldn't be able to find in large supermarkets. You won't be able to get all of the ingredients all year round (the blackcurrants in the crème brûlée, for example, are available only for a few weeks each year), but none of them are obscure or exotic.

Eggs

Wherever I use eggs in this book, they're large ones, but there are some instances where you can swap in medium eggs instead if that's all you've got. As a rule of thumb, I'd recommend that you don't fiddle with egg quantities in anything whisked (that includes whisked cakes and meringues), but in most other cakes, biscuits, pastries and bread doughs, you can use medium eggs, adding a dash more milk or water if the mixture looks a little dry as a result.

Whatever size you use, make sure the eggs are free-range at the very least, and organic if possible.

Milk

Always use full-fat or semi-skimmed milk for baking. Sometimes the higher fat content of full-fat milk is important for helping something to mix, set or bake as it should. Where this is the case, I have specified full-fat in the recipe.

Butter

Butter should always be unsalted. It doesn't keep as well as salted butter, but it gives you far greater control over the amount of salt you add to the food. This is particularly important in breads and buns, where too much salt will adversely affect both taste and texture, preventing the dough from rising properly. You really don't need to spend a fortune on the best quality butter for most cakes, biscuits or even butter-rich shortcrust pastries. I invest in good butter only for puff and Danish pastries — the lower water content of Continental-style butter gives crisper layers.

Sugar

I always specify the type of sugar to use, but do feel free to play around with it to achieve subtly different flavours and textures. Caster sugar, which has crystals much smaller than those of the slightly cheaper granulated sugar, is most commonly used in this book. It's quick to dissolve, versatile and won't distract from other flavours. Soft light and dark brown sugars are less intensively refined than white sugar, leaving them with a soft, crumbly texture and toffee flavour (the darker the sugar, the more intensely treacly it is). They are the taste of gingerbreads, damp chocolate cakes and sticky toffee puddings. Demerara is slow to dissolve — good for sprinkling on top of cakes or sweet pies for a crunch. Icing sugar is very finely ground and, as the name suggests, perfect for making smooth, glossy icing.

Flour

Most of the recipes here use plain flour, by which I mean the most common type of white, wheat flour. Note that it is different from strong white flour, which has a higher protein content and is better suited to breads, where it helps the dough to stretch as it rises. Wholemeal flour has the bran from the wheat grain left in, giving it a lightly nutty taste and coarser texture. There are also flours made from different grains, including rye and spelt. These have very different properties to wheat, and are

discussed further in the Bread chapter. You can buy self-raising flour, which is white flour with added raising agents. This usually does away with the need for separately-added baking powder or bicarbonate of soda, but I prefer not to use self-raising flour, and you won't find any recipes that use it here — adding your own raising agents affords you far greater control.

Baking powder and bicarbonate of soda

These are chemical raising agents — they help to produce the air bubbles that make a cake rise. Baking powder 'activates' upon contact with water and again when it enters the oven, meaning that even if you leave a cake batter standing for a while before you bake it, it'll have a second lease of life when it hits the heat. You don't have this luxury with bicarbonate of soda, which reacts the instant that it's mixed in (there's more on bicarbonate of soda on page 178), so make sure that you bake cakes leavened with bicarbonate of soda soon after the batter has been prepared.

Yeast

Yeast is a natural raising agent, and the force behind bread. It ferments bread dough, feeding on starches and producing tiny air bubbles as it works. It's these air bubbles that expand in the oven to give bread its rise. Yeast adds complex flavours, too. You can read more about it on page 73.

Cornflour

Cornflour is a pure starch, and a potent thickener. Added to liquids and then heated, it absorbs water and releases a network of starch molecules, which thicken sauces and creams. You can see it in action in the pastry cream on page 312. Don't confuse cornflour (also known as cornstarch) with cornmeal, which is yellow in colour, and has rather grittier particles.

Salt

Wherever salt is called for, I mean standard table salt. Although there's a romance to *fleur de sel* or crystalline flakes of sea salt, quick-dissolving table salt is far better suited to baking, and cheaper, too. You'll find that many of my recipes have a little salt added to them (even sweet dishes benefit from a pinch of salt to bring out their flavour).

MEASURING

There are as many ways of measuring ingredients as there are recipes: some modern, some archaic, some cruelly vague and some whimsical ('a scant thimbleful'). You can measure in metric or imperial, by weight or by volume, with cups, spoons, pinches and handfuls.

But I've endeavoured to keep things simple. You won't find any imperial units here (no ounces, pounds, pints or bushels). And because measuring by volume is notoriously inaccurate, I nearly always give measurements by weight — unless of course common sense dictates otherwise (½ teaspoon of ground cinnamon or 2 tablespoons of double cream, for example). If you're in any doubt at all, you can use the conversion chart on page 19, which lists some old-fashioned baking measurements and their metric equivalents.

MIXING

The way that you mix a pastry, batter or dough can be every bit as important as the way you actually bake it. There are a few different mixing techniques involved in baking, and you'll see these key words pop up again and again. Take a moment to run through the list and check that you know your beating from your whisking.

Beat

Use a wooden spoon to vigorously stir the mixture in a roughly circular motion. This combines two ingredients and incorporates air at the same time.

Cream
This is much the same as beating, but specific to the stage at the beginning of preparing a cake batter, when you mix softened butter with sugar until thick and creamy (see page 27).

Crumb
Rub cubes of butter into flour using your fingertips, continuing until no visible pieces of butter remain.

Fold
This is a delicate operation. When you fold two mixtures together, you're aiming to combine them without knocking the air out of them. Use a spatula or large metal spoon to cut across the middle of the bowl then sweep around the side. Twist the bowl slightly, then repeat. It's something like a figure-of-eight motion. Work quickly but lightly, and remember to dig right to the bottom of the bowl.

Stir
There's nothing difficult about stirring — just use a wooden spoon to mix the ingredients until combined.

Whisk
Use a wire whisk to rapidly beat the mixture. The point of whisking (sometimes referred to as 'whipping') is either to aerate the mixture or to break up clumps. If you're trying to incorporate air into the ingredients, it can help to hold the bowl at a slight angle and lift the whisk partially out of the liquid with every stroke.

A NOTE ON HEALTHY BAKING

The thought of baking a cake, or a stack of rubbly biscuits, or a bittersweet crème caramel with anything less than complete joy in the excess it embodies is, for me, a very sad one. There are plenty of areas in your culinary life where compromises can be made, but if you have a choice in the matter, baking shouldn't be one of them.

It's difficult to slim down baked foods. Where there isn't butter, you might find oil; where there's no cream, there could be half a dozen eggs; where flour is wholemeal, there'll still be salt. There is no such thing as a 'healthy' cake and you should be suspicious of anything that claims to be one. If what you're eating really is low in fat, sugar, carb and salt, it's probably a vegetable.

But that's not to suggest that you can't make health-conscious changes to your baking. Where one ingredient can be swapped for a healthier one, I do just that. Double cream, for example, can be left out in favour of single cream, or even full-fat milk, depending on the recipe (although, I beg you: hands off the skimmed milk). I've slimmed down certain recipes with this in mind, avoiding slathering icing on everything, and experimented with non-wheat flours. What I'm not willing to do is whittle down the calories (and taste) where the sensible option is just to cut oneself a slightly smaller slice.

CONVERSIONS

VOLUME

¼ teaspoon	1ml
½ teaspoon	2.5ml
1 teaspoon	5ml
1 tablespoon	15ml
1 dessertspoon	25ml
¼ cup	60ml
⅓ cup	80ml
½ cup	125ml
¾ cup	185ml
1 cup	250ml
1 pint	568ml
1 fl oz	28ml

WEIGHT

¼ oz	7g
½ oz	14g
1 oz	28g
1 lb (=16 oz)	454g
100ml water	100g
1 teaspoon instant dried yeast	3g
1 teaspoon table salt	6g

OVEN TEMPERATURES

Conventional oven °C	Fan oven °C	Gas oven gas mark
120	100	½
140	120	1
150	130	2
160	140	3
170	150	3-4
180	160	4
190	170	5
200	180	6
220	200	7
230	210	8
240	220	9

CAKE

LITTLE CAKES

LEMON & MARZIPAN CUPCAKES • HONEY MADELEINES

MORNING MUFFINS • CAMOMILE VANILLA CUPCAKES

LOAF CAKES

ORANGE & WHITE CHOCOLATE LOAF CAKE • DATE MALT LOAF

BANANA BREAD • FIG, ORANGE & STAR ANISE TEA LOAF

SOUR CREAM MADEIRA CAKE

FAMILY CAKES

LEMON SEMOLINA CAKE • RYE APPLE UPSIDE DOWN CAKE

CARAWAY CARROT CAKE WITH POPPY SEEDS

STOUT GINGERBREAD • GOOSEBERRY ELDERFLOWER CAKE

CHOCOLATE FUDGE CAKE

WHISKED CAKES

CHOCOLATE LIME MUD CAKE • TIRAMISU CAKE

PASSION FRUIT CURD SWISS ROLL

COFFEE BLACKCURRANT OPÉRA CAKE

A slice of birthday cake cradled in a greasy napkin — a thick layer of fondant over buttercream, over yellow cake with bright red jam sandwiched in the middle. This is my first definitive memory of cake, and I'm sure that it's the reason why, to this day, I feel a little cheated by anything less than the most cheerful, blandly saccharine of confections. Nonetheless, I've grown to appreciate a few more grown-up flavours, too: rye flour with crisp apples, marzipan (its sweetness tempered with a kick of lemon), black coffee, passion fruit and grassy caraway seeds. As you look through this chapter you'll notice that the cakes become slightly bigger and more complex as you progress, from small cakes to loaf cakes, family cakes and whisked cakes until the climactic opéra cake at the end. This isn't a rigid syllabus but a friendly guide. Tackle the recipes in whatever order you please and don't feel intimidated by the trickier recipes — it's only cake, after all.

WHEN'S MY CAKE DONE?

Sliding a tin of cake batter into a hot oven and tenderly shutting the door, it's tempting to turn the kettle on, kick back and congratulate yourself on a job well done. But, without wishing to scaremonger or to fuss: don't speak too soon. Far from being the closing credits in your cake's story, its time in the oven will prove pivotal: baked well, it'll rise to great heights; baked poorly, even the most fastidiously prepared cake batter will proceed to disappoint, emerging perhaps claggy, perhaps dry.

Cooking time and temperature are the important variables to consider at this point. Rapid, high-temperature cooking will set an airy sponge batter, whereas a deeper, heavier cake — a fruit cake, for instance — will be better suited to a longer, gentler stint in the oven. As I mentioned in the introduction, oven temperatures can be checked by using a cheap oven thermometer. The bake time, however, is slightly more difficult to pin down. Variations in tin sizes and thicknesses, different ambient and ingredient temperatures and oven peculiarities can all have an impact on how long it takes a cake to cook.

With this in mind, it's important to be able to look beyond the guide baking times and learn how to 'read' a cake, judging for yourself whether your creation is baked or not. If you can do this — by ogling, prodding and stabbing your cake — you'll be able to scale up or down or swap tins with confidence, making these recipes your own. Here are a few tests, which will, I hope, make the process more intuitive and less fraught.

KNIFE-TEST

This is the most used test, and the most effective. I always use a small knife for this, but you can use a proper cake-tester if you have one, or even a skewer or cocktail stick. If the cake is ready, a knife inserted into the middle will come out with no more than a couple of moist crumbs sticking to it. If the knife emerges coated with batter, the cake isn't yet done. This is the best way of being sure that the cake is cooked right through. Just don't be overzealous: the knife needs to come out clean-ish, but if you wait until it comes out bone dry then you will have baked the cake too long. Remember, the centre of the cake will continue to cook in its own heat for a short while after it's taken out of the oven, so it's better to bake slightly too little than too much.

CHECK THE EDGES

Large cakes, particularly whisked ones such as genoise sponges, will pull away from the edges of the tin when ready. Look out for the rim of the cake just starting to peel back from the cake tin. This won't hold true for all cakes, particularly very moist ones such as banana bread or dense chocolate cakes, but it's not bad as a rule of thumb.

SPRING

This test won't tell you definitively whether the cake is ready, but it will give you an indication. If, under the gentle press of a fingertip, the cake is left dented or feels fragile and spongy, it'll almost certainly need a while longer in the oven. If it's springy to the touch, it may well be ready, or very nearly there.

COLOUR

Recipes will often specify that a cake ought to be 'golden brown' when done. This is fair enough as an observation, but a very inaccurate way of actually judging the cooking time in practice. Some very thin cakes might cook through before they have a chance to brown on top; some cakes, such as gingerbread or chocolate cake, will remain much the same colour throughout; some have higher sugar content, so colour more easily. But the fundamental problem here is that most cakes will begin to take on a deeper hue long before their centre is cooked. The only time you need to heed the colour of your baking cake is if it's beginning to burn.

RISE

This test isn't very conclusive either. If the cake is well risen: fantastic. But that doesn't mean that it's cooked through just yet.

WHY IS MY CAKE...

Not all things in baking, as in life, can be foreseen. There will be times when even tried-and-tested, hand-me-down recipes fail. These disasters can, however, be explained. I can certainly relate to anyone who, as they despairingly attempt to salvage a burnt birthday cake in the early hours of the morning, doesn't much want to dwell on precisely when and how it all went wrong. But if you can face it, it's well worth taking a moment to look back and pinpoint the problem: not only will this make it less likely that the mistake will repeat itself, but you'll also be able to gain some peace of mind. More often than not, it will come down to something as seemingly inconsequential as a teaspoon of baking powder or an egg too many. Here are some of the most common cake problems, their causes and solutions.

...TOO DENSE?

— Too much liquid. Reduce the amount of liquid and be careful if adding any fresh fruit to the batter before baking.

— Under-baked, causing the cake to fall back on itself as it cools.

— Too little raising agent. In most standard butter-based cakes you'll need about 1 teaspoon of baking powder per 100g plain flour, but you might need more if the batter is laden with fruit, nuts or chocolate, and so on.

— In whisked cakes, you may have under-beaten or 'deflated' eggs. Make sure to whisk the eggs to the specified stage, whether ribbon, soft peak or stiff peak, and fold the other ingredients in very carefully to avoid bashing the air out and 'deflating' the mixture.

...TOO DRY?

— This will almost certainly be because your cake is over-baked. You can salvage a dry cake with a generous dose of syrup, though, or even by slicing it into thinner layers and sandwiching with buttercream.

...SUNKEN IN THE CENTRE?

— Too much raising agent. Believe it or not, too much bicarbonate of soda or baking powder can result in a cake that rises and then falls again in the oven. The cake starts off with too much energy, tiring itself out before it has had a chance to set, and slumps back down again, exhausted.

— Under-baked. The cake's structure hasn't had a chance to firm properly and so has fallen back on itself under its own weight. But you might just be able to hurry the cake back to the oven to finish baking before it collapses completely.

— Bear in mind that some cakes do sink in the centre as they cool — flourless cakes, for example, or very rich cakes such as the Chocolate Lime Mud Cake (see page 60) are particularly prone to this. Most standard flour-based cakes shouldn't suffer from this problem.

...STEEPLY DOMED OR CRACKED?

— Usually this happens when the oven temperature is too high, causing the crust to set before the inside of the cake has cooked through. The raw batter then erupts through the surface as it continues to heat and expand, resulting in a domed, ruptured top. Bake on a slightly lower temperature next time (160°C/fan 140°C/gas mark 3 will be sufficient for most cakes, with a longer cooking time factored in accordingly). One other novel solution to this problem is to wrap the outside of the cake tin in well-soaked kitchen towels or rags prior to baking. These shield the sides of the cake from the direct heat of the oven, slowing the setting and so ensuring a more uniform rise.

— Counter-intuitively, domed or cracked tops can also be caused by using too little raising agent. Raising agents slightly weaken the structure of the flour, resulting in a cake batter that can stretch and rise more before it begins to set. When there's too little of this weakening, the cake's growth and the crust will set too soon, as above.

...BROWNED OR BURNT OUTSIDE BUT RAW INSIDE?

— It's very likely that your oven temperature is too high. Turn the oven down low, to 140°C/fan 120°/gas mark 1, and continue to bake until just set inside. Next time, bake at a slightly lower heat or invest in an oven thermometer (they're inexpensive and worth their weight in burnt cakes) to check that your oven is operating at the right temperature.

— Too much sugar can also be at the root of this problem, causing the outside to caramelise too quickly. Some sugars brown more quickly than others, too — agave nectar, for instance.

LITTLE CAKES

CREAMING BUTTER & SUGAR

I'm guilty of laziness when it comes to beating together butter and sugar. The cold butter has barely combined with the sugar before I hold up my hands in defeat and add the rest of the ingredients. This way lie curdled batter and heavy cakes. It's a boring job but you mustn't cut corners: as the butter and sugar are mixed, air is beaten into the mixture and the sugar begins to dissolve. You'll really notice the difference if you do it properly: a transformation from a heavy, greasy lump to a fluffy mixture, far lighter in both colour and texture than before. This will take around 5 minutes if you work by hand, or as little as 2 minutes using a hand-held electric whisk or stand mixer. Dip a finger in and you'll notice that the mixture is almost mousse-like in texture now, and far less gritty. The millions of air bubbles held in suspension by the fat and sugar are responsible for this metamorphosis, and this is what makes the cake particularly light and tender once baked.

LEMON & MARZIPAN CUPCAKES

In Portugal, there is a drink called *amarguinha* — a light-coloured, bitter almond liqueur mixed with a very generous measure of lemon juice. Bitter almond and lemon partner together wonderfully and this very simple recipe is proof of that. To add even more of a lemony kick to these zingy cupcakes, feel free to heat the juice of the lemons mixed with a little sugar on the hob, to make a lemon drizzle.

Makes 12
120g butter, softened
75g caster sugar
½ teaspoon almond extract
Zest of 2 lemons
120g plain flour
60g ground almonds

1½ teaspoons baking powder
½ teaspoon salt
2 large eggs
3 tablespoons milk
200g marzipan, divided into 2 pieces

12-bun muffin tin

1   Line the tin with paper cases and preheat the oven to 180°C/fan 160°C/gas mark 4.

2   Cream the butter and sugar together until light and fluffy. Add the almond extract and lemon zest. Combine all the dry ingredients in a separate bowl. Break one egg into the butter mixture and then add a couple of tablespoons of the flour mix. Stir to combine and repeat. Add the rest of the flour along with the milk.

3   Grate in 100g of the marzipan, then break the remaining marzipan into small pieces and stir into the batter. Spoon the mixture into the paper cases and bake for 17-20 minutes. A knife test is tricky with these cupcakes as the melted marzipan inside looks suspiciously like the uncooked cake batter. But use your instincts — if the cakes are well-risen, golden, and spring back when gently pressed with a finger, they are ready.

BROWN BUTTER

Peel back the wrapper of a heavy, pallid block of butter. Place the butter in a small pan over a low heat and watch it slip and slide, leaving criss-crossing trails of yellow fat across the pan. Before long the last island of butter will disappear into the golden liquid. Milky specks will settle at the bottom, while the fat — this bit is now clarified butter — begins to sizzle. It'll grow fragrant and nutty, deepening to an amber colour. Snatch it off the heat now: this is brown butter. A few seconds later, the smell will turn bitter, the milk residue will char and it'll be too late. If you thought that butter was butter, plain and simple — think again.

Brown butter is most commonly found in recipes for *financiers*: little French cakes typically baked into tiny portions, each — fantastically, immodestly — the shape of a gold ingot. Used in place of 'normal' butter it will impart a welcome warmth and roundness of flavour, especially when showcased against the neutrality of milk, cream or simple sponge cakes. It has a natural affinity with nuts, too, hazelnut being a particularly good match. The madeleine recipe that follows uses brown butter to complement the flavour of the honey.

It's important to substitute with care, however, if using brown butter in place of the usual stuff. During the cooking process, brown butter loses almost all of its water content (up to 20% of its original weight). This moisture must therefore be reintroduced to the recipe, with a splash of milk, for instance.

HONEY MADELEINES

Quite enough florid food prose has been written on the subject of these delicate little French cakes already, so I'll resist the temptation to wax lyrical about them here. All I will say is that they really are every bit as good as Proust and co. would have you believe.

If you have a madeleine tray only large enough to make 12 at a time, don't worry: the batter won't suffer for being left standing while you cook the cakes in batches. And if you don't have a madeleine tin at all you can use a standard muffin one instead. The end result won't be any less delicious.

Chilling the filled tin seems to help the cakes develop their characteristic 'nipple'. I think it brings an element of interest to the teatime table...

**Makes 20–24 traditional madeleines
    or 12 in a muffin tin**
130g unsalted butter
75g caster sugar
2 tablespoons honey
2 large eggs
100g plain flour

½ teaspoon baking powder

**12-hole madeleine tray or 12-hole
    muffin tin**

📷 p28

1   Melt the butter over a low heat. As soon as it's melted, transfer 2 tablespoons of it to a small bowl. Return the remaining butter to the heat, stirring continuously while it sizzles. Before long it'll turn a light brown colour and smell slightly toasted — as soon as it reaches this stage, remove it from the heat or else it'll burn. Set this browned butter aside to cool for a few minutes.

2   Use the reserved couple of tablespoons of melted butter to brush the holes of the madeleine or muffin tin. You may not need all of it. Place the tin in the fridge (or freezer, if you have the space) while you make the cake batter.

3   Combine the sugar, honey and eggs in a bowl, whisking for a minute or so until foamy. In a separate bowl combine the flour and baking powder, and then add this to the egg and sugar mixture. Fold in the slightly cooled brown butter.

4   Remove the tin from the fridge or freezer. If making traditional shell-shaped madeleines, fill each hole no more than three-quarters full, with barely a spoonful of batter. Set the remaining batter aside until the next batch, remembering to grease and chill the tin again before using. If using a muffin mould, just divide all of the mixture between the 12 holes (they won't be anywhere near full — these are going to be dainty morsels, not full-sized cupcakes). Place the filled tin in the fridge for 20 minutes while you preheat the oven to 200°C/fan 180°C/gas mark 6.

5   Bake the shell-shaped madeleines for 8–9 minutes, or the cupcake ones for 9–12 minutes. Remove from the tin and leave to cool.

MORNING MUFFINS

These muffins are what I like to eat with a mug of black coffee on a lazy weekend, as the morning pushes into the afternoon. They're substantial without being stupefyingly rich: a welcome alternative to buttery pastries and full fry-ups, yet without the dour frugality of a bowl of porridge. The wholemeal flour lends them a reassuringly virtuous edge (although you can swap this for plain flour if you really must). Grapefruit, zested into the batter and decorating the tops of these muffins, gives a citrus kick. Don't be fooled into thinking that they're a healthy breakfast superfood, though: no matter how you dress it up, it's still cake for breakfast.

You can make the batter in the evening, ready to cook the morning after. Just leave in a cling film-covered bowl in the fridge overnight. But it is a quick batter to make, and not unfeasible for breakfast-time — you can have it prepared in 15 minutes, and the muffins freshly baked, slightly cooled and ready to eat within the hour.

These muffins are best eaten straight away (they're at their lightest and fluffiest while still slightly warm) which is why I have given the quantities for a batch of only 6 here — enough for three people. If you're feeding more, or those with very healthy appetites, the recipe can very easily be doubled or even tripled, according to your needs.

Makes 6
1 grapefruit (I use pink grapefruit)
50g unsalted butter, softened
100g caster or soft light brown sugar
1 large egg
175g plain yoghurt
40g porridge oats
60g plain flour
30g wholemeal flour

½ teaspoon baking powder
½ teaspoon bicarbonate of soda
¼ teaspoon salt
20g sugar (preferably demerara), to sprinkle on top

6- or 12-hole muffin tin

📷 p31

1 Preheat the oven to 180°C/fan 160°C/gas mark 4. Line the tin with paper cupcake or muffin cases (not fairy cake cases, which are far smaller).

2 Grate the zest of the grapefruit into a large bowl. Cut one half of the grapefruit into six segments, trim away the peel and pith from each and set aside. (You can wince your way through the remaining half grapefruit while you wait for the muffins to bake.)

3 Melt the butter in a small pan then add it, with the sugar, to the bowl containing the zest. Beat to combine. Stir in the egg, yoghurt and oats. In a separate bowl, combine the flours, baking powder, bicarbonate of soda and salt. Add all this to the wet mixture and stir briefly until just combined, being careful not to stir any more than is absolutely necessary, as any excess mixing can strengthen the structure of the batter, resulting in chewy, heavy muffins.

4 Divide the batter between the cases. It shouldn't reach any higher than two-thirds of the way up each case, otherwise the cakes will overflow while baking and you get far more muffin top than you bargained for.

5 Perch a grapefruit segment on top of each muffin and sprinkle on the extra sugar. Bake for around 25 minutes, or until well risen and springy.

Variations
If the thought of grapefruit sets your teeth on edge, swap it for a small handful of raisins stirred through the batter and possibly a little cinnamon, too. Blueberries could also be used for a more traditional morning muffin.

BAKING WITH TEA

I once worked in a small London tearoom. It was a steep learning curve for someone who, until then, thought that tea came in just four ways: with milk, sugar, both or neither. And so I learned about cups, saucers, strainers and brewing tea in dainty teapots rather than steeping it in a stained mug. The tea was loose-leaf, stored in heavy glass jars clustered on the shelves: fine Earl Grey, feathery camomile, grey-green Darjeeling ... The lid of the jar would open with a pop, and up came the smell of rose, fragrant jasmine, or smoky lapsang souchong. It was an education.

And, excitingly, the very things that make tea so good to brew — the aromatics, the concentrated flavour — also make it perfect to cook with. Earl Grey can complement a citrus tea loaf, green tea lends a bright green colour and delicate flavour to a shortbread biscuit. Even gentle camomile tea can be effective, as in the soothing camomile cupcakes opposite. It's a change from the usual flavouring formula of essence, spice or zest. Tea does, however, benefit from being infused in a liquid first if it's to release its flavour most effectively. This is best done in butter or milk, bringing the tea and liquid to the boil then leaving it to cool and infuse.

CAMOMILE VANILLA CUPCAKES

Camomile might not be an obvious flavour for a cake but it's one that works remarkably well. It is subtly grassy, fragrant and — bolstered by the vanilla — mellow and warm. On days when comfort food is called for, you could do worse than one of these sunny cupcakes. There's not an excessive amount of buttercream on these — just enough to cap each one. But if you have a very sweet tooth, you can of course make extra.

I've called for camomile tea bags here rather than the better-quality loose tea only because the bagged stuff is so much easier to source. But if you can get hold of the more aromatic loose leaves then by all means use those instead.

Makes 12
225g unsalted butter
160ml milk
6 camomile tea bags
160g caster sugar
3 large eggs
1½ teaspoons vanilla extract
210g plain flour

1½ teaspoons baking powder
Pinch of salt
200–300g icing sugar

12-hole muffin tin

📷 p35

1   Preheat the oven to 180°C/fan 160°C/gas mark 4. Line the tin with paper cases.

2   Place the butter, milk and tea bags in a small pan and set over a low heat. Once the butter has completely melted let the mixture simmer for a couple of minutes. Set aside to cool for 5 minutes then strain out the tea, collecting the camomile-infused liquid in a bowl. Some of it will have evaporated and some will get lost in the tea bags, but you should still have 240–300ml of the butter and milk mixture left. Divide the liquid into two bowls — the first bowl containing two-thirds (160–200ml), the other containing the remaining third. Set both bowls in the fridge for 20 minutes to slightly firm the butter.

3   Beat the larger portion of the butter and milk mixture with the sugar for a couple of minutes until slightly lighter in colour. Add the eggs and vanilla extract. In a separate bowl, stir the flour, baking powder and salt together, then fold this mixture into the wet ingredients (not the retained one-third) until all is combined. You'll be left with a thick batter, which drops softly off an upturned spoon. If it stays clinging to the spoon, a splash of milk can be used to loosen it until that 'dropping consistency' is reached.

4   Divide the batter between the cases and bake for 15–20 minutes, testing at the lower end of this interval and keeping a close eye on them until ready. Small cakes such as these move from under- to over-baked very quickly, so it's important to be present during the latter part of the cooking time.

5   To make the buttercream, beat the remaining third of the camomile-infused butter and milk mixture until smooth, gradually adding the icing sugar until the buttercream is thick. Buttercream shouldn't be hidebound by rules and ratios — just use enough icing sugar to give a good texture and flavour, balancing the

butter's richness with sweetness and testing as you go. Chill the buttercream in the fridge to set while you wait for the cupcakes to cool.

6   Once the cupcakes have cooked and cooled, top each one with a slick of buttercream. I like to go for maximum coordination, serving them (to myself) with a pot of matching camomile tea.

Variations
This recipe can be adapted to play host to almost any spin-off tea variation (Lady Grey with orange zest is a favourite).

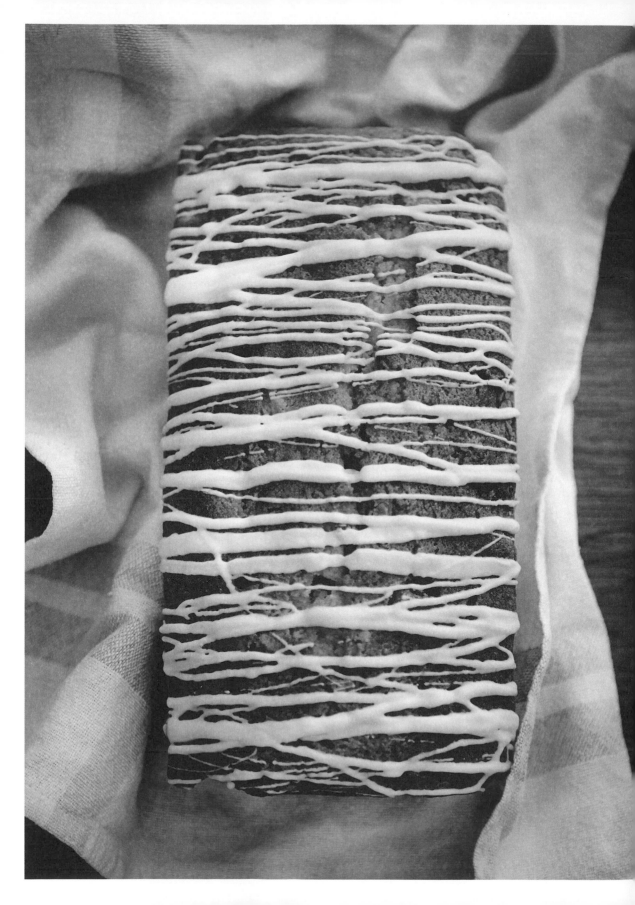

LOAF CAKES

ORANGE & WHITE CHOCOLATE LOAF CAKE

Sometimes a cake is a cake is a cake, not to be fussed over or tampered with. This is one such cake: moist, sweet and citrus-scented. It is worth it for the joy of zesting alone.

150g butter, softened
150g caster sugar
Zest of 2 oranges
Zest of ½ lemon
2 large eggs, lightly beaten
225g plain flour, plus a little extra
1½ teaspoons baking powder
¼ teaspoon salt
75ml milk
150g white chocolate chips, or a block
  chopped into small chunks

For the syrup:
Juice of 1 orange
Juice of ½ a lemon
50g caster sugar

To decorate:
50-100g white chocolate

900g loaf tin

📷 p36

1   Preheat the oven to 180°C/fan 160°C/gas mark 4. Grease and line the loaf tin with baking parchment.

2   Cream the butter and sugar together until light and fluffy (this takes some elbow grease or a food processor). Beat in the zests and gradually add the eggs. In a separate bowl, combine the flour, baking powder and salt, then gently fold this into the butter and egg mixture. Stir in the milk.

3   Make sure that the white chocolate is in quite small chunks — about 5mm cubes if chopping it yourself. Toss the chocolate chunks/chips in a couple of tablespoons of extra flour, to help ensure that they don't sink straight to the bottom of the tin, and then stir into the batter.

4   Spoon the mixture into the lined tin, smooth over and bake for 50-60 minutes. When ready, a knife inserted into the middle of the cake should come out with only a few crumbs sticking to it.

5   While the cake is in the oven, prepare the syrup by gently heating the orange and lemon juices in a pan, and then stirring in the sugar until dissolved. As soon as the cake is out of the oven, pierce all over with a small, sharp knife, cocktail stick or skewer, and spoon the syrup over. You may not need to use all of it, but do be generous. Leave the cake to cool in the tin before turning out.

6   Heat the white chocolate for the drizzle in 10-second bursts in the microwave, or in a bowl suspended over a pan of simmering water, stirring regularly. Don't let the bowl touch the water. Drizzle over the top of the cake, using either a spoon or a piping bag.

DATE MALT LOAF

This is more a bread than a cake in spirit, I suppose: there's little lightness or refinement to it. It's possibly the only cake that ever survived my childhood raiding of the kitchen cupboards, regarded with the same suspicion reserved for things like brown rice and fresh fruit. But when it comes to not judging a book by its cover, this squat, heavy little loaf is a case in point. It is densely chewy, deeply malted, heavy with fruit and with an almost toffee flavour... forget the tiered, turreted, palatial centrepieces of the cake kingdom: it's this cake — all substance and no style — that really steals the show.

Malt extract is everywhere. It creeps into breads, beers, cereals and chocolates, bringing with it a unique flavour, which I can really only describe, apologetically, as 'maltiness'. It's a taste somewhere between roasted, toasted, caramel and coffee, and it's delicious. Yet for something so quietly ubiquitous in our foods, malt extract can prove tricky to find in its most basic state: thick, brown syrup, as viscous as black treacle, sold by the jar. But thanks to a folkloric belief in the nutritional power of the stuff (a power which I'm not convinced would stand the scrutiny of nutritionists nowadays) you should be able to find it in high-street health food shops.

60g unsalted butter
120ml strong black tea
150g malt extract
120g soft dark brown sugar
2 large eggs, lightly beaten
260g plain flour
2 teaspoons baking powder

¼ teaspoon salt
150g dates, roughly chopped

900g loaf tin

📷 p39

1   Preheat the oven to 160°C/fan 140°C/gas mark 3. Grease and line the loaf tin with baking parchment.

2   Place the butter, tea and malt extract in a small pan over a low heat, just until the butter is melted. Take off the heat, stir in the sugar and add the beaten eggs to the mix. Stir to combine.

3   Mix the flour, baking powder and salt in a bowl, then pour in the wet ingredients and stir lightly to combine. Add the dates. The satiny batter might be slightly runnier than you're used to, but this is no cause for concern.

4   Pour the mixture into the prepared loaf tin and bake for 1-1¼ hours, or until a knife inserted into the centre comes out with nothing but a crumb or two on it. Let cool completely before eating, if you can resist it. And for those with powers of moderation and restraint that I can barely dream of: wrap the loaf tightly in foil and leave for a couple of days before eating, during which time its flavour will deepen and mature.

Variations
You can swap the dates for sultanas, raisins or currants if you want, although I quite like the caramel flavour of the dates here. You might also try using brown ale, porter or even stout instead of the tea — it's an unusual but completely logical combination,

the mellow maltiness of the ale bolstering the malt flavour of the cake. Some things, however, are not up for negotiation, and when it comes to the eating there is only one sensible way to proceed: cut the malt loaf into generous slices, spread each thickly with salted — always salted — butter and eat with your fingers.

BANANA BREAD

Banana bread has a magnetic pull. Don't be surprised if its sweet, deep banana scent draws you nose-first into the kitchen as it bakes. This is one of the best-smelling cakes I've made. The misty sugar glaze is an inessential but delicious afterthought. You can, of course, omit it if sugar levels are a concern.

This banana bread is made with agave nectar: it's an alternative to traditional sugars and syrups but does call for some fine-tuning of the other ingredients to get the ratios right. Although light, agave has its own distinctive taste, which in a plainer cake might be an unwelcome distraction, but here subtly complements the banana.

If you'd rather make this with 'normal' sugar, just swap the agave for 140g of caster or soft light brown sugar and add 50ml milk with the rum or brandy. Similarly, you can omit the cardamom if it's not to your taste, although I really like the citrussy spice alongside the banana's creamy sweetness.

125g unsalted butter, softened
110g agave nectar
2 medium bananas, well mashed
2 tablespoons rum or brandy
2 large eggs
190g plain flour
1½ teaspoons baking powder
½ teaspoon ground cinnamon
¼ teaspoon salt

4 cardamom pods, seeds only, crushed

For the glaze, if desired:
25ml water
100g icing sugar

900g loaf tin

📷 p40

1   Preheat the oven to 180°C/fan 160°C/gas mark 4. Grease and line the loaf tin with baking parchment.

2   Cream the butter then stir in the agave nectar. Beat in the bananas and rum or brandy, then the eggs and a couple of tablespoons of the flour. Beat until smooth, but don't worry if it looks a little curdled at this stage. Combine the remaining flour with the baking powder, cinnamon, salt and cardamom in a separate bowl then add this to the wet mixture. Fold the ingredients together then stir lightly until fully combined.

3   Spoon the batter into the prepared tin and bake for 45–55 minutes, or until a knife inserted into the centre of the cake comes out clean. While the cake is in the oven, make the glaze: stir the water into the icing sugar, a teaspoonful at a time, until combined. Set aside.

4   Once the cake is done let it cool in its tin for 5 minutes, then turn out onto a wire rack set over a tray (to catch any drips). Spoon the icing over the top of the cake while it's still hot. The glaze will cover the top and run down the sides in thick rivulets, but will set to a cracked sugar crust as the cake cools.

FIG, ORANGE & STAR ANISE TEA LOAF

This is my favourite recipe in this book. If you buy dried figs just once in your life, let it be for this. It's a headily perfumed loaf that is, quite impossibly, at once floral, citrus, liquorice, spice and caramel and yet not definitively any one of those things. It sits happily outside the tea loaf status quo. I love it.

300ml milk
250g dried figs, coarsely chopped
75g soft light brown sugar
Zest of 1 orange
1 teaspoon finely ground star anise*
1½ teaspoons vanilla extract
2 large eggs
275g plain flour
2½ teaspoons baking powder

1 teaspoon ground ginger
¼ teaspoon salt

900g loaf tin

* grind 3-4 whole star anise, sift out the grit and measure what you need

📷 p43

1 Preheat the oven to 180°C/fan 160°C/gas mark 4 and grease and line the tin with baking parchment.

2 In a large mixing bowl, combine the milk, figs, sugar, orange zest, star anise, vanilla extract and eggs.

3 In a separate bowl, combine the flour, baking powder, ginger and salt. Add the dry ingredients to the wet mixture and stir lightly until combined. Spoon into the loaf tin and bake for 50-60 minutes. Once baked, allow to rest in the tin for 15 minutes or so before turning out onto a wire rack to cool completely.

SOUR CREAM MADEIRA CAKE

This unadorned cake doesn't need any drizzle, dusting or decoration — any such messing around will only distract from the meltingly soft, yellow sponge itself. The sour cream works wonders here, offsetting the buttery richness and creating a tender texture. It's a firmer cake than some but this is precisely what makes madeira cake, allowing it to be cut cleanly into proud, even slices.

150g unsalted butter, softened
150g caster sugar
2 large eggs
Zest of 1 lemon
150ml sour cream

175g plain flour
1½ teaspoons baking powder
¼ teaspoon salt

900g loaf tin

1 Preheat the oven to 180°C/fan 160°C/gas mark 4. Grease and line the tin with baking parchment.

2 Beat the butter and sugar together for about 5 minutes. Although stubbornly heavy to start with, the butter will soon become soft, light and fluffy as the sugar

dissolves into it and air is incorporated. Stir in the eggs, lemon zest and sour cream, beating well until the mixture is completely combined.

3 Combine the flour, baking powder and salt in a separate bowl then stir this into the butter mixture. Don't mix for any longer than is necessary, or you risk a heavy, chewy cake.

4 Spoon the mixture into the prepared tin and bake for around 45 minutes, or until a knife inserted into the middle of the cake comes out with no more than a crumb or two on it. Leave to cool completely in the tin before serving.

FAMILY CAKES

LEMON SEMOLINA CAKE

Lemon drizzle cake should teasingly tread the sweet-sharp line: if it doesn't make your mouth pucker just a little then, to my mind, it's all wrong. For this, a generous hand with the syrup is essential and using both the juice and zest of the lemons helps, too. The use of semolina makes for a far more interesting texture and leaves the cake exuberantly, sunnily yellow.

125g unsalted butter, softened
125g caster sugar
2 large eggs, lightly beaten
Zest and juice of 2 large or 3 smaller lemons
100g semolina
60g plain flour
1 teaspoon baking powder
Pinch of salt

For the syrup:
60g caster or granulated sugar
Lemon juice
20g icing sugar (optional), to dust

20cm loose-bottomed or spring-form cake tin

1   Preheat the oven to 170°C/fan 150°C/gas mark 3–4 and grease the tin. If not loose-bottomed, be sure to base-line with baking parchment.

2   Cream the butter and sugar until pale and fluffy then add the eggs, lemon zest, semolina and a tablespoon of the lemon juice. Reserve the remaining juice for the syrup, to be made later. In a separate bowl, combine the flour, baking powder and salt. Add the flour mixture to the wet ingredients and stir to combine. Spoon into the prepared tin, smooth the top and bake for 25 minutes (or until a knife inserted into the middle comes out clean).

3   While the cake is in the oven, combine the remaining lemon juice and the 60g sugar in a pan over a low heat. Let bubble for just a couple of minutes, or until it looks a bit more... well, syrupy. Then take it off the heat.

4   As soon as the cake is out of the oven, pierce deeply through the top with a fork or skewer a few times and spoon over the syrup, giving it time to seep into the cake. Leave to cool slightly then remove from its tin and move to a wire rack to finish cooling. A liberal dusting of icing sugar is a glorious (but admittedly unnecessary) finishing touch.

RYE APPLE UPSIDE DOWN CAKE

A nutty, caramel-crusted apple cake. This is only a single-tier cake by design: why go to such pains to achieve a layer of toffee-apple splendour if it's going to be dwarfed by the mass of cake underneath? The rye flour enhances the flavour and gives a more interesting texture, too. If your 20cm round tin is quite shallow, with sides less than 5cm high, I'd recommend making two-thirds of the quantity to avoid overspill.

For the caramel layer:
100g caster or granulated sugar
2 tablespoons water
10g unsalted butter
1–2 medium dessert apples (I use Cox's),
   peeled, cored and thinly sliced

For the cake:
160g unsalted butter, softened
150g caster or light brown sugar
3 large eggs, lightly beaten
2 medium dessert apples, peeled and
   coarscly grated

90g plain flour
90g rye flour
1½ teaspoons baking powder
1 teaspoon ground cinnamon
¼ teaspoon salt
100g chopped nuts
100g raisins or sultanas

20cm round deep cake tin

📷 p46

1 Preheat the oven to 180°C/fan 160°C/gas mark 4. Grease and line your cake tin with baking parchment.

2 Combine the sugar and water for the caramel in a small pan (preferably one that isn't non-stick) over a low heat. Stir occasionally until the sugar is dissolved and then — and this really is important — do not touch it. Turn up the heat and let it simmer until the sugar has turned golden. (See page 316 for advice on making caramel.) Add the butter once the caramel is ready (careful — it may spatter!), and stir until melted. Pour the caramel into the prepared tin, covering the entire base.

3 Arrange the apple slices in concentric circles on the caramel while it's still warm and sticky. Set aside while you prepare the cake batter.

4 Cream the butter and sugar until light and fluffy then gradually add the eggs. Stir in the grated apple. Don't worry if the mixture seems slightly curdled.

5 Combine the flours, baking powder, cinnamon and salt in a separate bowl then add all this to the wet ingredients. Finally, stir in the nuts and dried fruit. Spoon the batter into the cake tin, very carefully levelling it with the back of the spoon,

6 Bake for 35–45 minutes, or until a knife inserted into the middle comes out with no more than a crumb or two sticking to it. Leave to cool in the tin for a few minutes before turning out onto a wire rack, turning it upside down (or the right way up now, I suppose). Peel back the baking parchment to reveal the caramelised apple top.

CARAWAY CARROT CAKE WITH POPPY SEEDS

Despite being an unusual addition to a carrot cake (typically flavoured with cinnamon), caraway seeds work very well in this recipe. They're not much to look at — tiny, banana-shaped brown seeds — but their taste is unique. If you haven't ever done so, chew on a seed before you get to work on this cake: you'll find it sharp yet earthy, bitter but surprisingly bright. It's often used in rye breads. You can increase the amount of caraway here to taste, or even leave a few of the seeds whole, for a bolder flavour. Be sure to use good-quality cream cheese — cheaper ones will have a higher water content, leaving the icing runny and thin.

150g unsalted butter, softened
150g soft light brown sugar
125g grated carrot (from approx.
    2 medium carrots)
2 large eggs
30ml milk
150g plain flour
Pinch of salt
1½ teaspoons baking powder
1 teaspoon ground coriander
1½ teaspoons caraway seeds, coarsely
    ground or crushed
25g poppy seeds

For the icing:
300g full-fat cream cheese
75g icing sugar
Zest of 1 lemon
25g poppy seeds

**Deep 20cm round cake tin, preferably
    spring-form or loose-bottomed**

📷 p49

1   Preheat the oven to 180°C/fan 160°C/gas mark 4 and grease the tin.

2   In a large bowl, beat the butter and sugar until fluffy. Add the carrot, eggs and milk along with a tablespoon or two of the flour. Mix the remaining flour, salt, baking powder, coriander, caraway seeds and poppy seeds in a separate bowl then add all to the wet ingredients. Stir until just combined.

3   Pour the batter into the prepared tin and bake for 25– 35 minutes, or until a knife inserted into the centre of the cake comes out with no more than a crumb or two stuck to it. Let cool for a few minutes in its tin before unmoulding and leaving to cool completely on a wire rack.

4   For the icing, strain any excess liquid from the cheese – this is to avoid a runny icing. Stir the cream cheese until smooth then add the icing sugar, lemon zest and poppy seeds, mixing just until combined.

5   Halve the cooled cake horizontally, using a large, serrated knife. Perfectly even layers aren't always easy to achieve — I tend to just remedy the inevitably wonky cake with extra icing to balance it.

6   Dollop half of the icing on the bottom circle of cake and spread gently to cover the layer. Sandwich with the upper layer, and spread the remaining icing over the top and sides.

LIQUID FLAVOURINGS

Using liquids to add flavour to a cake is a difficult manoeuvre. They can't simply be added to a standard cake mix, skewing the ratios of ingredients and potentially resulting in a dense, claggy texture in the finished cake. It's often safer and easier to use dry flavourings or highly concentrated liquid ones, hence lemon zest rather than juice, a dash of ground spices or a scant teaspoon of potent vanilla extract.

But there are some cakes that have a more liquid batter, among them gingerbreads, malt loaves, banana breads, some chocolate cakes and heavy fruitcakes. With these cakes, you're freer to experiment. If a fruited loaf cake calls for a cupful of milk, perhaps try strong black tea instead. It's not unusual to find recipes for chocolate cake that use Guinness to deepen the flavour. The gingerbread below works on exactly this principle. Have a go with your own substitutions — tea, ale, spirits, cordial, coffee. Just steer clear of acidic liquids such as fruit juice, which can curdle the batter.

STOUT GINGERBREAD

This isn't the brittle, biscuit type of gingerbread — this one is moist, cakey and deliciously dark. It's a very wet batter, easier to pour than to spoon into the tin, so don't be alarmed. The smooth, almost chocolatey stout rounds the flavour of the cake and keeps it beautifully tender. You can use milk instead, if you prefer, but the result won't have quite the same treacly depth.

This cake tastes even better in the days after baking: a little self-restraint will really pay off if you can bear to leave it untouched for a day or two. That said, it rarely lasts longer than a few hours in our house.

60g unsalted butter
80g treacle
60g soft dark or light brown sugar
5–6cm piece root ginger, grated
100ml stout, porter or brown ale
1 large egg, lightly beaten
120g plain flour

2 teaspoons ground ginger
½ teaspoon bicarbonate of soda
¼ teaspoon salt

20cm round cake tin

📷 p50

1   Preheat the oven to 180°C/fan 160°C/gas mark 4. Grease and line the tin with baking parchment.

2   Combine the butter, treacle and sugar together in a pan over a low heat just until the butter is melted. Stir in the fresh ginger and ale. Using a whisk or fork, beat in the egg.

3   Mix the flour, ground ginger, bicarbonate of soda and salt together in a large bowl. Add the wet ingredients to this gradually, whisking all the time, and continue to mix until the mixture is combined and clump-free.

4   Pour the mixture into the prepared tin and bake for 25–30 minutes. It's done when the top is springy and a knife inserted into the middle comes out clean.

WHIPPING CREAM

That's the act of whipping cream, not 'whipping cream'. The latter — that strange, not-quite-double-cream hybrid — isn't something I can endorse. When I whip cream, it is always double. Whipping cream is at once very simple and unexpectedly tricky: it's dangerously easy to move from smooth, proud crests of cream one moment, to a grainy mess the next. If you really bully the cream it'll separate, clump and turn into butter. To avoid a cream calamity, go slowly when whisking and stop just before you think it's thick enough, particularly if you plan to pipe the cream (forced through the nozzle of a piping bag, even loosely whipped cream can, bewilderingly, churn itself). Although it's hard work, I like to whip cream the old-fashioned way with a wire whisk — it gives you a far keener sense of the texture of the cream as it thickens than an electric mixer does, and minimises the risk of over-whipping. And let's face it: if you're going to be eating any of this gloriously thick, whipped cream, a little preliminary workout can't do any harm.

GOOSEBERRY ELDERFLOWER CAKE

The archetypical summer fête cake: two thick layers of buttery cake sandwiched with cream and fruit. It's an old-fashioned slice of our collective nostalgia.

If you can't get your hands on fresh gooseberries (they're best from June to August, and even then aren't always easy to find) you could try tinned gooseberries, reducing the amount of sugar they're simmered with, but they're rarely very good. Or opt for a different filling altogether (see the variations below).

175g unsalted butter, softened
175g caster sugar
175g plain flour
Pinch of salt
1½ teaspoons baking powder
3 large eggs
1 teaspoon vanilla extract
50ml milk
100ml elderflower cordial

For the filling:
250g gooseberries, topped and tailed
    if fresh

40–100g caster sugar
150ml double cream
45ml elderflower cordial
Caster sugar, to dust

**Two 20cm round cake tins, preferably
    loose-bottomed or spring-form**

 p53

1   Preheat the oven to 180°C/fan 160°C/gas mark 4. Grease the tins and line the bases with baking parchment.

2   Cream the butter and sugar until light and fluffy. In another bowl, combine the flour, salt and baking powder. Add a third of the flour and one of the eggs to the butter mixture and stir to combine. Repeat until all of the flour and eggs are incorporated, then stir in the vanilla extract and milk.

3   Divide the batter between the two tins and bake for around 15–20 minutes, or until golden brown and just starting to shrink away from the sides of the tin. The cakes should feel springy to the touch.

4   Leave the cakes to cool in their tins for 5 minutes, then carefully turn them out onto a wire rack. Drizzle over the 100ml elderflower cordial. Leave to cool completely.

5   While the sponges rest, simmer the gooseberries with the 40–100g sugar over a low heat. If tinned, the gooseberries will need only about 40g of sugar, but fresh gooseberries will need quite a bit more to balance their sharpness. Just add the sugar to taste, and cook for as long as it takes for the berries to split their skins, release their juices and soften — about 10 minutes for fresh gooseberries and only a couple of minutes for tinned ones. Set aside to cool.

6   Whisk together the cream and the 45ml elderflower cordial until just thick enough to spread. This will take anywhere between 2 and 5 minutes, depending on whether you use a manual wire whisk, a hand-held electric whisk or a stand mixer.

7   Once the cake and the gooseberry mixture are at room temperature, spread one half of the cake with the gooseberries, dollop the cream on top then sandwich with the other layer. Dust with caster sugar. It is best not to make this too far in advance — the cream will turn if left at room temperature for too long, but the cake will go stale if stored in the fridge. The only option is to guzzle it quite soon after baking. That shouldn't be too hard.

Variations
Strawberries also complement the delicately floral elderflower. Fill the cake with a few tablespoons of good-quality strawberry jam — better still, make your own (see page 323) — instead of the gooseberries. If elderflower isn't your thing, omit the elderflower drizzle and spread with raspberry jam for a timeless Victoria Sandwich.

CHOCOLATE FUDGE CAKE

'Suddenly the Trunchbull exploded. "Eat!" she shouted, banging her thigh with the riding-crop. "If I tell you to eat, you will eat! You wanted cake! You stole cake! And now you've got cake! What's more, you're going to eat it! You do not leave this platform and nobody leaves this hall until you have eaten the entire cake that is sitting there in front of you!"' Roald Dahl, *Matilda*

Bruce Bogtrotter's triumph over the chocolate cake was perhaps my most read passage in any book throughout my childhood. It's the cake that stands for cake itself, with two thick layers of moist, dark chocolate sponge smothered in fudgy frosting. And if you can turn eating it into an act of defiance against the Trunchbull, or diet culture, or whatever: all the better.

Chocolate is the very essence of this cake, so using a reasonable-quality bar will make a big difference. I do not, however, subscribe to the rather priggish school of cooking that blusteringly dismisses anything but the finest single-origin, artisanally-crafted Peruvian chocolate. I've made many a chocolate cake with nothing more fancy than a couple of bars of Bourneville and had no complaints thus far.

200g dark chocolate
200g butter, cubed
4 large eggs
200ml milk
100g soft dark brown sugar
160g caster sugar
50g cocoa powder
200g plain flour

2 teaspoons baking powder
½ teaspoon bicarbonate of soda
¼ teaspoon salt

Two 20cm round cake tins, preferably loose-bottomed or spring-form

📷 p56

1   Preheat the oven to 180°C/fan 160°C/gas mark 4. Grease and line the tins with baking parchment.

2   Melt the chocolate either in short bursts in the microwave or in a bowl suspended over (but not touching) simmering water in a pan. Take off the heat then stir in the butter until melted. Whisk in the eggs, milk and both types of sugar.

3   In another bowl, combine the cocoa powder, flour, baking powder, bicarbonate of soda and salt. Add all this to the wet ingredients, gently whisking in for just as long as it takes to combine. The batter will be thick and satiny, inviting you to take first a little finger, then a teaspoon, then a ladle to it.

4   Divide the mixture between the prepared tins and bake for 25-30 minutes. Chocolate cakes suffer for being even slightly over-baked, so be vigilant: test at 25 minutes and keep a close eye on it thereafter. If a knife inserted into the centre of the cake comes out with no more than a couple of crumbs sticking to it, it's ready.

5   Let the cakes cool for a few minutes in their tins before turning them out onto wire racks to finish cooling to room temperature. Sandwich and ice with one of the following types of frosting.

CHOCOLATE FUDGE GANACHE

This dark, fudgy ganache is an event in itself. The same goes here for the chocolate as in the cake recipe above: one with a high percentage of cocoa solids (65% or more) will give a richer, more chocolatey ganache while a lower-quality chocolate will create a frosting with a very different (but no less interesting) flavour — more mellow, caramelised and sweeter.

Makes enough to fill and cover one 20cm sandwich cake
200g dark chocolate
200ml double cream

100g soft dark brown sugar
Pinch of salt
4 tablespoons golden syrup

1   Finely chop the chocolate and set aside in a large bowl.

2   Heat the cream, sugar and salt in a pan over a low heat until scalding — it needs

to be steaming hot but you mustn't let it boil. Pour it slowly over the chopped chocolate, let the mixture sit for a minute, then stir to combine. The chocolate should have melted into the cream, leaving a smooth, shiny ganache mixture. If any chunks of chocolate remain, heat very gently over a pan of simmering water or in the microwave. Stir in the golden syrup.

3   Let the ganache cool to room temperature before using some to sandwich the cake layers together. Then spread the rest on the top and sides. It'll set too firm to use if you keep it in the fridge, but you can put the whole cake in the fridge once iced if you want a firmer set.

BUTTERSCOTCH FROSTING

It seems laughable that a buttercream could be a 'light' alternative to anything, but that's exactly what this is: a lighter, brighter, sweeter alternative to the rich chocolate ganache above. If you're nervous about working with caramel, there's more information on page 316.

**Makes enough to fill and cover one
   20cm sandwich cake**
150g caster sugar
3 tablespoons water

75ml double cream
125g unsalted butter, softened
250-300g icing sugar

1   Combine the sugar and water in a small pan, set over a low heat and very occasionally stir until the sugar has just dissolved. Now increase to a medium-high heat and let bubble, without stirring, until it reaches a rich amber colour. Immediately take off the heat and stir in the cream and 20g of the butter. Set aside to cool.

2   Cream the remaining butter. Slowly beat in the cooled caramel then gradually add the icing sugar until thick, smooth and a workable consistency. Spread over the layers and sides of the cooled cake.

WHISKED CAKES

This next group of cakes is a little different. Rather than using chemical raising agents such as baking powder or bicarbonate of soda, these sponges rely solely on whisked eggs for their rise. The ratios of flour, egg, fat and sugar are very different, too: in order to keep the cake light, only a small amount of butter is used, while the higher volume of egg means that only a little flour is required to set the batter. These cakes are a little trickier than the earlier recipes but they're well worth the effort: they are generally lighter, less crumbly and more versatile. They're therefore well-suited to use in desserts such as trifles and fruit puddings, where the sponge's role is not to provide richness, but to absorb and marry the other flavours in the dish, whether inky fruit juices, punchy liqueurs or rich egg custards.

WHISKING EGG WHITES

Whereas egg yolks are rich, gloriously yellow, neatly spherical, delicious, the whites are near tasteless, slimy, translucent. But the ugly duckling egg white is nothing short of a baking miracle. When introduced to a whisk and a little sugar, the white will slacken, hold bubbles, grow thick with foam and slowly expand to a great billowing cloud of meringue. It really is a sight to see.

But egg whites are tricky things. They won't perform this culinary magic without a little wooing. They'll refuse to whip up to stiff peaks unless the bowl and whisk used are scrupulously clean. There can be no moisture, no dirt or grease, and not a single drop of yolk. For this reason it's often best to use a metal or glass bowl as grease can cling to plastic after even the most thorough clean. I used to be sceptical about whether this egg white paranoia was strictly necessary, but after my fair share of failed meringues I can assure you it really does make a difference. Taking five minutes now to clean and dry your equipment will save you fifteen minutes of futile whisking later.

It may seem like a lot of fuss, but the difference that a few well-beaten egg whites will make to a cake is huge. The air incorporated as you whisk is caught in the egg's protein structure in millions of tiny pockets. During baking, the fierce heat of the oven causes the air in these bubbles to heat and to expand, and the cake will rise. In the Chocolate Lime Mud Cake below, this happens very quickly in the first half of the cooking time: the cake rises impressively and the uppermost layer sets to form a sugar crust. But the mixture underneath, though aerated, won't set as firm as the crust, meaning that as it cools, the bubbles won't be able to support the weight of the cake and it'll sink in the centre. This creates a sublime contrast of texture: a crisp, fractured crust and a gooey inside.

CHOCOLATE LIME MUD CAKE

This is more or less a glorified brownie, I suppose, but I prefer the name mud cake. Unlike a brownie this isn't something to be cut into fat squares, picked up in paper napkins and doled out at a children's party — this is a cake to be eaten with reverence, with a fork. It is moist, almost mousse-like and elegantly dark.

120g dark chocolate
100g unsalted butter, cubed
Zest of 3 limes
Generous pinch of salt
3 large eggs, separated
150g caster sugar

50g plain flour

20cm round cake tin

📷 p58

1   Preheat the oven to 180°C/fan 160°C/gas mark 4. Grease the tin and line its base with a circle of baking parchment.

2   Gently melt the chocolate, either in short bursts in the microwave or in a bowl perched over a pan of simmering water, taking care not to let the bowl touch the water. Off the heat, stir in the butter, allowing it to melt. Add the lime zest and salt. Set aside to cool a little.

3   Whisk together the egg yolks with 50g caster sugar for a couple of minutes until thick and creamy. It's the right consistency when the mixture falling from the whisk leaves a 'ribbon' on the surface of the mix. (See opposite for more information on this elusive 'ribbon stage'.) Make sure you whisk the yolks and sugar together promptly — if the sugar just sits on top of the yolks it will 'cook' the egg, resulting in rubbery bits of yolk, which you'll have to sift out later.

4   In a clean, dry bowl, with an equally clean, dry whisk, beat the egg whites until completely foamy. Continue to whisk, adding a tablespoon of the remaining 100g caster sugar at a time. Whisk well between each addition of sugar. The mixture will become thicker and glossier until, after several minutes of elbow grease, slowly lifting the whisk out of the mixture will leave a 'soft peak' — a tapering curl of meringue, slightly droopy at its tip.

5   Fold the egg yolk mixture into the chocolate with a large spoon. Now fold a third of this chocolatey mixture into the egg whites. As soon as this is basically combined but still marbled, add the next third, and so on. Sift in half the flour. Gently fold until nearly combined, then sift in the remaining flour and fold until just combined. The most important thing here is to keep as much air as possible in the batter — gently cut through with the spoon, don't beat it and mix only for as long as is necessary.

6   Spoon the batter — it should feel light, aerated, wobbly — into the prepared cake tin and bake for 30 minutes. It should be well risen and crisp on top, and a knife inserted into the centre should come out barely clean. Let it cool in its tin before carefully releasing. It's very good while still warm, served with a scoop of good-quality ice cream.

RIBBON STAGE

When whisking sugar into whole eggs or yolks — whether for a custard, cake, or cream — you'll often be told to keep going until the 'ribbon stage' is reached. Ribbon stage is the point at which, when you lift the whisk from the egg and sugar, the mixture is sufficiently thick and creamy that a 'ribbon' of it will sit for some seconds on the surface before sinking back in. If the mixture sinks immediately into the vat, it's not yet ready. You'll notice other changes en route, too: the eggs will grow paler and their texture will move from slimy, to foamy, to velvety thick.

It can take a good ten minutes (depending on the ratio of egg to sugar) to reach ribbon stage if whisking by hand, but it'll be quite a bit quicker if you have an electric whisk. The process is catalysed somewhat by suspending the bowl over a pan of simmering water to gently heat it as you whisk, but it's not a method I've recommended here. It's easy to accidentally cook the mixture if the water is at too vigorous a simmer, and I find it's not much of a 'shortcut' at all once you've gone to the effort of finding the right size pan and bringing the water to the boil. Whisking at room temperature works just fine — it just takes a little patience.

You might start wondering, halfway through the whisking process when the mixture is still resolutely liquid and your arm is beginning to cramp, whether it's really that important to reach ribbon stage. You might convince yourself that I'm either a pedant or a sadist for insisting upon it. But I promise that all the whisking isn't for nothing: it dissolves the sugar and, crucially, aerates the mixture. The result will be springy cake with impressive rise and open structure. The alternative is a pancake-flat disappointment.

TIRAMISU CAKE

All of the elements of tiramisu — thick mascarpone cream, coffee-sodden sponge, a scattering of chocolate — rearranged, neatened and stacked into this impressive dessert cake. A whisked sponge (this one is called a genoise) is the perfect base for this: it's easily cut into thin layers; it absorbs the coffee and is light enough that, miraculously, this cream-slathered, boozy cake still manages to resist feeling stodgy. This certainly feels like a special sort of cake, one to be cut into slender slices, eaten with the good cutlery and washed down with a strong coffee. Somehow, it's a cake that commands respect.

For the sponge:
40g unsalted butter
4 large eggs
125g caster sugar
125g plain flour

For the filling:
400g mascarpone
75g caster sugar
150ml double cream

150ml sweet dessert wine, such as
    muscat or marsala
200ml strong black coffee
50g dark chocolate

**Deep 20cm round cake tin, preferably
    spring-form or loose-bottomed**

📷 p62

1   Preheat the oven to 180°C/fan 160°C/gas mark 4 and grease and line the cake tin with baking parchment.

2   Melt the butter and set aside to cool slightly.

3   Whisk the eggs and sugar together in a large bowl until very thick and creamy. The mixture needs to reach the stage where, as the whisk is lifted out, it will leave a thick ribbon trail that sits on the surface for a short while before sinking back in. This will take a good 10 minutes with a hand-held electric whisk and much longer by hand.

4   Sift a third of the flour into the beaten egg and very gently fold in, taking care to sweep right to the bottom of the bowl as the flour can easily sink through. Sift and fold the next third, and then the final third. Drizzle the butter over the mixture and carefully fold it in.

5   Lightly spoon the batter into the prepared tin and bake for 25–30 minutes. When it's ready it'll be well risen, golden brown, springy and — most importantly — shrinking away from the sides. Let it cool completely in the tin, then unmould.

6   For the filling, beat the mascarpone with the sugar until smooth. Add a little of the double cream to slacken the mascarpone mixture and stir to combine. Pour in the remaining cream, whisking for a minute or two, until smooth and luxuriantly thick. Gradually add the wine and stir in.

7   Using a large, serrated knife or specialist cake-cutting wire, cut the cake horizontally into three thin layers. It can be tricky to cut them evenly, but just go

slowly and breathe deep. It's not an issue if the layers are slightly irregular or even if they break: they'll be smothered in cream soon enough, masking all manner of sins. If you have a completely flat baking tray (one with no rim), a sturdy sheet of plastic or thin chopping board, you can use this to help move each fragile cake layer: just shimmy it underneath the sponge, and slide the cake off afterwards. This is far less risky than using your hands, risking puncturing or tearing the cake in the process. If the thought of cutting the cake into three makes you nervous, just settle for dividing it into two, thicker layers — it won't taste any worse for it. Just use slightly less of the mascarpone cream filling if you do.

8   Drizzle a third of the coffee over one of the layers then spread with a quarter of the cream. Grate a third of the chocolate over the cream then stack the next cake layer on top. Repeat with these layers then spread the final quarter of the cream around the sides of the cake. Use a peeler to scrape thin curls of chocolate for on top.

Variation
Layer the simple genoise sponge above with thick cream, amaretto and punnets of very ripe raspberries. A handful of toasted, flaked almonds wouldn't go amiss either.

PASSION FRUIT CURD SWISS ROLL

This is another variant of the genoise sponge used on page 63, this time rolled around a startlingly sharp, tropical passion fruit curd.
    You can make the components of this cake in whatever order best suits you but I prefer to get the curd made first so that it has ample time to thicken and set in the fridge before using.

For the curd:
5-6 passion fruit
70g caster sugar
1 large egg
25g butter

For the sponge:
20g unsalted butter

3 large eggs
85g caster sugar
80g plain flour
A little icing or caster sugar, to dust

**Swiss roll tin or rimmed baking tray,
    approximately 22x33cm**

1   Halve the passion fruits, scoop out the seeded pulp and strain through a sieve, collecting the juice in a large heatproof bowl. It's well worth taking time to squeeze as much juice out of the seeds as you can — you'll need 60-75ml.

2   Add the sugar, egg and butter to the passion fruit juice. Set the bowl over a pan of barely simmering water, making sure that the bottom of the bowl doesn't touch the water. Patience is critical here: the curd will take a good 10-15 minutes to thicken and it's best to keep stirring it continuously. The curd is ready when it thickly coats the back of the spoon (see page 325 for more on this). The curd will thicken more as it cools so don't worry that it's still quite liquid at this point. Once ready, set aside to cool to room temperature and then refrigerate until thick.

3   Preheat the oven to 200°C/fan 180°C/gas mark 6. Line the tray or swiss roll tin with baking parchment.

4   Melt the butter then set aside to cool. Whisk the eggs and sugar for the sponge until very, very thick and creamy. The mixture needs to be thick enough that when the whisk is lifted out it leaves a ribbon trail that sits on the surface of the batter for several seconds before sinking back in.

5   Sift half of the flour over the surface of the egg mixture, very gently fold in then repeat with the remaining flour. Be sure to dig right to the bottom of the bowl when folding in the flour, as it tends to clump and sink through the mixture unless carefully incorporated.

6   Spoon the batter into the tin and bake for 9–11 minutes, or until well risen, just golden and springy. Take care not to over-bake, which could result in a dry, shrunken cake.

7   Let the baked sponge cool for a minute or two then turn out onto a sheet of baking parchment dusted all over with sugar. Peel the original piece of parchment off the sponge. Now roll the sponge, along with its dusted baking parchment — the parchment will stop the cake layers sticking to each other. Roll from short end to short end, creating a roll around 22cm long. Sit with the join underneath to stop it unfurling then let cool. Cooling it this way helps the sponge to 'remember' this shape and stay tightly rolled later, once filled.

8   After around 30 minutes the sponge should be cool. Unroll it, spread thickly with the passion fruit curd and carefully roll it up again, this time without the layer of baking parchment. If you've got a particularly sweet tooth you could spread with a layer of buttercream, too, to curb the sharpness of the curd.

COFFEE BLACKCURRANT OPÉRA CAKE

After a crescendo of cakes, a symphony of crumbs, layers, frostings, and bar upon bar of butter, we reach this, the most complex of the cake recipes in this book and the most refined. It's a take on a French patisserie classic, comprising four layers of light almond sponge alternating with coffee, inky blackcurrant jam, whipped chocolate buttercream and mirror-shine ganache to top. Coffee and blackcurrant are natural partners: both are deeply fruity, robust, dark. It's an unlikely but seductive flavour combination — the stronger, sultrier cousin of chirpy strawberries-and-cream.

The sponge used here is a joconde sponge. Unlike a genoise sponge, this one has ground almonds as its base and uses whisked egg whites as well as whole eggs. It's doubly whisked, feather-light and — unlike the genoise — quite delicious to eat by itself. You could even add a drop or two of almond extract to bolster the almond flavour if you want but it's a flavour which can overwhelm, so take care.

Because the joconde sponge calls for more egg whites than yolks in total, I've used the remaining yolks for the buttercream to save them from going to waste. This is a traditional French buttercream — a far cry from the simple butter-and-sugar blend we're used to. Egg yolks are cooked with hot sugar syrup and whisked to an unctuously thick cream before you add butter, and butter, and more butter. Melted

chocolate is folded into this mousse-like mixture and the chocolate buttercream is born. Because of the whisked egg base for this type of buttercream it doesn't require vast quantities of icing sugar to thicken it, meaning that it's actually not nearly as sickly sweet as the heavy, lazy British buttercreams.

Scan through the recipe before beginning, to familiarise yourself with the components and get a clear idea of the order in which you'll be making them. Neither the individual elements nor their eventual assembly are particularly difficult; organisation is the key.

Makes one 20x15cm opéra cake, serving 10-12 in suitably elegant slices

For the joconde sponges:
25g unsalted butter
100g ground almonds
100g icing sugar
3 large eggs
3 large egg whites (reserve the yolks for the buttercream)
25g caster sugar
50g plain flour

For the buttercream:
100g dark chocolate
3 large egg yolks
100g caster sugar
2 tablespoons water
100g unsalted butter, very soft
1 teaspoon vanilla extract

For the filling:
150ml very strong black coffee
200g blackcurrant jam

For the ganache:
150ml double cream
100g dark chocolate, finely chopped
1 tablespoon golden syrup

Two 22x33cm rimmed baking trays or swiss roll tins

📷 p66 / p68

For the joconde sponges:

1   Preheat the oven to 200°C/fan 180°C/gas mark 6 and line the tins with baking parchment.

2   Melt the butter and set aside to cool. Meanwhile, whisk the ground almonds, icing sugar and whole eggs together in a large bowl until doubled in volume and very, very thick and creamy. After about 10 minutes of hand-whisking, the mixture should just be getting really thick and voluminous.

3   In a separate, scrupulously clean and dry bowl (preferably not plastic, which tends to retain grease even after the most fastidious clean) and with an equally spotless whisk, whisk the egg whites until completely foamy. Add the caster sugar, half at a time, whisking well between each addition. Continue to whisk until the whites just about hold stiff peaks. Take care not to over-whisk, which can easily happen with such a low proportion of sugar in the mix.

4   Sift the flour into the almond-egg mixture and gently fold in. Watch out for any pockets of flour that may have sunk to the bottom of the bowl. Fold in the melted, cooled butter then, a third at a time, fold in the egg whites.

5   Divide this delicate, airy batter between the cake tins, pushing it gently towards the edges to cover the bottom of each tin. Bake in the preheated oven for 5-7 minutes or until risen, spongy and just beginning to colour in parts. Leave the sponges to cool in their tins.

For the buttercream:

6   Gently melt the chocolate — either in short bursts in the microwave or in a heatproof bowl perched over a pan of simmering water. Set aside to cool a little while you prepare the other ingredients.

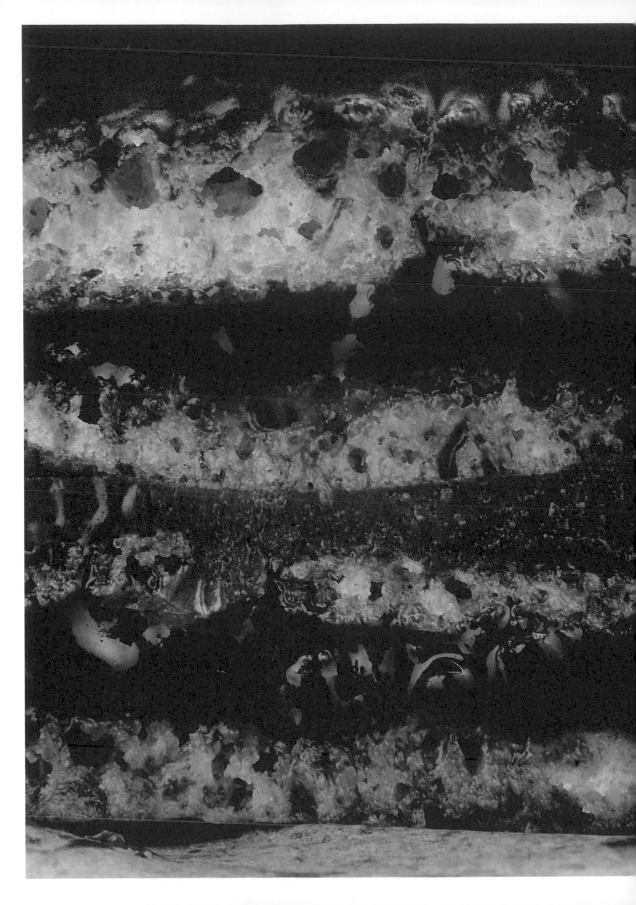

7   Place the egg yolks in a large heatproof bowl. Combine the sugar and water in a small pan and heat, stirring occasionally, very gently. The moment that the sugar has dissolved, stop stirring and let the syrup come to the boil. Let it simmer on a medium-low heat for 30 seconds (you don't want it to colour at all — you're not making caramel!).

8   Pour the hot sugar syrup in a very thin stream into the egg yolks, whisking all the time. Don't add the syrup too quickly, and make sure the mixture is kept constantly moving, otherwise the yolks will cook in parts and the sugar will cool in clumps. Continue to whisk until the mixture is completely cool to the touch. This will take 10 minutes or so. By the time it's cool, the egg mixture should be thick, creamy and pale.

9   Cream the butter until completely smooth and soft, then whisk it, bit by bit, into the egg yolk mixture. Keep beating well between each addition until all of the butter has been incorporated. Add the vanilla extract and stir in the slightly cooled melted chocolate.

To assemble the cake:

10 Halve each sponge crossways to give four rectangles of approximately 22x16cm. Place one piece of sponge on a sheet of baking parchment (this will make it easier to move later) and drizzle a quarter of the coffee over it. Spread with half of the blackcurrant jam.

11 Stack the next rectangle of sponge on top. Drizzle with another quarter of the coffee then spread with three-quarters of the buttercream. Stack the next sponge on top. Drizzle over another quarter of the coffee and spread with the remaining blackcurrant jam.

12 Add the final layer of sponge, soak with the rest of the coffee and spread the remaining buttercream on top. This layer of buttercream is the undercoat for the ganache glaze to come, so it's good to get it as smooth as possible. Transfer the whole thing to the fridge for around an hour to set the layers.

For the ganache:

13 Once the cake is thoroughly chilled and set, prepare the ganache. Heat the cream either in a pan over a low heat or (vigilantly!) in the microwave until scalding but not boiling. Pour the cream over the finely chopped chocolate, let the mixture sit for a moment to melt then stir gently until smooth. Add the golden syrup and combine. The ganache needs to be at pouring consistency — let it cool for a few minutes if it's too runny, or heat gently in a water bath if it's too thick.

14 Pour the ganache over the top of the chilled cake. Some of it will run down the sides — this is no problem. Put the cake in the fridge for 30 minutes.

15 With a large knife, trim the edges of the cake by around a centimetre. This will remove any ganache overflow and expose the spectacular layers. Cut into slender pieces. And it's done!

BREAD

EVERYDAY LOAVES

DAILY BREAD • TIGER BREAD • MILK LOAF

SEEDED TIN LOAF • SODA BREAD

WHOLEMEAL WALNUT COBS

OLIVE & ORANGE CROWN • CHERRY SPELT LOAVES

SWEDISH CARAWAY RYE BREAD • LEEK & CHEESE TART

SMALL BITES & FLATBREADS

GARLIC DOUGH BALLS • RYE CARAWAY BAGELS

CHICKPEA & CUMIN SEED BUNS • SOCCA

CHORIZO & KALE FLATBREAD • PARATHAS

SLOW & STEADY

THREE-CHEESE BRIOCHE

FRENCH COUNTRY BREAD • CIABATTA

There's something deeply cathartic about baking bread. Some like kneading away their frustration (bread is perhaps the only food that works better for being cooked in a foul mood); while for others there's a calm that comes with falling into step with the languorous rhythms of the dough. You might simply find relief in the comforting aroma of the bread as it bakes. But, for me, it's the unpredictability of bread that's so seductive. Yeast is a living organism — it must be fed, watered, treated with care, waited for and worked around, and even after all this it might create a loaf that's denser, squatter, fatter or sweeter than you'd hoped for. There's something liberating about having control wrested from your hands like this: perfectionism takes a back seat and you're left with no choice but to shelve your neuroses, roll up your sleeves and bake.

THE FOUR ELEMENTS

FLOUR

The very essence of bread. Bread calls for something more robust than the very fine, soft flours that we use in our cakes and biscuits. The sort of chewiness that would mark a truly awful cake is the key to a sublime loaf of bread. For this we use — quite literally — strong flour: one higher in protein and gluten than plain flour, resilient in the face of the kneading, pummelling and stretching that bread dough must endure. You can even find very strong flours on the supermarket shelves now, but in my experience these are rarely necessary. For most breads, a canny balancing of flours and careful handling should suffice.

As for the quality of the flour, I have to take issue with those who insist that you source your flour organic and stoneground from your local mill, farming cooperative or similar. Such standards are unrealistic at best. I rarely use anything more exciting than the £1-a-bag strong white you get from the supermarket for the majority of breads and that works perfectly well. Of course, the fewer chemicals in your flour, the better: unbleached, organic flours are fantastic if you can afford them, but bread is no snob and it'll bloom all the same even with the cheapest flour fuel.

Yet there's far more to flour than wheat and white. Take a moment to scan the shelves next time you shop: you'll notice brown, granary, malthouse and wholemeal flours making the most of wheat, to varying degrees, plus barley and rye flours and ancient varieties such as spelt, einkorn and kamut. Gram, rice, soya and potato flours are health-conscious and gluten-free, and in very well-stocked suppliers you might find yet more unusual varieties: teff and amaranth, for example. Each one of these flours is very different and can't be straightforwardly substituted in bread making. For this reason it's well worth learning about each flour's properties (is it high or low in gluten? How absorbent is it? How does it behave?) before heading straight for the fancy stuff in the brown-paper packets. There are few kitchen disappointments more keenly felt than the sticky, heavy failure of a loaf several hours in the making. You'll find more about spelt and rye flours, and their bread-making qualities, preceding the bread recipes that make use of them on page 100 and page 102 respectively.

YEAST

Yeast is bread's beating heart. It is the secret to its flavour, texture and rise. The science of it is difficult, and its mastery an exceptional challenge, but in a nutshell: yeast feeds on the flour, producing carbon dioxide and other by-products. The gases released by the feeding yeast collect in tiny air pockets in the dough. When the dough is baked, the rapid increase in temperature causes these air pockets to expand, pushing the dough upwards and outwards, accounting for the impressive 'oven spring' in the early stages of baking. Yeast develops gluten and so strengthens a bread's structure. But yeast's role in bread making isn't a purely mechanical one — it's also crucial for good flavour. Enzymes in yeast break down complex starches in the flour (starches that have little flavour in themselves) into more basic molecules: sugars. These sugars deepen the flavour of the bread and the colour of the crust — you can often tell if a baked loaf was left to prove for too long by an unusually dark colour, the crust having browned too rapidly.

Yeast is sensitive to its environment, acting more quickly, slowly or not at all depending on the temperature, acidity and hydration of the dough, amongst other factors. I'll go into greater depth about these variables a little later, but for now it'll suffice to say that yeast works well at room temperature; very slowly at cool temperatures; is dormant in the fridge and is dead at anything above 40°C.

Fresh yeast

Fresh yeast, sold in little blocks, is a sandy beige colour, distinctively yeasty in smell and rubbery to touch. There are many who argue that it produces a better-tasting loaf, or at least a more authentic one. I disagree. I've never been able to discern any difference in flavour between loaves made with fresh or with dried yeast. Fresh is also harder to source, shorter-lived and less straightforward to use than the alternative. You're welcome to use it if you prefer, however — there's certainly a charm to it.

To substitute fresh yeast into any of the recipes in this book, swap in 20g for every 7g of instant dried yeast. The fresh yeast should first be crumbled into a couple of tablespoons of lukewarm water with a little sugar or honey and left to stand for about 5 minutes, or until bubbles begin to form on the liquid's surface. You can then add this mixture to the flour along with the rest of the water. Any leftover yeast will keep in the fridge for a few days. Once it starts to look blotchy or dry, it is past its best. If in doubt about the liveliness of your yeast, just 'activate' it by dissolving it as above — if after 5-10 minutes there's no sign of bubbles or any action, it's probably dead.

Active dried yeast

This is most often sold in little tins: small granules of yeast ready to be 'activated' by rehydration in a little warm water with sugar. Prepare it as per the above instructions for fresh yeast. You might want to use slightly more than you would instant dried yeast: approximately 10g (3 teaspoons) for every 7g of instant dried yeast. If you don't increase the amount, be prepared to wait a little longer for the dough to rise.

Instant or fast-action dried yeast

This is the type of yeast called for in every one of the bread recipes in this book. You can find it in small tins, similar to those containing active dried yeast, but it's most commonly sold in boxes of 7g sachets — 7g being conveniently just the right amount to leaven one large loaf of bread. It takes the form of very small, beige-coloured granules. The reason that this is my yeast of choice is quite simply because it is easy to use. Unlike both the fresh and the active dried yeasts above, instant — or fast-action — yeast requires no pre-soaking, no extra stages, no special treatment. Just mix the yeast straight into the flour. One piece of advice: when adding the yeast and salt to the flour in the early stages of the recipe, take care not to pour the salt directly on top of the yeast, or vice versa, as the salt may 'kill' the yeast.

Natural leaven

Some things money can't buy. Natural leaven, spontaneous fermentation, sourdough starter — whatever you'd like to call it — isn't something you'll find in the supermarket baking aisle. Natural leaven makes use of yeasts found naturally in flour and in the air to create a culture that, given plenty of time and a lot of food, will naturally ferment — no added yeast required. Breads made with natural leaven are called sourdoughs and have in recent years spawned a devout following of their own among bread enthusiasts.

WATER

There's no mystery here: plain tap water is all bread needs. If you really want to pamper your loaf, you can feed it mineral water, filtered water and so on, but it'll ultimately taste no better for the fuss.

Water is crucial for yeast to grow, for the dough's gluten to develop, for the rise and spring of the bread and its soft crumb. And the precise amount of water used can make the difference between a chewy, close-textured bagel, a soft sandwich loaf, an open focaccia and a featherweight ciabatta. In general — and of course without taking into account the effects of different flours and so on — the wetter the dough, the more open the crumb. Naturally there are limits to this: too dry and a dough will barely rise at all and will be crumbly and fragile; too wet and it'll be near impossible to shape and bake.

Bakers typically calculate bread ingredient quantities based on the ingredients' weights as percentages of the weight of the flour in the recipe. For example, a bread that uses 300ml water, 500g flour and 10g each of salt and yeast would have a water percentage of 60%, based on the water being three-fifths of the flour weight. For most breads you can expect the amount of liquid to be around 60–70% of the flour weight.

SALT

This can be a contentious issue in bread making. It's sensible to be concerned about salt intake and reasonable to cut excess salt from your diet — ready meals, cheese and cured meats all contain a great deal of the stuff. But there are some foods where salt really can't be omitted, and bread is one of them. Salt strengthens the gluten in bread, stabilising its structure. It also regulates the yeast's activity, preventing the dough from fermenting too quickly. It's an essential component of any loaf (there are one or two exceptions to this rule, but they're unimportant here).

The amount of salt called for in the recipes that follow might seem excessive but it's in line with, and often less than, the amount specified in the majority of bread recipes. A teaspoon of salt weighs approximately 6g: this amount would render a pasta sauce inedible or be disgusting in a cake, but spread through an entire bloomer loaf, where the base ingredients are so bland, it is hardly detectable. And to put it into perspective: one medium slice of that bread would contain just 0.3g of salt — less than you'd find in most supermarket brands. Moderation of consumption is the key to enjoying bread healthily — a salt witch-hunt is not.

As for the type of salt: I always use table salt in my breads and have developed these recipes accordingly. It is practical, potent and easily dissolved. I can't see the use of pretty, crystalline flakes of sea salt in bread unless scattering for flavour, with a splash of olive oil, on top of focaccia or flatbread.

A LOAF'S LIFE

1 MIX

Fat bags of flour poured into the mixing bowl, yeast sachets torn open, a sprinkling of salt and — to rouse the dormant yeast and nudge the dough into action — a couple of mugfuls of lukewarm water. There's no trick to this part of the process, just take care not to empty the yeast directly on top of the salt, or vice versa, and don't be afraid to get your hands dirty.

Bear in mind that the temperature of the ingredients will affect the activity of the yeast: freezing cold water will dramatically slow the rise; too much heat risks stressing the yeast. Unless otherwise specified, all ingredients should be at room temperature, with the exception of the liquid, which should lie somewhere in between tepid and lukewarm. Don't feel too hidebound by rules, though. Respond to the needs of the dough (will it be proved warm and quickly, or cool and slowly?) and the demands of your environment (on a hot day, tap-cold water may suffice), balancing the temperatures of your ingredients accordingly.

2 REST

This stage isn't always necessary but can be useful in wholemeal breads or for a particularly wet dough. It gives the flour a chance to absorb more water before you start kneading. During this time the gluten in the flour will also begin to develop, making kneading easier still. Simply leave the dough to rest for 20-30 minutes after mixing.

3 KNEAD

There's plenty of contradictory advice out there on the importance of kneading. For some, it's crucial; others suggest that you can replace a traditional knead with a less intensive one; and there are those who insist that we can do away with kneading altogether. I'd love to be able to pick a side in this dough debate but unfortunately there isn't a straightforward answer.

The aim of kneading is to develop and strengthen the dough, building a complex network of gluten strands that will underpin the structure of the bread. Vigorous kneading does just this. But so can a less intensive method of stretching and folding the dough at regular intervals. And so too can doing nothing at all: for some breads, an extended rest (as above) is all it takes. As the yeast swings into action, it begins to develop the gluten itself, relieving you of a job. No-knead bread won't tend to rise quite as high as a well-kneaded one, but you may well be happy to make that sacrifice. There are some breads, however, where kneading is non-negotiable — ciabatta (see page 120), for instance.

With that in mind, I'll leave it to you to decide when and how to knead. I've given kneading guidelines for all of these recipes and suggested a couple of techniques on page 80 but if it's a step that you choose to omit: no harm done.

4 RISE OR FIRST PROVE

The least fraught, lowest-maintenance stage of your loaf's life is when you incubate it in a covered bowl and let it ferment. Enzymes in the yeast will begin to break down some of the flour's starches, feast on its sugars and release — amongst other things — carbon dioxide into microscopically small pockets in the surrounding dough. The dough will relax and rise, doubling or even trebling in size. How long this takes depends on the temperature of the dough and its surroundings, the amount and type of yeast and whether the dough contains any enrichment. Butter- or egg-heavy dough will rise more slowly, as will dough left to rise at cool temperatures.

At normal room temperature (18-21°C) the average bread will take 1-1½ hours to complete its first rise. You can speed this up at slightly warmer temperatures but this will come at the expense of good flavour: dough that has proved too rapidly has little flavour and risks tasting yeasty. Conversely, the rise can happily be slowed by moving the dough to a cooler environment or by using colder water. This won't adversely affect the loaf's flavour — in fact, in the majority of cases a slower prove will yield a better bread. Take this one step further by moving the dough to the fridge overnight for this first prove, factoring in a little extra time for the dough to regain momentum to complete its second, post-shaping prove at room temperature.

5 SHAPE

A midway point. There's still a way to go until the loaf is finished, but this is the stage at which the dough — now happily fermenting and active — will finally begin to look something like bread. It's important to shape the dough smoothly and tightly for a good rise, even if baking a simple tin loaf. When it's done well, shaping will create tension across the surface of the bread to act as a sort of skin, controlling the rise and giving an even shape. That said, a lopsided loaf will still taste every bit as good as the most exquisitely plaited wreath or platonic hemisphere cob, so I wouldn't worry too much. See pages 80–82 for more on how to shape.

6 PROVE

Consider this the tumultuous teenage stage: it's during this proving period that the dough will go the rest of the way towards developing the texture, flavour and shape that it'll have as a fully baked loaf. It's not always an easy stage to manage. An under-proved loaf will still feel firm as it enters the oven and will bake to a heavy, close-textured and pale bread. Prove too long and the dough will feel fragile, on the verge of collapse, and it'll emerge from the oven sunken, crumbly and dry. A perfectly proved, oven-ready loaf should be 1½-2 times its original size, springy and soft to the touch yet not fragile. A little finger pressed 1cm into the dough's surface should leave an indentation that slowly fills out again.

7 SCORE

There's far more to scoring a loaf than just gratuitous decorative flourishes. Scoring the dough is a tactical manoeuvre, affording the baker some control over how the loaf rises in the oven. The sudden increase in temperature as a loaf hits the preheated oven causes a tremendous surge in yeast activity and a rapid 'oven spring'. If the crust begins to set before this rise is complete, the swelling dough will break through the crust at a point of weakness, resulting in bulging, asymmetric loaves. But a carefully scored loaf can channel this energy constructively. A deep incision along the length of a tin loaf, for instance, will be a natural site for the dough to rise from, giving a tall, domed shape. See page 84 for more advice on scoring.

8 BAKE

The finish line is now in sight. During the first 10 minutes of the bake, the yeast will have a final surge of energy, working ever faster as the dough's temperature increases until, at around 40°C, the yeast begins to die. This is no sprint finish, though. Even after the bread ceases to rise it must continue to bake until its interior is cooked, setting the crumb. And still, after that, it'll need a while longer if you want a good, thick crust and deep colour. Confronted with the heady aroma of baking bread, and with several hours of mixing, kneading and proving already behind you, patience can be difficult, but it's well worth the wait if you can bear it.

In terms of temperature, a good blast of heat as the bread first enters the oven can maximise the oven spring, which is why many of the recipes here call for 10-15 minutes at a high temperature before decreasing the heat.

And how to tell when the loaf is ready? The most common test is to tap on the underside of the baked loaf — if it sounds hollow, its time is up. The test is far from perfect but it's not bad, either. Look at the colour and thickness of the crust, too — it'll usually be golden brown by the time the crumb inside has set, although small breads and rolls will be cooked through long before a real crust has had the chance to form.

9 COOL
The bread will continue to cook and set as it cools. Resisting the temptation to eat the steaming loaf straight from the oven will pay off in the long run.

HOW TO KNEAD

— Always use as little flour on the work surface as possible. I prefer to use none at all: excess flour incorporated into the dough at this stage risks leaving the bread heavy and uneven.

— Most dough will be sticky, heavy and frustrating at first. This is to be expected. It's only after a vigorous knead that it'll feel smoother and be easier to handle.

— Be prepared to spend a good 10-15 minutes kneading: the dough is ready when it feels robust and elastic and has a satiny sheen to it. The windowpane test (see photo on page 79) is a good indicator of how well kneaded it is. Tear off a small piece of dough and gently stretch it as far as possible between your fingers. If it can be stretched thinly enough that it'll let light through, it's ready. If it tears along the way, knead for slightly longer.

FOR DRIER DOUGH

Using the heel of your hand, push the dough down and out, stretching out a 10-15cm flap of dough. Fold this piece of dough back over on itself then rotate the dough by 90 degrees and stretch, fold and turn again. The key is to keep rotating the dough in order to fully develop the gluten.

FOR WETTER DOUGH

Very wet doughs need a different approach. Kneaded the traditional way, as above, they'll cling to the work surface, weld to your hands and remain flabbily lifeless in the face of even the most enthusiastic knead. Quick, light handling is needed. The photos opposite and the following instructions offer a step-by-step guide.

With splayed fingers, slide both hands underneath the dough from either side. Lift it slightly above the work surface. Stretch the dough outwards, pulling sideways until it feels tighter. Fold the elongated dough in half, rotate by 90 degrees (leaving the fold running horizontally) and set down on the work surface. Again with fingers splayed, scoop your hands back under the dough from either side then stretch, fold and turn again. You should feel it become gradually more resistant and less sticky.

HOW TO SHAPE

— Surface tension is the most important thing here. Gather any excess dough underneath, leaving the top taut and firm.

— Use only as much flour on the work surface as is absolutely necessary.

— Swift, decisive movements when shaping will minimise sticking.

COB 📷 p83

1 Shape the dough into a very rough ball.

2 Fold the dough in on itself a few times, almost as if lightly kneading it. By doing this, you'll be gathering the loose dough at the top, leaving the underneath smooth and taut. You don't want to overdo this, as it'll result in the dough becoming too tight and rupturing as it rises. A few folds should suffice.

3 Turn the ball upside down, hiding the gathering and joins underneath and exposing the neater surface on top.

4 The next stage is to tighten the 'skin', smooth out any wrinkles and ensure even rising. Lay your hands, palms facing upwards, either side of the dough. Bring your hands quickly together to meet underneath the dough then move them outwards in opposite directions — one sliding forwards, one sliding back — out from underneath the dough. It's a difficult action to describe, but it's best thought of as a slicing motion, gathering the dough tightly underneath then deftly sliding your hands back out again before the dough has a chance to stick to them.

BAPS AND BUNS

1 Shape each portion of dough into a rough ball.

2 For perfectly risen buns, fold the dough over on itself (as described above) before proceeding. Otherwise, just roll the dough around in a circle, under a roundly cupped palm, on a clean surface. The aim is to keep the ball roughly upright, just gently smoothing its shape using this motion.

TIN LOAF OR BLOOMER

1 Form the dough into a rough oval shape, about as long as the loaf tin, if using.

2 Gather any loose dough underneath, either by folding the dough in on itself or by 'slicing' it with your hands (see Cob, steps 2-4, above).

3 Tuck the tapered ends of the oval neatly underneath to give the dough a smooth upper surface.

BATONS OR BAGUETTES

1 Using both hands, roll the dough backwards and forwards on a clean (or very lightly floured) surface until it forms a long sausage shape. Remember that it will grow far fatter as it rises, so it's best to start with a piece of dough significantly thinner than the size you envisage for the finished bread.

2 Tuck the tapered ends of the dough underneath, to give a clean, blunt shape.

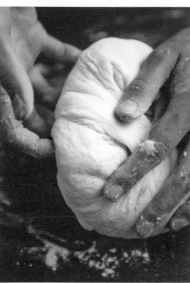

HOW TO SCORE

— A very, very sharp knife is crucial: alternatively you could use a razor blade or a lame (a double-edged blade made precisely for scoring dough).

— Use firm, decisive strokes and move quickly: hesitation and a shaky hand will cause the blade to stick and the dough to snag and tear.

— Hold the blade at a slight angle to the dough's surface — not perpendicular to it. The aim is to cut a sort of flap of dough that will open slowly as the bread rises and bakes.

— Cater the type and depth of incision to the loaf being scored: a loaf that won't rise much in the oven, such as a dark rye, can be given a quite decorative, shallow scoring pattern. Other loaves will require greater pragmatism, scoring a little deeper and with just a few strokes.

— Always dust with flour before scoring, never after. This is only for the sake of the aesthetic, mind you, not practicality.

WHY IS MY BREAD...

Here are a few of the most common pitfalls encountered when baking bread. You'll notice that for every complaint, there are a number of potential explanations. A dense loaf, for example, could have started with problems in the ingredients, or could have developed during the kneading, the proving or the cooking — with so many stages and techniques involved, it can be difficult to pinpoint exactly where and when a loaf went wrong. Yeast's unpredictability and sensitivity — so exciting when they work to your favour — can quickly become infuriating. And yet bread isn't an unsolvable riddle or a sorcerer's trick: both good and bad loaves can be explained. I hope that the problems, causes and solutions below will help.

...DRY AND DENSE?

— A dry, heavy loaf has likely sunk in the oven, having been over-proved. The yeast has exhausted itself before the loaf reached the oven. Try proving in a cooler place or for a shorter time.

— Too little water in the dough. Most dough should be slightly sticky when you begin to knead it — if it's already perfectly dry and smooth pre-kneading you should add a little more water.

— Too much flour incorporated during the kneading or shaping stages. Keep dusting to a minimum.

...WET AND DENSE?

— Under-proved breads tend to be very close-textured, particularly at the base of the loaf, with a sticky, claggy feel. You could bake for slightly longer to help dry it, but to prevent this in future, give the bread a longer second prove.

— Under-baked — return the loaf to the oven on a medium heat until it sounds hollow when tapped underneath.

— A wet and dense texture might just be a side effect of the types of flour used. A high proportion of rye (30% upwards) can do this and it's common in all-wholemeal loaves, too. A dose of strong white flour in these loaves will go a long way towards lightening the texture.

— If you don't develop the gluten enough, particularly wet doughs might struggle to rise. A vigorous kneading period ought to prevent this.

...CRUST TOO DARK?

— A good, deep golden-brown crust is a fantastic thing, but if it tips over from bronzed to burnt, it may be that the oven temperature was too high, or the bake time too long.

— Over-proved loaves have a greater proportion of their starches broken down into sugars, which then brown very quickly in the oven.

— Some glazes darken very quickly; egg washes are applied with just this in mind.

...CRUST SO PALE?

— Too few sugars in an under-proved loaf leave the crust looking pasty and sad. Wait longer on the second prove before baking next time.

...POORLY RISEN?

— This is nearly always due to expired or spoiled yeast. Always check the expiry date on the packet, be careful if using fresh yeast (which spoils quickly) and if in any doubt, 'activate' the yeast in a little warm water to test it (see page 74).

— It could also be that the yeast has been affected by one of the ingredients added to the dough: if the water was too hot, for instance, or if the salt was added directly on top of the yeast.

...UNEVENLY SHAPED OR TORN?

— Bread that is not scored, or scored too shallowly, is likely to rupture in the oven as it rapidly expands.

— Under-proved loaves rise very quickly, tearing as they bake. Leave for slightly longer, or in a warmer spot, before baking.

...YEASTY?

— A little yeast goes a long way, it's powerful stuff. Too much yeast will leave a loaf tasting distinctively yeasty and put it at risk of over-proving.

— The dough was proved too quickly, or in too warm an environment. Yeast will work just fine at room temperature: don't be tempted to stash the sensitive dough in an airing cupboard, proving drawer or top oven.

...DOUGH RISING SO SLOWLY?

— Bread takes time, and slowly proved bread tastes better, so it's important to be patient. But if the dough is rising very slowly it may be that the temperature — either of the room or the ingredients used — is too low. Using cold tap water in the depths of winter will naturally slow the action of the yeast.

— Enrichments in the dough, including butter, eggs or oil, will slow the action of the yeast and result in a lengthier rise. In this case, you will just have to allow extra time for the dough to rise.

— Too much salt will also inhibit the yeast and slow down the rise. A certain amount of salt is necessary to regulate the yeast's growth, but too much — anything over 10g per 500g flour — can result in a longer rising period.

— Too little yeast. It makes sense that the more yeast there is working on the dough, the faster the job of rising will get done. Preferments (see page 118), for instance, which are allowed to ferment in advance to give the dough extra flavour and a better structure, use only a fraction of a teaspoon of yeast and therefore take up to 18 hours to double in size.

EVERYDAY LOAVES

DAILY BREAD

This is a basic loaf, perfect for the novice bread baker. It's a recipe stripped back to its bare bones with just five ingredients, a simple method and speedy execution. The only flourish is the addition of a little oil, giving a more tender finished bread and a more malleable, less sticky dough in the meantime. But for all its simplicity this daily bread still delights: watch it transform from putty, to supple dough, to soft-skinned cob, to crusty loaf. There's nothing quotidian about it.

Makes 1 large cob loaf
500g strong white flour
7g instant dried yeast
1½ teaspoons salt

310ml lukewarm water
2 tablespoons olive oil

 p88

1   Combine the flour and yeast in a large bowl. Stir in the salt, followed by the water and oil. Bring the dough together into a sticky mass then let it sit for 20 minutes or so at room temperature. You can skip this resting time if you want, but the dough will be less sticky to knead if you do wait.

2   Knead the rested dough for a good 10–15 minutes. It ought to feel elastic, smooth and robust by the time you're done. (See the kneading techniques on page 80 for more guidance.) Put the dough in a large, lightly greased bowl, cover with cling film or a dampened kitchen towel and leave to double in size — either 1–1½ hours at room temperature or overnight in the fridge.

3   Shape your dough into a cob or bloomer shape (see page 82 for instructions on how best to shape the dough) and let prove at room temperature in a draught-free spot until doubled in size. I usually leave mine in the kitchen. How long this takes will depend on the temperature of your room and of the dough, but it'll usually be just under an hour. If your dough had its first rise in the fridge overnight, the yeast will still be lethargic from the residual cold. In this case, the proving period could be as long as 1½–2 hours. Meanwhile, preheat the oven to 220°C/fan 200°C/gas mark 7.

4   Lightly dust the top of the dough with flour and, using a sharp knife, score either a deep cross or a row of slits into the loaf. Bake in the preheated oven for 15 minutes before reducing the temperature to 190°C/fan 170°C/gas mark 5 and leave for a further 30 minutes. It'll be baked by around a total of 35 minutes, but the extra 10 minutes helps to form a good, deeply coloured crust. Give the loaf plenty of time to cool completely before eating, as the inside will still be gummy and moist when first baked.

FLOURY BAPS

Makes 8 baps
1 quantity of Daily Bread dough (see page 89)

1   Prepare the dough and let it rise as given in the recipe. Divide the risen dough into 8 portions. Shape each piece into a ball shape by rolling under your cupped palm on a clean surface (see page 82 for further shaping instructions). Place the balls a few centimetres apart on a large baking tray and lightly pat each one down to a fat circle of dough just under an inch thick.

2   Let the baps prove at room temperature in a draught-free place until visibly puffy and almost double their original size. This should take 45-60 minutes, possibly a little longer if the dough had its first prove in the fridge overnight. Meanwhile, preheat the oven to 180°C/fan 160°C/gas mark 4.

3   Liberally sprinkle the risen baps with flour and bake in the preheated oven for 20 minutes. For golden, soft-crusted buns, leave out the dusting of flour and brush instead with full-fat milk or even single cream before baking.

BATONS

With batons, crust is key: it should be golden and firm, cracking into thick shards under the bread knife, in contrast to the soft, white crumb within. A hot and steamy oven, together with a generous baking time, will help to achieve this. If crust isn't your thing, a 180°C/fan 160°C/gas mark 4 oven for 20 minutes will suffice, and you needn't worry about the water tray, either.

Makes 3 batons
1 quantity of Daily Bread dough (see page 89)

1   Prepare the dough and let it have its first rise. Divide the risen dough into three pieces. On a very lightly floured work surface, roll each piece of dough into a sausage shape, around 20cm long. Set the batons on a large baking tray.

2   Let the batons prove at room temperature until just over 1½ times their original size. This should take around 45 minutes, possibly a little longer if the dough had its first rise in the fridge overnight, or shorter in a particularly warm environment. Meanwhile, preheat the oven to 240°C/fan 220°C/gas mark 9 (or as high as your oven will go). Place another baking tray on a low shelf in the oven.

3   Score each risen baton with three or four diagonal slits (see page 84) and put them in the oven. Pour a few tablespoons of water onto the now hot tray on the lower shelf of the oven. Bake for 10 minutes before reducing the temperature to 200°C/fan 180°C/gas mark 6 and baking for a further 15 minutes. Surprisingly, the sauna conditions created in the early stages of the bake help to create a crustier crust. Just watch out for the blast of steam when you open the oven door.

CRUST

Crust is a deeply subjective thing. Some like a very thin, almost papery crust. Others prefer the thick, chewy sort that must be quite forcefully sawed through with the bread knife. Having spent a childhood pushing even the flimsiest crusts to the side of plates, hiding them deep in coat pockets and throwing them to the ducks, I've now embraced the crust. For me, it must be thin but beautifully crisp, prone to shattering into golden, jagged shards.

The ingredients in a bread will have some bearing on the calibre of the crust — fat in the dough, for instance, will inhibit crust formation — but most of the magic is in the baking. Most breads will feel crusty immediately after leaving the oven, but all too often they deteriorate as they cool, the escaping steam from the loaf's centre softening the crust. Quite simply, crust that lasts requires a long cooking time to dry the crumb and thicken the crust, while a softer crust can be achieved by baking for a shorter time at a slightly higher temperature.

And a loaf baked just right will, quite literally, sing: whispering, snapping and crackling as it cools and the red-brown crust splits tectonically into an intricate jigsaw. It might just be the most beautiful sound in the world... or in the kitchen, at least.

TIGER BREAD

There's something instantly inviting about the fractured, volcanic surface of a loaf of tiger bread. It's an easy finish to achieve and an impressive upgrade from a simple dusting of flour. A paste of rice flour is brushed over the surface of the dough during its final prove prior to baking. This paste cooks more quickly than the bread, splintering into its characteristic crags and rifts as the dough continues to expand beneath it. It also browns quickly, though, so you may have to decrease the oven temperature or reduce the cooking time slightly, especially for larger loaves, if the crust begins to look ominously dark.

1 quantity of Daily Bread dough
  (see page 89)

For the paste:
½ teaspoon instant dried yeast
1 teaspoon sugar

¼ teaspoon salt
60g rice flour
100ml lukewarm water
1 teaspoon oil, preferably sesame

📷 p92

1   Prepare, rise and shape the dough into a cob (see page 82). During the second prove prepare the paste: combine the dry ingredients then stir through the wet ingredients to give a thick batter. Brush the rising dough generously with this paste and leave until fully risen (the dough ought to approximately double in size), preheating the oven to 220°C/fan 200°C/gas mark 7 in the meantime. Bake according to the instructions given for the Daily Bread (page 89) reducing the oven temperature to 190°C/fan 170°C/gas mark 5 after 15 minutes. You may need to take the loaf out of the oven before the standard 45-minute baking time is up, because this crust will brown quickly. As long as a loaf of this size has had 30 minutes in the oven, it will be sufficiently cooked.

THE TIN LOAF

For all the versatility and artisanal aesthetics of free-form loaves, I can't help drifting back to the standard tin loaf. There was always a parade of proud, muffin-topped tin loaves queued neatly along the back wall of the bakery near our family home in Essex, each destined for a whirlwind romance with shades of jam, cheese and pickle, Marmite or even, on weekends and birthdays, sausages and brown sauce. I like their ungainly top-heaviness, I like the simplicity, I like that my tin at home — free with some promotion or other — suggestively emblazons 'Lurpak' across the side of each loaf. Couronne, croissant and *kugelhopf* all you like — I know what my desert island loaf would be.

MILK LOAF

I worry we're in danger of forgetting the simple pleasures of the plain sandwich loaf. This isn't a loaf that confronts you on those fragile, bleary-eyed mornings with an impenetrable crust and sterling sourdough lineage. It's a gentler sort of bread: thin-crusted and pillowy soft inside. Toast it, mop up gravy with it or cut it into neat sandwich triangles. Best of all, and incidentally the best hangover cure I have ever had, make French toast with it, dipping in beaten egg, milk and cinnamon, frying in a little butter and dredging with icing sugar.

I've called for full-fat milk here — the higher fat content helps to give a more tender crust and crumb. You can use semi-skimmed if you really want but the resulting bread won't be quite as delicately soft. Soya milk also works very well.

450g strong white flour
7g instant dried yeast
1 teaspoon salt
330ml full-fat milk, plus extra to glaze

Butter or oil, to grease

900g loaf tin

1   Combine the flour and yeast in a large bowl then stir in the salt. Over a very low heat, warm the milk in a small pan until just lukewarm. Add the milk to the flour mixture and use your hands to mix the ingredients. Once combined, turn the dough out onto the work surface and knead for a good 10 minutes, possibly nearer to 15 minutes, until smooth and elastic. It should pass the windowpane test (see page 80).

2   Place the dough into a large bowl, cover with cling film or a plate and let it rise for 60–90 minutes. Exactly how long this takes will depend on the temperature of the room and of the ingredients. It's ready once it has doubled in size.

3   Very lightly grease the loaf tin. Shape the loaf into a rugby ball shape (see page 82 for shaping tips), making sure that you fold it over into itself with a join underneath, creating a tight 'skin' on the exterior. This will help it to keep a good shape as it rises and bakes.

4   Let the dough prove in the tin for 45–60 minutes, or until it has almost doubled in size again. Meanwhile, preheat the oven to 180°C/fan 160°C/gas mark 4.

5   Once the loaf has risen, brush it with milk and score, slightly off-centre, along its length using a razor blade or a very sharp kitchen knife. Bake for 50 minutes, brushing with milk again halfway through. Let cool completely before slicing.

SEEDED TIN LOAF

If you're suffering from the endemic carb-concern that's blighting our mealtimes, I beg you to shelve it just for a moment. This loaf is wholesome without being joyless, filling but not heavy. It's packed with goodness. There are of course carbohydrates in here, but there's also a hefty dose of fibre plus linseeds, pumpkin seeds, nutty sunflower seeds... Eating a slice ought to be all pleasure, no guilt. Relish it with cheese and a thick spread of mango chutney. It's a meal to make princes of paupers.

300g strong white flour
100g wholemeal flour
7g instant dried yeast
¾ teaspoon salt
270ml lukewarm water
150g seeds (sunflower, pumpkin,
    linseed or sesame are all good)

Oil, to grease

900g loaf tin

◻ p95

1   Combine the flours and yeast then stir in the salt. Add the lukewarm water. Mix with your hands until the liquid is well integrated and leave the dough to rest for 20 minutes, during which time it'll absorb more of the water. Now knead for 10 minutes before adding the seeds and kneading lightly to combine. Set the dough aside in a large, covered bowl to rise at room temperature. It'll need around 1½ hours — it's ready when it has doubled in size.

2   Lightly grease the loaf tin with oil. Turn the dough out and shape into a fat log shape and set it in the tin. Leave to prove at room temperature in a draught-free spot for approximately 1 hour, or until the loaf is between 1½ and 2 times its original size. Meanwhile, preheat the oven to 200°C/fan 180°C/gas mark 6.

3   Score the risen loaf with a very sharp knife: cut an incision about 1.5cm deep straight along its length. Bake for 10 minutes then reduce the oven temperature to 180°C/fan 160°C/gas mark 4 and bake for a further 40 minutes.

SODA BREAD

For days when time is short, soda bread — leavened only with bicarbonate of soda — makes a fine alternative to slow-moving yeasted breads. The buttermilk leaves a bright acidity, the bicarbonate of soda a slight tang, and the sugar a gentle sweetness to round it all off. It is so delicious that I often wonder, as I greedily eat it in thick wedges, why I ever bother with yeast at all.

330g plain wholemeal flour, plus extra,
    to dust
1 teaspoon bicarbonate of soda
½ teaspoon salt

2 tablespoons soft dark brown sugar
300ml buttermilk

 p96

1   Preheat the oven to 180°C/fan 160°C/gas mark 4. Combine the dry ingredients in
    a large bowl then stir through the buttermilk. Knead the sticky dough just very
    lightly and then shape — using plenty of flour to dust — into a rough ball. Sit this
    on a floured tray, score a deep cross into its top and bake in the preheated oven
    for 50 minutes. It couldn't be simpler.

THE WHOLE STORY

Not quite as easy to work with as white flour, but roughly ten thousand times more interesting, wholemeal flour is a miracle cure for all blandly anaemic white loaves. Swapping as little as 10% of the white flour for wholemeal will begin to yield a more interesting, rounded flavour, while at amounts approaching half the bread will develop a deeply savoury taste.

Because wholemeal flour contains all parts of the grain — endosperm, germ and bran — it has a coarser texture than white flour and higher water absorbency. The percentage of fibrous bran in the flour also means there's less gluten here than in white flour. As such, loaves made with only wholemeal flour can tend to be heavy. I prefer to lighten the texture by using a blend of wholemeal and white flours.

WHOLEMEAL WALNUT COBS

Nutty wholemeal flour and a double dose of walnut are the secrets to this mellow, flavourful bread. It puts paid to the old myth positioning austere, cardboard wholemeal opposite the saintly Sliced White. It has even seduced one of my most stubbornly wholemeal-phobic friends.

Once cut, this bread stales quickly, so I've given directions here for baking two small cob loaves rather than a large loaf. Made this way, they can be relished one at a time. It also means a higher ratio of crust to crumb, which to my mind can't be a bad thing. If you'd rather make a single loaf, bake for 45-50 minutes and be extra conscientious when shaping to ensure an even rise.

Makes 2 small cob loaves
200g walnuts
250g strong white flour
150g wholemeal flour
7g instant dried yeast

1 teaspoon salt
250ml lukewarm water
1 tablespoon honey
1 egg, lightly beaten, to glaze (optional)

1   Grind 100g of the walnuts in a food processor or coffee grinder. Stop as soon as the nuts resemble coarse sand, as over-grinding will prompt the nuts to release their natural oils, creating a greasy paste.

2   Mix the ground walnuts with the flours and yeast in a large bowl then stir in the salt. Add the water and honey and combine. Let the dough rest for 20 minutes before kneading for 10 minutes (see page 80). The kneaded dough won't become quite as smooth and elastic as you might be used to, due to the ground nuts and proportion of wholemeal flour. Roughly chop the remaining walnuts and knead them into the dough. Set aside in a large, covered bowl to rise for approximately 1½ hours, or until roughly 1½ times its original size.

3   Halve the dough and shape into two small, round cobs (see page 82 for tips on shaping) on a lightly floured work surface. Leave to prove on a baking tray at room temperature for 45-60 minutes, during which time the loaves should increase in size by half as much again. Meanwhile, preheat the oven to 180°C/ fan 160°C/gas mark 4.

4   Brush the top of each loaf with the egg, if using. With a very sharp knife, score
     a 1cm-deep criss-cross pattern, much like a noughts and crosses grid, into each.
     Bake for 35-45 minutes, depending on how thick you'd like your crust.

Variation
It's not an innovative idea, but the addition of just a handful of raisins will make a big
difference to these loaves. The toasted, slightly bitter taste of walnut will be balanced
by the sweet raisins, and the bread will take on a slightly caramelised flavour. It
makes a fine tea bread.

OLIVE & ORANGE CROWN

A happy glug of olive oil here is the secret to a rich, tender loaf. Orange and olive
might not be an obvious pairing but they strike a delicate balance, an echo of citrus
playing off the punchy saltiness of the olives. Though I'm loath to descend into food
snobbery, it has to be said: the quality of the olives really is paramount. Olive bread
made with rubbery, briny cheap olives really won't be the same. That said, olive bread
is arguably — like pizza — good even when it's bad.

350g strong white flour, plus extra to dust   Zest of 1 orange
1½ teaspoons instant dried yeast   100g Kalamata olives, chopped and
¾ teaspoon salt   patted dry
60ml olive oil
175ml cool water   📷 p99

1   Combine the flour and yeast in a large bowl then stir in the salt. Add the oil, water
     and orange zest and mix roughly to combine. Knead the dough. It'll be wet and
     uncooperative to start with but the high oil content should stop it from sticking
     too much. Persevere until it is elastic and no longer sticky — this will take about
     10 minutes. Knead in the chopped olives and set the dough in a large, covered
     bowl to rise at room temperature for 1½-2 hours, or until doubled in size.

2   On a lightly floured work surface, divide the dough into 5 pieces and roll each into
     an oval shape — a little like a rugby ball. Arrange the portions in a circle shape on
     a large baking tray, each piece of dough very close to, but not quite touching, its
     neighbours (they will swell and join as they rise and bake). Leave to prove for
     40-50 minutes at room temperature — it ought to almost double in size.
     Meanwhile preheat the oven to 220°C/fan 200°C/gas mark 7.

3   Dust the risen dough with flour, score lightly along the length of each oval
     of dough and bake for 10 minutes before reducing the temperature to 200°C/
     fan 180°C/gas mark 6 and baking for a further 25 minutes.

SPELT FLOUR

Spelt, an ancient cousin of wheat, is an easy way to ring the changes in your bread baking. It brings with it a light nutty taste, slight sweetness and moist texture. Its relation to wheat means that it's reasonably easy to substitute into most normal wheat bread recipes — there are just a couple of things to bear in mind.

Firstly: spelt, though reasonably high in gluten, is far less resilient than wheat flour. It needs to be handled sympathetically. When kneading all-spelt dough it's crucial not to overdo it: after just a couple of minutes of kneading you'll notice the dough tighten and soon after it'll begin to tear. I find it best to knead spelt dough for only a minute or so, enlivening it without overworking it.

This weak gluten also means that spelt loaves run the risk of 'flowing', even after shaping. The dough may seem flabby; the loaf may spread apathetically across the baking tray — it certainly won't stand as proud as an average white wheat loaf. However, there are things that can be done to combat this. Proper shaping technique will do wonders (see pages 80–82), as will pre-shaping: after the first rise, shape the dough into a ball as usual, then leave for 5 minutes and shape again. The dough will 'flow' a little in the 5 minutes following the pre-shape but should hold better after the second shaping. It's also worth noting that small loaves will hold their shape better than very large, heavy ones.

But beyond that there's little point trying to work against the grain. If spelt spreads, it spreads: intricately shaped loaves may be out of the question, but you'll still be able to bake a fine cob or bloomer. So what if it's a little squat?

Secondly, and it's an important point: spelt flour ferments faster than wheat flour, putting your dough at great risk of over-proving. To minimise the possibility of the dough exhausting itself, it's best to let shaped spelt loaves prove for only as long as it takes for them to increase in size by half as much again. The loaf will quite quickly begin to feel fragile so it's useful to have the oven preheated to a high temperature slightly in advance so that you can transfer the loaf into the heat the moment it's proved.

CHERRY SPELT LOAVES

Coffee gives this bread a subtle darkness against which the cherries taste all the more excitingly tart. If you can't find white spelt flour (it seems to be less easy to source than its wholemeal counterpart) you can use strong white wheat flour instead.

Spelt flour has a far shorter window for baking than wheat flour: it'll very quickly turn from oven-ready to over-proved. For this reason, the rise and proving times specified are a little shorter than for many of the other breads in the book. You'll also notice that the dough needs very little kneading.

Makes 2 small loaves
150g wholemeal spelt flour
360g white spelt flour or strong
    white flour
7g instant dried yeast
1 teaspoon salt

2 tablespoons caster or soft light
    brown sugar
360ml black coffee, lukewarm
100–150g whole dried cherries

📷 p101

1 Combine the flours and yeast in a large bowl then stir in the salt and sugar. Pour in the coffee, working the dough with your hands until fully mixed. Lightly knead the cherries into the dough, working it for no longer than a minute. Place the dough into a clean bowl, cover and leave to rise at room temperature for around an hour. By the end of this hour it should be at least 1½ times its original size.

2 Divide the risen dough into two, shaping each piece into a neat cob or rugby ball shape and spacing well apart on a large baking tray (or use two trays, if necessary — spelt dough tends to spread). It's important to shape tightly and neatly to ensure a decent rise from these fragile loaves. (There's more information on correct shaping technique on page 82 should you need it.) Let the loaves prove at room temperature in a draught-free spot for 30-40 minutes if using 100% spelt flour or up to an hour if you swapped strong white flour for a portion of the spelt. Preheat the oven to 240°C/fan 220°C/gas mark 9 in the meantime. The loaves are ready to bake as soon as they're 1½ times their original size; if you wait until they've doubled you will have waited too long, and the loaves risk collapsing.

3 Dust the risen breads with flour, score their tops and bake for 10 minutes before reducing the temperature to 200°C/fan 180°C/gas mark 6 and baking for a further 20-25 minutes, depending on how crusty you like your bread. Once completely cool, enjoy the loaves cut into slices no more than 1cm thick, toasted and spread liberally with butter and a good cherry jam.

RYE FLOUR

Rye is one of the most exciting and difficult flours in the baker's arsenal. You can find dark, medium or light varieties (corresponding to the varying percentages of bran and germ left in the flour) if you look hard enough, but the standard kind on British supermarket shelves is dark rye, the most wholemeal version. It's not thrilling to look at — greyish, speckled with dark, ashy flecks of bran — but rye bread is a pleasure to eat: sweeter than wheat, nutty and very slightly sour.

Unfortunately this remarkable flavour comes at a cost. Rye has little gluten, and the gluten it has is very weak, resulting in dense loaves. If this were the extent of rye's difficulties I wouldn't much mind — there is, after all, something uniquely satisfying about a slim slice of treacly, heavy rye bread. But there are other problems to be overcome: enzyme overload in 100% rye breads can lead to something called (rather dramatically) 'starch attack'. To take away the apocalyptic spin, this is just what happens when the enzymes break down the rye flour, resulting in a slurry of sugars that will remain resolutely sticky, almost cement-like, even after baking.

There are ways to combat the decline and fall of rye breads, among them fostering a slightly more acidic environment in order to inhibit the overactive enzymes. Sometimes this might mean adding an acidic ingredient such as treacle or honey. Alternatively, sourdoughs naturally provide that sort of acidic microclimate, which is why you'll find that many rye breads are some days in the making. But you needn't be a martyr to your rye if you can be savvy with flour combining. By using just a small proportion of dark rye flour in a loaf made primarily of strong wheat flour, you'll be able to counter the self-destructive tendencies of rye while still enjoying its inimitable flavour.

SWEDISH CARAWAY RYE BREAD

Here in the UK, bread tends to be something of a wheat-wash; the mild climate is so perfect for cultivating wheat that it often means our other grains are overlooked. Yet if we turn to northern Europe (with cooler climes where wheat struggles to grow) there's a rich culture of rye bread, from heavy German *vollkornbrot* to Danish *rugbrød* and crisp Norwegian *knekkebrød*.

Here's a chewy Swedish rye bread that carries on that tradition. I'm a big fan of its dark, grungy density. Grassy caraway, black treacle and rye mean that this is a bread that packs a punch. Because bread would be very dull indeed if it began and ended with airy sandwich loaves.

Using three different flours for one loaf might seem a lot like hard work but it's the key to a full-flavoured bread that, though close-textured, avoids becoming claggy. You can switch the wholemeal flour for an equal weight of strong white flour if you want, increasing the gluten levels to give a lighter, spongier texture.

Makes 2 small loaves
350g strong white flour
125g wholemeal flour
125g dark rye flour
7g instant dried yeast
1 teaspoon salt
1 tablespoon caster or light brown sugar

1 teaspoon caraway or fennel seeds
Zest of 1 orange
4 tablespoons orange juice
300ml lukewarm water
2 tablespoons black treacle

📷 p103

1 Combine all three flours and the yeast in a large bowl then stir in the salt, sugar and the seeds. In a separate bowl, beat together the orange zest and juice, water and treacle. Add this to the dry ingredients, mix and then knead for 10 minutes until it's stronger, stretchier and no longer sticky.

2 Let the dough rise in a large, covered bowl at room temperature for 1–1½ hours, or until just under double its original size.

3 Divide in half, shaping each half into a ball then patting down to a fat, round disc of dough, about 5cm thick. Place the two loaves on lightly floured baking trays and let prove again at room temperature for 45–60 minutes, until 1½ times their original size. Take care not to over-prove the dough. Meanwhile, preheat the oven to 200°C/fan 180°C/gas mark 6.

4 Dust the tops of the loaves with a little flour then score using whatever pattern you want — use swift, firm strokes and use a very sharp knife. There are some more tips on scoring on page 84.

5 Bake for 40–45 minutes. Let it cool completely before slicing.

LEEK & CHEESE TART

This French tart, properly called *flamiche*, combines soft leeks and hard cheese in an enriched dough. Bread provides a far more substantial case than the shortcrust pastry we're used to. It's an exceptional foil to the richness of the filling, too — when one is confronted, blissfully, with a forkful of quivering crème fraîche, cheese and leek, a traditional butter-heavy pastry case can feel like overkill. Serve this with nothing more than a handful of peppery salad leaves.

   You'd usually chill brioche-type dough such as this prior to its second prove, thus setting the butter and making shaping easier, but I'm not convinced it's necessary here: I've used less butter than in a standard brioche, yielding a dough that, though rich, acts in much the same way as a 'normal' bread dough might.

The filling puffs up quite magnificently in the oven, so take care not to overfill. The amount of crust and filling is just right for my deep pie dish at home, but should it be too much for your dish or tin, just use less accordingly. Any leftovers also make a fine sauce when tossed through linguine.

Serves 6
250g strong white flour
1 teaspoon instant dried yeast
½ teaspoon salt
110ml lukewarm water
1 large egg
50g unsalted butter, softened

For the filling:
50g unsalted butter
400-500g leeks, trimmed and sliced
300ml crème fraîche

2 large eggs, lightly beaten
Pinch of nutmeg
150g Cheddar, Comté or Gruyère cheese, coarsely grated
Salt and pepper, to taste
1 egg, beaten, to glaze (optional)

Large pie or tart dish, 25-30cm in diameter at the rim

📷 p105

1   Mix the flour and yeast in a bowl before stirring in the salt, followed by the water and egg. Work with your hands to roughly combine then knead for 5-10 minutes, or until the dough is stronger and elastic. Once it has gained a little strength, knead in the soft butter until fully incorporated. Set aside to rise in a large, covered bowl at room temperature for 1-1½ hours until doubled in size.

2   Meanwhile, start preparing the filling. Melt the butter in a large pan, add the leeks and stir together. Put a lid on the pan and cook on a low heat for 25 minutes, stirring occasionally. The cooked leeks should be meltingly tender. The leek mixture can be left to cool at this point.

3   When the dough has doubled in size, tip it out onto a lightly floured work surface and roll to a large circle — big enough to line the base and sides of your dish. Let the dough relax for a minute or two after rolling: it'll shrink back slightly thanks to the gluten developed during kneading. Roll out a little more until it's the required size again. Line the pie dish, pressing the dough into the corners and pushing up a little around the sides to give a slight overhang. I go one step further at this point, folding a little dough back over the rim of the dish and tacking it down against the outside by pressing firmly. This stops the dough from sliding down the inside of the dish during its proving time. Set aside to prove for 30 minutes. Preheat the oven to 200°C/fan 180°C/gas mark 6.

5   While the dough proves for a second time, complete the filling. Stir the crème fraîche, eggs, nutmeg, cheese and seasoning through the now cool leek and butter mixture. A generous hand with the pepper is crucial here to cut through the creamy richness of the filling. Once the dough has proved, spoon in the filling.

6   Brush the rim of the dough, which by now should be risen and puffy, with the beaten egg to glaze, if using. Bake for 40 minutes. The cooked tart should be mottled golden and brown on top and well risen. For a yet more enticing tart, sprinkle on an extra 30g cheese in the final 10 minutes of the baking time.

SMALL BITES & FLATBREADS

Bread is far too exciting to be limited to predictable slicing, buttering and sandwiching. These next recipes show how varied the methods of shaping and serving bread can be. Some are leavened, others are not; there are breads here to wrap, to split or to eat in just one mouthful.

GARLIC DOUGH BALLS

Forget the greasy, half-baked dough balls that you find in cheap pizza chains and takeaway boxes. Make these at home and revel in the chewy, unashamedly garlicky joy of them.

Makes 30-36
4 medium cloves garlic, unpeeled
4 tablespoons olive oil, plus extra for
    roasting
250ml water
500g strong white flour
7g instant dried yeast

1 teaspoon salt
30-40g parsley, finely chopped

Large baking trays

📷 p108

1   Preheat the oven to 180°C/fan 160°C/gas mark 4.

2   In an oven dish, roast the garlic cloves in their skins with a splash of olive oil for around 15 minutes, or until soft and fragrant. Peel off the papery skins and mash to a purée. Stir in the 4 tablespoons olive oil and the water. Switch off the oven.

3   In a separate bowl, combine the flour and yeast. Stir in the salt, followed by the garlicky liquid mixture and the chopped parsley. Once all is incorporated, knead for 5 minutes or so, until the dough is just beginning to feel less sticky. There's no need to agonise about reaching windowpane stage (see page 80) with this dough: the balls are very small so they don't need a perfectly developed, impressively elastic dough in order to rise and hold their shape.

4   Let the dough rise in a covered bowl at room temperature for approximately an hour, or until doubled in size. Gently deflate the dough, divide into 30-36 pieces and roll each of these, on an unfloured work surface, into a small ball. Spread the dough balls out across a couple of well-greased baking trays. Prove for a further 30 minutes, during which time the balls will puff up slightly. Meanwhile, preheat the oven again to 180°C/fan 160°C/gas mark 4.

5   Bake for 13-15 minutes, until well risen. The dough balls will still look a little anaemic at this point, but they'll be cooked through nonetheless. Pile them into a bowl and eat while they're still warm. I like to drizzle over a little melted butter, too. I can't officially recommend this for fear of reprisals from doctors and the health-conscious, but what I will say is that it's buttery, garlicky ambrosia.

Variation

Forget the garlic and parsley, swap in 150g grated Cheddar cheese and reduce the salt to ½ teaspoon to make warm cheese dough balls. Dangerously moreish.

RYE CARAWAY BAGELS

Toasted then topped with cream cheese and smoked salmon, these make an exceptional breakfast. But for more frugal days they're fantastic with just a slick of butter, too.

This recipe might seem a little laborious at first glance — individually shaping each one, boiling them in batches and then baking — but these bagels merit the extra work. The shaping, though repetitive, is very simple and barely takes ten minutes. The boiling is crucial for the bagel's characteristically chewy texture. The addition of bicarbonate of soda to the boiling water helps to give a deeper colour to the crust as the bagels bake (thanks to the Maillard reaction — see page 178) but it's by no means essential.

If you want to bake these ready for breakfast, prepare the dough the evening before and let it rise, covered, in the fridge overnight. In the morning, shape and let rise again then proceed with the boiling and baking.

Makes 8
325g strong white flour
125g dark rye flour
7g instant dried yeast
1¼ teaspoons salt
1 tablespoon sugar
250ml lukewarm water
1 tablespoon oil
2 tablespoons caraway seeds

Flour or polenta, to dust
2 tablespoons bicarbonate of soda
  (optional)
4 tablespoons water
½ teaspoon salt
30-50g poppy seeds (optional)
Oil, to grease

📷 p110

1   Combine the flours and yeast in a large bowl, stir in the salt and sugar and then add the lukewarm water and oil. Using your hands, vigorously mix until the dough comes together into a ball, then knead for 10 minutes. It's a drier mix than most of the other breads here, and so will be tighter and less sticky. Gently knead in the caraway seeds. Cover the bowl with cling film and leave to rise for approximately 1½ hours, or until it has doubled in size.

2   Turn out the risen dough, divide into 8 pieces and shape into bagels. There are two ways of doing this. The first way is to roll each lump of dough into a small ball, as you would for a bread roll, then push through the centre with your finger. Twirl the dough around your finger, gradually widening the hole. The other method is to roll the dough into a long sausage shape, tapered so that it is thinner at each end. Slap the dough lightly against the work surface to allow it to shrink back a little then let it rest for a minute. It needs to be 30-35cm long once rested. Curve the dough round into a circle shape, twisting the tapered ends around each other and pinching at the joins to secure. I prefer this second method: the intertwined ends and asymmetry of the bagel are really very pretty.

3   Let the bagels prove for 30-45 minutes at room temperature until puffy and almost
    1½ times their original size, on a baking tray dusted with either flour or polenta,
    which gives a good crunch. Meanwhile, preheat the oven to 180°C/fan 160°C/gas
    mark 4 and bring a large pan of water to the boil.

4   If using, add the bicarbonate of soda to the boiling water. Turn the heat down
    so that the water is simmering and boil the bagels in batches. They'll bob at the
    water's surface as they cook, half-submerged. Leave them to simmer for 60 seconds
    before carefully turning over and cooking for a further minute. It's important not
    to leave them in the water for too long so do have a watch/timer on hand for this.
    Remove with a slotted spoon and place on well-greased baking trays.

5   Combine the 4 tablespoons water and the salt, and brush the bagels with this.
    Sprinkle over the poppy seeds, if using. Bake in the preheated oven for 25 minutes.

CHICKPEA & CUMIN SEED BUNS

Who says that a bun should play second fiddle to its burger? Traditionalists would
have it that a bun is little more than a bland, cursory vessel. Toss that notion aside.
These ones are suffused with a bold, earthy flavour, complementing even robust
fillings. Try them with falafel, beanburgers or even spiced lamb.

Makes 12
3 tablespoons olive oil
1 tablespoon cumin seeds
400g can chickpeas (240g drained
    weight), drained

300ml lukewarm water
480g strong white flour, plus extra,
    to dust
7g instant dried yeast
1 teaspoon salt

1   Heat the olive oil in a pan and fry the cumin seeds for barely a minute (any longer
    and they may become bitter). Put the chickpeas into a large bowl, add the oil and
    cumin seeds and mash until no whole chickpeas remain. Beat in the water.

2   In a separate bowl combine the flour and yeast then stir in the salt. Add these
    dry ingredients to the chickpea mixture, bring together with your hands then
    knead for 10 minutes, building elasticity and reducing stickiness in the dough
    (see page 80). Leave to rise in a covered bowl at room temperature for
    approximately 1½ hours, or until doubled in size.

3   Shape the dough into 12 rolls and arrange the rolls on a large baking tray so that
    they're closely spaced (within 2cm of one another), but not touching. Let prove,
    preferably loosely covered with a piece of cling film, for around 45 minutes.
    Meanwhile, preheat the oven to 180°C/fan 160°C/gas mark 4.

4   Dust the risen rolls (they should now be at least 1½ times their original size, and
    just about touching one another) with flour and bake for 25 minutes.

SOCCA

These French chickpea flour flatbreads are arguably more pancake than bread, but I don't feel too conflicted about including them here. They're nutty, intensely savoury and versatile: think improvised pizza bases, wraps and even — if cooked for a little longer — dipping chips and crackers. But I prefer them, partly in the name of simplicity and minimal washing-up, eaten with just a grind of pepper, straight from the sizzling pan.

In Nice and along stretches of the south coast of France they are *socca*; further east and curving down the coastline into Italy they're *farinata*. They're usually found on street corners at vendors' stalls, to be bought cheaply and eaten greedily while on the move. Most of us here don't have the pleasure of having a local *socca* vendor (although who knows where the street food movement will take us) but luckily these are easy, cheap and quick to make at home. This is a simplified stove-top version although the thicker, more substantial, oven-baked *socca* are also popular.

You can find gram flour (sometimes labelled chickpea flour) in the 'World Cuisine' sections of some larger supermarkets, in health food shops or in most Indian or Pakistani food stores. Raw gram flour can have a bitter, astringent aftertaste but this is remedied by toasting the flour first, which is exactly what I've suggested here.

Makes 12 *socca*
300g gram/chickpea flour
½ teaspoon salt
Pepper, to taste
500–600ml water
4 tablespoons olive oil, plus extra
    for frying

Additions (optional):
2 teaspoons paprika

or 1 onion, finely sliced and fried
or 2 tablespoons rosemary needles, briefly
    fried in oil
or 2 tablespoons dried oregano or thyme
or 2 cloves garlic, finely chopped and
    gently fried in oil

📷 p112

1   Toast the gram flour over a medium heat in a large, dry pan, stirring continuously for 5–10 minutes, or until the flour has slightly darkened in colour. It should begin to smell nutty and rich. Don't overcook the flour or let it sit unstirred: burnt flour will slide back into exactly that bitterness that we're trying to lose. If it begins to look brown rather than just golden, whip it straight off the heat. Let it cool slightly before proceeding, using this time to prepare any additions, if using.

2   Combine the flour, salt, pepper and about a half of the water in a bowl until a thick paste is formed. Add all but 100ml of the remaining water and the olive oil. The batter ought to be thick but not gloopy: add the final 100ml water if necessary to reach the right consistency. Stir in any additions that you're using at this point.

3   Preheat a small non-stick frying pan on a medium-high heat, grease with oil and add a ladle of batter — enough to form a roughly 15cm circle. Cook for 1½–2 minutes, lifting the edges occasionally to prevent sticking, then carefully turn over and cook for a further minute or two. Repeat with the remaining batter, re-greasing the pan before each of the *socca*.

CHORIZO & KALE FLATBREAD

Not one to be shoved to the sidelines, this bold flatbread combines spicy chorizo and iron-rich kale to become very much a meal in itself. Although hearty chorizo is the flavour powerhouse here, for me it's the kale that steals the show: it essentially fries in the oil from the meat, the once-virtuous greens growing crisp, salty and delicious. This is a big flatbread: it's big enough to share, but I won't judge you if you don't.

Serves 2
250g strong white flour
1 teaspoon instant dried yeast
½ teaspoon salt
175ml lukewarm water
5 tablespoons olive oil
100g chorizo, diced

125g kale or cavolo nero, stalks removed and finely shredded

Large baking tray, swiss roll tin or roasting dish, approximately 22x33cm

📷 p115

1   Combine the flour and yeast in a large bowl, stir in the salt and add the water along with one tablespoon of the olive oil. Mix with your hands until well combined then tip out onto a clean surface and knead for 10 minutes, or until the dough is elastic and less sticky. Let it rise for an hour until doubled in size.

2   While waiting for the dough to rise, bring a pan of water to the boil and add the kale or cavolo nero. Boil for just 1 minute then drain and run through with cold water. Once cool, gently press out any excess water from the greens.

3   Knead just under half of the kale into the risen dough. It'll be a little tricky due to the residual moisture on the leaves, but don't worry about it being perfect. Preheat the oven to 190°C/fan 170°C/gas mark 5.

4   On a floured surface, roll out the dough to around 20cm in diameter. Use your hands to stretch the dough the remaining distance. It will shrink back a little as it rests, so carry on stretching the dough until it's approximately the size of the tin after shrinkage. Don't worry if some bits are a little thicker than others. It's not a disaster if there are one or two holes in the bread — think of it as rustic. Grease the bottom of the tin with two tablespoons of the remaining olive oil and lay the dough down.

5   Let the bread prove at room temperature for 15 minutes then sprinkle over the remaining kale and then the chorizo. Gently pat the toppings down then dimple the dough using your fingertips. This is particularly useful here as it helps to semi-embed some of the topping, securing it to the dough.

6   Let prove for a further 5 minutes then drizzle over the final two tablespoons of olive oil and bake for 20 minutes.

Variations
You might wince at the idea of carb-upon-carb potato bread, but it is really very good. Just replace the chorizo with a few peeled, boiled and diced potatoes. Lightly toasted cumin seeds work well with this, too, or even some crumbled goats' cheese.

PARATHAS

These are soft, multi-purpose flatbreads that — at around 20 minutes to make — are as close as bread comes to fast food. And what sets these apart from the tortilla bread, pancake, chapatti or pitta? Butter: melted, brushed lavishly on and folded in, creates a flaky, golden bread. Some days, when baking spills over into the sombre early morning hours, I wearily make a batch of these and eat one (or two, or more), plucked straight from the heat of the frying pan and slathered in raspberry jam. Let the purists protest.

You can make these less indulgent if you prefer: just forget the melted butter and don't fold the dough. Missing out this stage will, granted, make these much less work. But without this characteristic layering of butter and dough these are no longer parathas, and you won't achieve that same melting flakiness.

Makes 6
250g flour, plus extra for dusting
¼ teaspoon salt

75g salted butter
135ml water

1   Stir the flour and salt together in a mixing bowl then rub in 1 tablespoon of the butter until completely integrated. Add the water and very lightly knead for just a minute or so, or until the dough is well combined. Set aside to rest for 15 minutes. During this time the dough will absorb more water, making it less sticky and so easier to roll out. The gluten will relax as the dough rests too, again aiding the rolling process. While the dough's having its break, melt the remaining butter.

2   Divide the dough into 6 pieces and roll each into a rough ball. Using a floured rolling pin on a well-floured work surface, roll the dough portions to circles around 20cm in diameter. Brush lightly with the melted butter. There should be a little butter left over after this stage, to be used later when frying the parathas.

3   Fold the buttered dough into thirds as you would if you were folding a letter: bottom third folded up towards the middle, then top third folded down over this. Rotate the dough in front of you by 90 degrees (so that the folds are now running vertically), and fold again: bottom third up, top third down. You'll be left with small square(ish) parcels of buttery dough. Roll these out again, flouring the surfaces as you go, so that they're 15–20cm in diameter. I find it easiest to go for roughly square parathas, although you could make circles of them if you're more artful with the rolling pin than I am.

4   To cook, brush one side of a bread lightly with some of the remaining butter and fry for 2 minutes, buttered-side down, while brushing the top. Flip over and cook for a further minute or two. Repeat with the remaining breads. These breads are best eaten freshly cooked.

SLOW & STEADY

So far, the breads included here have been the sort that can be made over the course of an afternoon, leisurely fitted around the odd hour of calm during a hectic day or even thrown from mixing bowl to griddle to plate in just a few minutes. The next few breads are a little different. It's time that sets these apart: an unhurried rise leading coolly into deep flavour and a chewy texture. To rush these loaves would be to miss the point entirely.

THREE-CHEESE BRIOCHE

How grown-up (or otherwise) this bread turns out is dependent entirely on your choice of cheese. My combination lies at the less-sophisticated end of the spectrum: a cheesy but not overpowering bread, prettily flecked with Red Leicester. For something a little more refined, try Gruyère, Taleggio or Gouda.

The butter in this dough makes it a pleasure to knead and an even greater pleasure to eat. It'll be soft, extensible and smooth as you work and shape it, and tender once baked. It pays to be patient, though: all the enrichment makes the dough slower to rise than you might expect.

This can be made without the overnight stint in the fridge if you're in a hurry; it'll be trickier to shape but it'll taste good nonetheless. Give the dough its first prove as usual, then skip straight to shaping and the second prove. The second prove will take far less time this way, starting as it does from room temperature.

Makes 1 large brioche, enough for 8
400g strong white flour
7g instant dried yeast
½ teaspoon salt
100ml milk
3 large eggs, lightly beaten
175g unsalted butter, softened

50g Red Leicester, grated
50g strong Cheddar, grated
50g Parmesan or Grana Padano,
   finely grated
1 egg, lightly beaten, to glaze

Deep 20-23cm round tin or 900g loaf tin

1   Combine the flour and yeast in a large bowl then stir in the salt. In a small pan over a very low heat, warm the milk until barely lukewarm. Beat together the milk and the three eggs, add this all to the flour mixture and knead for 10 minutes until smooth and elastic.

2   Knead in the butter. This is a messy job — the very different textures of the dough and the soft butter will have you believing, at the outset, that this is an impossible task but I promise that after just a few minutes it'll come together smoothly — scrunch, squelch or squeeze the butter into the dough if need be. Once the butter is well incorporated, knead for a further 5 minutes then add all the cheese.

3   Leave the dough to double in size at room temperature in a large, covered bowl. Once doubled, gently push down, re-cover and place in the fridge for 8-10 hours (I usually leave it overnight).

4   Now for the shaping:

— If using a deep (sides of 6cm or taller) 20-23cm round tin, you can shape your dough rather impressively. Divide it into seven equal pieces. Roll five pieces into balls, and space evenly around the edge of the tin base. Roll the remaining two pieces together into one larger ball and place this in the circle's centre.

— Alternatively, if you're averse to unnecessary faffing around, shape into one large ball and pat this down to fill the tin.

— There's too much dough here really for a 900g loaf tin (sometimes it just about works for me, but the swelling dough teeters precariously over the tin rim), so if you don't have a deep 20-23cm round tin, shape three-quarters of the dough into a log shape, place in a 900g loaf tin and mould the rest into little bun shapes to be baked separately. The buns will bake in 20-25 minutes, leaving you just enough time to enjoy them and clean up the crumbs before the big loaf emerges from the oven.

5   Let the dough prove at room temperature, until nearly doubled in size. This can take up to 2 hours for a large brioche, depending on the temperature of the room. Covering the tin loosely with cling film will help to prevent the dough's surface from drying during this time, although you'll have to watch out that the rising dough doesn't stick to it. Preheat the oven to 200°C/fan 180°C/gas mark 6.

6   Brush the risen brioche with the beaten egg glaze and bake for 40 minutes, whether in the round or the loaf tin. Thanks to the egg wash, it'll colour quite deeply on top — this is not at all a problem, but if you're concerned that it might be colouring too much, try placing a 'hat' of tin foil over the bread for the remainder of the bake time.

WHAT IS A PREFERMENT?

A preferment is a clever way of improving the taste and texture of your loaf. A small amount of dough — the preferment — is made with just flour, water and a tiny amount of yeast, and allowed to ferment for 8 hours or more before being incorporated into the final dough. During this time, the yeast will work slowly on the flour, developing gluten and intensifying flavour.

The exact proportions of the preferment will vary depending on its purpose, how long it's to be left to ferment and the type of bread in which it will be used. A stiff preferment, for example, can help to develop gluten strength in very wet dough such as the Ciabatta on page 120. A wetter preferment, perhaps made with equal weights of water and flour, will develop a slight acidity over the course of a long fermentation, giving more flavour to even the simplest bread. It's a leap towards achieving some of the open-texture, chewiness and good flavour of a sourdough.

It's easier than it sounds, too: just a few minutes of mixing and then the preferment can be left to its own devices for 8-16 hours until you're ready to make the bread.

FRENCH COUNTRY BREAD

This rustic, French-style loaf uses just a small amount of rye flour to add depth and balance to the white flour's sweetness. Between the rye, the preferment and the long proving periods, this recipe yields a robust, full-flavoured, crusty bread that will thoroughly trounce any flimsy pre-sliced sandwich white you might find in the shops.

You only need a very small amount of yeast — one-sixth of a teaspoon — in this preferment. The easiest way to measure such a small amount is by dissolving some yeast in water and using just a fraction of this yeast solution in the preferment, as I've suggested below. Such fastidiousness isn't strictly necessary though, and if you can't be bothered (and I wouldn't blame you), a generous pinch of yeast will do just fine.

Makes 1 boule loaf
For the preferment:
½ teaspoon instant dried yeast
30ml lukewarm water
75ml cool water
100g strong white flour
50g dark rye flour

For the final dough:
325g strong white flour
1 teaspoon instant dried yeast
1 teaspoon salt
250ml lukewarm water
Preferment, from above

1 Sprinkle the ½ teaspoon of yeast into the 30ml lukewarm water, stirring well to dissolve.

2 Add two teaspoons of the yeast mixture to the 75ml cool water (the remaining yeast mixture can be discarded). Combine the flours then stir in the liquid. It will form a reasonably stiff dough: knead this very lightly for just a few seconds to help to integrate the ingredients then place in a bowl, cover tightly with cling film and

leave at room temperature for 12–16 hours. If, towards the end of this time, you're not yet ready to make the final dough, you can place the preferment in the fridge for a few extra hours until you're ready. The preferment is ready when it is 2–3 times its original volume and the surface is pockmarked with little holes.

3   Combine the flour, yeast and salt in a large bowl, then pour in the water and mix to a loose dough. Knead in the preferment — this can be a little tricky as the preferment and the new dough are so different in consistency, but it shouldn't take long. Once basically combined, set the dough aside to rest for 20 minutes or so. This rest isn't crucial but it is helpful: during the resting time the dough will absorb more water and the gluten will begin to develop, making kneading easier.

4   Knead the rested dough for at least 10 minutes, but preferably closer to 15 minutes. It's quite a wet dough, so don't be discouraged if it feels sticky, heavy and lifeless to begin with, and don't be tempted to add more flour. I promise that as you continue to knead (I'd recommend the kneading technique for wetter doughs on page 80) the dough will become easier to handle, and by the time you've finished kneading it'll be virtually unrecognisable: silky, supple and smooth.

5   Set the dough to rise in a large, covered bowl until it has doubled in size. This will take a little longer than usual because there's a comparatively small amount of yeast in this dough: anywhere between 1½–2½ hours, depending on the room temperature in your house. This slower rise will result in a more flavourful, chewy bread in the end, so don't worry too much if your dough is dragging its heels.

6   Shape the risen dough to a cob shape (see page 82 for more in-depth shaping techniques) and let it prove again at room temperature in a draught-free spot for around an hour, or until nearly doubled in size. Meanwhile, preheat the oven to 240°C/fan 220°C/gas mark 9.

7   Dust the risen dough with flour and, using a very sharp knife, score the top with a cross. Bake for 15 minutes before reducing the temperature to 200°C/fan 180°C/gas mark 6 and baking for a further 35–40 minutes. For an even crisper finish, put a little water in a tray on a low shelf in the oven for the first 10 minutes of the bake. The resulting steam will, counter-intuitively perhaps, give a wonderful crust.

CIABATTA

After recipes using a variety of flours, as well as nuts, spices, herbs, fruits and seeds, I'll conclude with this simple and spectacular bread. I can't think of a better illustration of the shape-shifting versatility, chemistry or alchemy of that magic four: flour, yeast, salt and water.

In the French Country Bread recipe above, the preferment is included to add flavour. Its primary function here, however, is structural. The stiff preferment develops strong networks of gluten over the course of its 10–12-hour rest. When kneaded into the rest of the dough, this gluten helps to lend strength and resistance to an otherwise very, very wet dough. It is then further developed by the long period of kneading and the subsequent stretch-and-folds through the first rise. The result: one of the most impossibly light loaves you'll ever eat.

Admittedly, this is a high-maintenance bake. It needs a good 10-hour head start, 20 minutes vigorous kneading, attention throughout its first rise and a vigilant eye cast over it as it bubbles up precariously during its second prove. That said, as a chronically lazy baker I can reassure you that I wouldn't dream of going through this ciabatta saga if the results were anything less than sublime.

Makes 2 ciabatta loaves
For the preferment:
¼ teaspoon instant dried yeast
150g strong white flour
80ml cool water

For the final dough:
300g strong white flour, plus extra,
    to dust

1 teaspoon instant dried yeast
1 teaspoon salt
280ml lukewarm water
Oil, to grease

 p123

1   To make the preferment, mix the ¼ teaspoon of yeast with the 150g of flour in a mixing bowl, then add the water, stir and knead very briefly just to combine. You should be left with a stiff dough. Let rest in a small, covered bowl at room temperature for 10–12 hours. After this time the preferment should be well risen with bubbles pockmarking its surface.

2   Combine the flour and yeast for the final dough in a large bowl then stir in the salt. Add 200ml of the water, mix then knead for 5 minutes. Work in the preferment and knead for a further couple of minutes. Now's time to add the remaining 80ml water: return the dough to the bowl, work in the water with your hands and then knead in the bowl for a full 15 minutes. It'll be far too wet to knead normally — instead, use a stretching and slapping motion, repeatedly pulling the dough upwards and slapping it back down, folding it over itself. As you continue to stretch the dough, you'll notice it become gradually stronger and more elastic. Fifteen minutes will feel like a long time to be kneading, but it's essential for the proper gluten development. The kneaded dough will still be sticky but should be supple, shiny and strong. Whatever you do, resist the temptation to add any more flour: this dough is supposed to be very wet.

3   Divide the dough in half, putting each piece in a large, lightly oiled container. (It's far kinder on the dough to divide it at this point, pre-rise, than to butcher it later and risk deflating it.) Cover the containers and let the dough rise at room temperature. After 30 minutes, give the dough its first stretch. Lightly oil your hands, slide them underneath one of the pieces of dough and pull to stretch the dough outwards horizontally. Fold one stretched side back into the centre then the other one over. Rotate the bowl 90 degrees and repeat once more. Do the same with the other piece of dough. Repeat this process after a further 30 minutes, and then leave to rest again for a further 45 minutes. By this point the dough will have risen for a total of 1¾ hours, with stretches at 30 minutes and an hour.

4   Generously dust two baking trays with flour. With lightly oiled hands, carefully scoop one of the pieces of dough out of its bowl and stretch it out to around 30cm long. The aim here is to interfere with the dough's structure as little as possible,

so don't fold or squeeze the dough, just stretch gently and lay it down on the baking tray. Repeat with the other piece. The dough won't be perfectly neat and it will 'flow' a little across the tray but this isn't a problem.

5   Let the loaves prove for around an hour at room temperature in a draught-free spot, preheating the oven to 240°C/fan 220°C/gas mark 9 in the meantime. The loaves will be tremulous and visibly bigger after the hour has elapsed. Sprinkle with flour then put the risen loaves in the hot oven, splashing a little water against the base and sides of the oven when you do so (creating steam, for a better rise). Bake for 10 minutes before reducing the oven temperature to 190°C/fan 170°C/gas mark 5 and baking for a further 20 minutes. Have a bowl of olive oil and balsamic vinegar at the ready: as soon as the loaves are cool, tear into chunks, dip and enjoy.

SWEET DOUGH

BUNS

BASIC SWEET DOUGH

CORNISH SPLITS (THUNDER & LIGHTNING BUNS)

SCANDINAVIAN ALMOND CREAM BUNS

BLUEBERRY SWIRLS • GLAZED SAFFRON BUNS

RASPBERRY MASCARPONE VATRUSHKA

DOUGHNUTS

CUSTARD DOUGHNUTS • OLIEBOLLEN

GLAZED CAKE DOUGHNUTS

TO SHARE

COCONUT LIME LOAF • MONKEY BREAD

CRUMBLE-TOPPED PEAR & ALMOND SLICE • BRIOCHE

CHERRY STOLLEN WITH PISTACHIO MARZIPAN

WHITE CHOCOLATE HAZELNUT COURONNE

Bread, but better. Sticky blueberry swirls, custard doughnuts, brioche and cream-filled splits, sweet coconut loaves and golden saffron buns: this chapter is a hymn to sweet dough. These buns — often bulbous, messily iced, generously proportioned — don't have the refinement of pastries or cakes, but there lies their appeal. They're my favourite things to bake and to eat, laced with butter, sugar, milk and eggs to leave them sweet and tender. And, unlike more basic breads, these don't need any dressing up, spreads or accompaniments — they're delicious just as they are.

BREAD WITH A DIFFERENCE

These breads are enriched versions of bread dough, so the techniques involved — mixing, kneading, rising, shaping, proving and baking — are the same as those in the Bread chapter (page 77-79). The finished breads however are very different: because they're laced with milk, eggs, butter and sugar, they're richer and more tender.

MILK

Milk is around 90% water, so can be almost directly substituted for water in most bread recipes. It's the remaining 10% that makes the difference, though: in full-fat milk, this is a mixture of sugars, protein and fat. The sugar lends a slight sweetness while the fat helps to keep the bread tender and the crust soft. You'll also notice that breads made with milk rather than water tend to cook to a deeper colour. Semi-skimmed milk, as you'd imagine, has half the fat and so creates a marginally less delicate texture. As for skimmed milk — I never use it.

Milk can have a slight tightening effect on the structure of bread, due to proteins that interfere with gluten development. Some argue that this can be prevented by scalding the milk prior to use, breaking down these problem proteins, but I've made breads with both scalded and unscalded milk and although the former produced a very slightly better texture, it won only by a hair's breadth. I'm not convinced that it's worth the time spent heating and cooling the milk. If you want to make prize-winning buns, by all means scald the milk first, but if you can't be bothered: don't worry. You can achieve a similar effect in a fraction of the time by simply increasing the amount of milk used by a couple of tablespoons (as discussed in the previous chapter, the wetter the dough, the more open the crumb).

BUTTER

This is the secret to soft, rich bread. Quite aside from the fact that it lends a deep, buttery flavour, the fat has an important structural role. Fat coats the flour particles and disrupts the formation of gluten, leaving enriched breads with a softer texture and crust than in a more basic flour-yeast-salt-water dough. It might seem self-defeating to undermine the gluten structure in this way, having so diligently developed it by kneading, but in truth it's a balancing act: a certain amount of gluten development is crucial for good structure, but fat is necessary for tenderness. Most of the time, you won't be adding enough fat to completely sabotage the gluten. But in very butter-heavy doughs, such as brioche, a compromise is reached by kneading before the addition of the butter, to give the gluten a head start.

Butter also affects the way the dough feels and behaves during its preparation. Dough made with plenty of butter is a joy to handle: soft, supple and less sticky than usual. It is, however, far slower to rise and prove than other doughs, the enrichment slowing the action of the yeast. As such, you'll find that the breads in this chapter take a little longer to make than those without butter.

Even after the bread has been baked, butter continues to play an important role: breads made with added fats are slower to go stale.

EGGS

Eggs are complex cocktails of water, fats and proteins, so their effects on bread are very similar to those of milk and butter. There are a couple of differences, however. Firstly, egg is very good at binding ingredients together, which means that breads made with egg will be less crumbly. Secondly, and more excitingly, the yolks give the bread a delightful yellow hue.

SUGAR

This is the obvious addition to a dough to make it sweet. Yeast will happily feed on sugars, so a small amount of sugar in dough can aid fermentation, meaning a faster rise. You can, however, have too much of a good thing: very sweet doughs actually rise more slowly, as the excess sugar inhibits the yeast. This shouldn't be too much of a problem for the recipes here, however, as I've kept sugar to a minimum in the dough itself, instead adding sweetness in extra fillings and toppings.

SPICE & ZEST

Because spices can slow or even kill yeast, it's advisable to use them sparingly in yeast doughs. A small amount is usually unproblematic, but for a more intense hit of flavour, try adding the spice separately, perhaps rolled up with the dough, as in cinnamon buns, or mixed into a glaze. The same goes for zest, although you shouldn't have to worry when including it in relatively modest quantities.

GLAZING

A matt, rugged finish can be appealing on top of a country loaf or a rustic bloomer, but in these more aesthetically-aware breads and buns, it can help to plump for a more polished appearance. This needn't be anything difficult, costly or time-consuming: more often than not, a simple lick of egg-wash or milk is all it takes. Different glazes will leave the breads with slightly different finishes. Milk will leave a faint sheen; butter gives a very tender crust; egg gives a richly coloured, shiny finish; a mixture of sugar and water will brown quickly on small buns, helping them to colour during their short bake. I usually suggest an egg glaze, but you can of course change or omit the glaze as you please.

SHAPING

There is no end to the ways you can shape a bun. Whichever one you choose — whether traditional or off the top of your head — make sure you shape with conviction and consistency, sealing any joins, smoothing any wrinkles and ensuring that the top of the dough is kept taut for an even rise.

BUNS

BASIC SWEET DOUGH

The following three recipes — Cornish splits, almond and cardamom buns and fruity blueberry swirls — all use versions of this sweet dough recipe. That three such different breads can be made from one basic mixture only goes to show the versatility of sweet dough. It can metamorphose from sticky cinnamon rolls to behemoth Belgian buns with as little as a dusting of spice or a handful of dried fruit. Feel free to make your own additions, too.

500g strong white flour
7g instant dried yeast
1 teaspoon salt
40g caster sugar

200ml full-fat milk
2 large eggs
60g butter, softened

1   In a large bowl, combine the flour, yeast, salt and sugar. Add any spices or zest at this point.

2   Heat the milk very gently in a small pan over a low heat until barely warm to the touch. It shouldn't be any warmer than tepid. Add the milk, eggs and butter to the dry ingredients and bring together using your hands. There's really no way to avoid getting your hands dirty unless you're fortunate enough to own a stand mixer: you need to stretch, squelch and squash the dough until the ingredients are all incorporated. Once combined, leave the dough to rest for 15 minutes or so in the bowl, during which time it will absorb some more of the liquid and begin to strengthen, becoming less sticky.

3   Knead the rested dough for 10–15 minutes. (There's some advice on kneading on page 80 if you need it.) It will feel sticky and heavy to begin with, but resist the temptation to add flour to the dough or to the work surface: I promise that the dough will become easier to handle the more you work it. It's particularly important to be thorough when kneading enriched dough such as this as you'll need to counteract the weakening effects of the butter and sugar on the dough's structure. Mix in any dried fruit or nuts you might be including once you've finished the main bulk of the kneading.

4   Once the dough is elastic, smooth and with a slight shine to it, set it aside in a large, covered bowl to rise at room temperature until doubled in size. This could take anywhere between 1 and 2 hours, depending on the initial temperatures of the ingredients and the temperature in your kitchen.

5   Use the risen dough in one of the recipes on the following pages or invent one of your own. For a back-to-basics bun, just shape into 12 small balls, leave to rise again at room temperature until doubled in size and bake for 20 minutes at 180°C/fan 160°C/gas mark 4.

CORNISH SPLITS (THUNDER & LIGHTNING BUNS)

Is the boldly dark treacle the thunder and the bright cream the lightning? Or is it the other way round — with jagged streaks of treacle against the muffling heaviness of the cream? Either way, these traditional Cornish buns are spectacular. Unlike some recipes (Red Velvet Cake, I'm looking at you), their charm doesn't begin and end with the intrigue of their name, but instead carries through to the buns themselves: full of drama, contrast and darkness.

The tradition of serving cream tea with sweet, yeasted buns is unfortunately one that doesn't seem to have taken hold beyond the south-western tip of the country. It's a shame: I find that the soft buns provide a far better counterpoint to the richness of clotted cream than scones do.

Makes 12
1 quantity of Basic Sweet Dough
  (see page 130)
1 egg, lightly beaten, to glaze

For the filling:
4 tablespoons golden syrup

2 tablespoons black treacle
225g clotted cream

📷 p132

Sweet Dough

131

1   Mix and knead the dough as instructed opposite, leaving it to rise until doubled in size. Line a large baking tray or roasting dish with baking parchment.

2   Turn the risen dough out of its bowl and divide into 12 pieces. Shape each piece into a small ball (for more information on good shaping technique, see pages 80–82). Arrange the balls on the prepared tray — they should be spaced within a couple of centimetres of each other. As the buns prove and bake, they'll grow enough to bridge this gap, fusing together in the oven to give soft-sided, fluffy rolls to be torn apart.

3   Leave the buns to prove for 45–60 minutes, or until approximately doubled in size. Meanwhile, preheat the oven to 180°C/fan 160°C/gas mark 4.

4   Brush the tops with beaten egg then bake for 20–25 minutes, or until golden brown and well risen. Let them cool completely on a wire rack before splitting and filling.

5   Mix the golden syrup and treacle in a small bowl. Tear the buns apart and make a very deep incision into the top of each one, from end to end, almost-but-not-quite reaching down to the bottom of the bun — you want to split them, not bisect them. Open up along this split and dollop a tablespoon of clotted cream into it. Drizzle with the golden syrup and treacle mixture to give a shock of black against the bright cream.

Variations
If you're dubious about forgoing the more traditional jam for treacle, use a good-quality strawberry jam instead or — my favourite — sharp blackcurrant compote. (But I'd encourage you to give the treacle a go — balanced with the golden syrup, the treacle becomes sweeter and less bitter.)

SCANDINAVIAN ALMOND CREAM BUNS

These differ slightly from the authentic Swedish *semlor*, or Norwegian *fastelavnsboller*, but they do share the same basic concept: sweet, cardamom-scented dough, cream and almond filling. If you don't like cardamom you can leave it out, but its citrussy fragrance really does offset the sweetness of the almond cream.

Makes 12
1 quantity of Basic Sweet Dough
    (see page 130)
8 cardamom pods, seeds only, finely
    crushed

For the filling:
150g almond flakes (or ground
    almonds — see below)

150g unsalted butter, very soft
150g caster sugar
300ml double cream

📷 p135

1   Prepare the sweet dough according to the instructions on page 130, adding the cardamom to the flour along with the yeast and salt. Leave the dough to rise in a covered bowl at room temperature until doubled in size — about 1½ hours. Line a large, deep tray or roasting dish (roughly 20x30cm) with baking parchment.

2   Gently push down the dough, turn out of its bowl, and divide into 12 pieces. Shape each piece into a ball, rolling in circles under a cupped palm on a clean surface. For more in-depth guidance on shaping turn to page 82. Arrange on the lined baking tray so that each bun sits a little apart from its neighbours.

3   Let the buns prove on their tray at room temperature for 45-60 minutes, or until nearly twice their original size, meanwhile preheating the oven to 180°C/ fan 160°C/gas mark 4. Once the buns have risen, bake them in the preheated oven for 20-25 minutes.

4   While the buns are baking, toast the almond flakes on a tray on another oven shelf for 10 minutes until light golden. Grind the almond flakes in a coffee grinder or food processor. If you have neither of these, use ready-ground almonds instead, but add ¼ teaspoon almond essence, for extra flavour.

5   Beat the butter and sugar together and add the cooled, ground almonds. In a separate bowl, whip the cream to soft peaks. Slacken the almond mixture a little by beating in a couple of tablespoons of the cream, and then fold in a quarter of the remaining cream.

6   Once the buns are cool, halve them, spread the bottom half with almond cream, spoon in some whipped cream, sandwich with the top half, and enjoy.

BLUEBERRY SWIRLS

Slide out of the winter rut of heavy, hibernation foods and make these buns at the first stirrings of spring — full of bright, fruity blueberries, delicate pistachio and orange zest. Granted, they're hardly light, but we can't be expected to just snap lithely into shape at the turn of the spring equinox. Consider these buns a transitional treat, somewhere between stollen stodge and summer salads.

Makes 12
1 quantity of Basic Sweet Dough
   (see page 130)
Zest of 1 orange

For the filling:
80g butter, softened

120g soft light brown sugar
Zest of 1 orange
150-200g blueberries
100g pistachios, roughly chopped
1 egg, beaten, to glaze

1   Prepare, knead and rise the Basic Sweet Dough as specified on page 130, adding the orange zest to the flour, yeast, salt and sugar mixture.

2   Gently press down the risen dough and, on a lightly floured surface, roll out to a rectangle approximately 50x30cm. Thanks to the gluten developed during the kneading and rising stages, the dough will tend to shrink back as you roll it. This elasticity can be annoying but with patience and persistent rolling you should be able to get the dough to a point where it's the required size, even after shrinkage.

3   Beat together the butter, sugar and orange zest for the filling and spread this mixture carefully over the rectangle of dough, taking care not to tear it. The filling needn't be perfectly even — it will level itself as it's rolled up and during cooking. Scatter over the blueberries and pistachios, pressing down very gently to lodge them in the dough.

4   Roll up the rectangle of dough from long edge to long edge — that is, to give a roll 50cm long. Roll reasonably tightly and don't be afraid to slightly squeeze the dough as you go to ensure a uniform thickness. When you've nearly finished the rolling, tack the remaining long edge to the work surface using a slightly dampened finger. Smear the dough downwards and outwards, just at the very edge, so that when the dough log is rolled over on to that edge, it will stick to itself. Leaving the roll join-downwards, trim a couple of centimetres off each end to even them up, then divide the rest into 12 equal slices.

5   Line a large baking tray or roasting dish with baking parchment. Arrange the slices, cut sides facing up, so that they're close but not touching one another. Leave to prove for 45-60 minutes at room temperature, or until almost doubled in size. If you have rolled tightly and tacked the dough to itself, you shouldn't find that the rolls come undone, but if any do begin to unfurl during the proving time, just gently press back into shape. Preheat the oven to 180°C/fan 160°C/gas mark 4.

6   Once proved, the swirls should be almost touching each other and visibly puffier. Brush the tops with the beaten egg and bake for 20-25 minutes.

Variations

Spread a few tablespoons of lemon curd over the dough instead of the butter filling and drizzle with a zesty water icing (see page 320) for easy lemon swirl buns. Alternatively, for something a little more autumnal, you could of course make more traditional cinnamon buns, beating the butter, sugar and zest as above, but swapping the blueberries and pistachios for a teaspoon or two of ground cinnamon.

GLAZED SAFFRON BUNS

Saffron is at once heinously expensive and ambrosially delicious. At around £7 per gram, it's hardly a budget ingredient. Fortunately, a little goes a long way: a pinch is enough to dye an entire batch of dough a glorious yellow and infuse it with a fragrant, honeyed taste. It works equally well in custards, rice puddings and almond cakes.

To show the saffron in its best light, I've avoided adding too much butter to this dough — such richness would mask the delicate flavour of the spice.

Makes 20 small or 12 large buns
330ml full-fat milk
2–3 pinches of saffron threads (no more than ½ teaspoon)
500g strong white flour
7g instant dried yeast
1 teaspoon salt
30g caster sugar

50g unsalted butter, softened

To glaze:
150g icing sugar
2 tablespoons water

📷 p138

1 In a small pan, heat the milk and saffron together until the milk is scalding. As soon as the saffron threads hit the milk you'll notice them bleeding an ochre colour into the pale milk. Before long, the milk will have first turned creamy, then barely yellow before settling on a colour close to the golden hue of a block of good butter. You can squeeze even more colour from the saffron by pressing it against the pan with the back of a spoon, as you might wring the flavour from a brewing teabag. Set the mixture aside to cool until tepid. If you dip a teaspoon into the infused liquid at this point you'll be able to taste the saffron: nuanced, faintly metallic and very slightly bitter.

2 In a large bowl, combine the flour, yeast, salt and sugar. Add the now-tepid milk and the butter, combine using your hands and then knead for 10 minutes, until smoother, less sticky and elastic. Leave the dough to rise in a large, covered bowl for 1–1½ hours, or until doubled in size.

3 Line a large baking tray with baking parchment. Roll the risen dough out to a rectangle approximately 50x30cm, lightly flouring the work surface as you go. Cut into strips of equal width, each 30cm long. Cut 20 strips if making small buns or 12 wider strips for the larger buns. One by one, roll the strips up from the bottom to their midpoint, then turn over and roll the top down to the middle, creating an S-shape. Leave the shaped buns to prove on the prepared baking tray for 45–60 minutes, or until almost doubled in size, Preheat the oven to 200°C/fan 180°C/gas mark 6 while you wait.

4   Bake for 12–15 minutes for the small buns, or 20 for the bigger ones, rotating the tray halfway through the cooking time to ensure an even bake. Prepare the glaze by adding the water to the icing sugar a little at a time, until smooth and thick, but slack enough that it will run from a spoon. Once the buns are cooked and while they're still hot, use a pastry brush (or a small, very clean paintbrush) to brush them all over with the glaze. Leave to cool on a wire rack.

Variations
A handful of currants could be added, too. Saffron also goes very well with almonds: chopped almonds kneaded into the dough, flaked almonds sprinkled on top or even a little marzipan (grated over the rolled-out dough before shaping).

RASPBERRY MASCARPONE VATRUSHKA

These Russian buns are fat discs with hollows at their centres, heaped with sweetened mascarpone and topped with raspberries. The traditional versions use quark instead of the far richer mascarpone, but I find that this version better balances the brightness of the fruit. Use blackberries, blueberries or blackcurrants if you'd prefer.

There's mascarpone in both the dough and the filling of this *vatrushka*, ensuring the buns are tender without any of the greasiness that butter can bring. A mixture of plain and strong white flours means that the bread is particularly soft.

Makes 6
125g strong white flour
125g plain flour
1½ teaspoons instant dried yeast
½ teaspoon salt
2 tablespoons caster sugar
100g mascarpone
120ml full-fat milk

For the filling:
150g mascarpone

1 large egg yolk
40g caster sugar
1 tablespoon cornflour
1 teaspoon vanilla extract
100–125g raspberries
1 large egg, lightly beaten, to glaze

📷 p141

1   Combine the flours and yeast then add the salt and sugar. In a separate bowl, beat the mascarpone for the dough until smooth. Heat the milk in a pan over a low heat until lukewarm then whisk it, a little at a time, into the mascarpone. Once combined, add this to the flour mixture and mix together with your hands.

2   Knead the dough for 10 minutes, or until smoother and more elastic. Don't add extra flour to the dough or work surface — just have a spatula on hand to scrape up any dough that sticks to your hands or the surface, and knead with speed and conviction. This dough might not feel quite as robust as some others, thanks to the proportion of lower-gluten plain flour in it, but it will grow supple nonetheless. Transfer the kneaded dough to a large, covered bowl and leave to rise at room temperature for 1½–2 hours, or until doubled in size. It may take less time than this if your kitchen is particularly warm.

3   Divide the risen dough into six pieces and roll each into a ball. One by one, use a rolling pin to flatten the balls to discs around 1cm thick, then use your hands to stretch them until they're around 12cm in diameter. You'll need to stretch the centres quite a bit thinner than the edges, in order to leave a rim of dough around the perimeter.

4   Leave the dough shapes to prove on a large, lined baking tray (you may need to use two trays if yours aren't very big) for around 45 minutes, or until visibly puffy and risen. While they prove, preheat the oven to 180°C/fan 160°C/gas mark 4 and prepare the filling by beating the mascarpone until smooth then stirring in the egg yolk, sugar, cornflour and vanilla extract.

5   Once the buns have risen, neaten their shape by very gently pressing down around the centre to define the indentation and ensure that the rim is well above the level of the hollow. Fill with a spoonful of the mascarpone mixture and press a few raspberries into the middle of each one.

6   Brush all over the buns with the egg, to glaze. This will be easy on the dough rims, but you'll have to be very gentle when brushing over the surface of the filling and raspberries. Bake in the preheated oven for 20 minutes. Let cool on the tray to room temperature before eating. The centres will remain soft-set even when completely cooled, but this rich, quivering custard is precisely what makes these buns special.

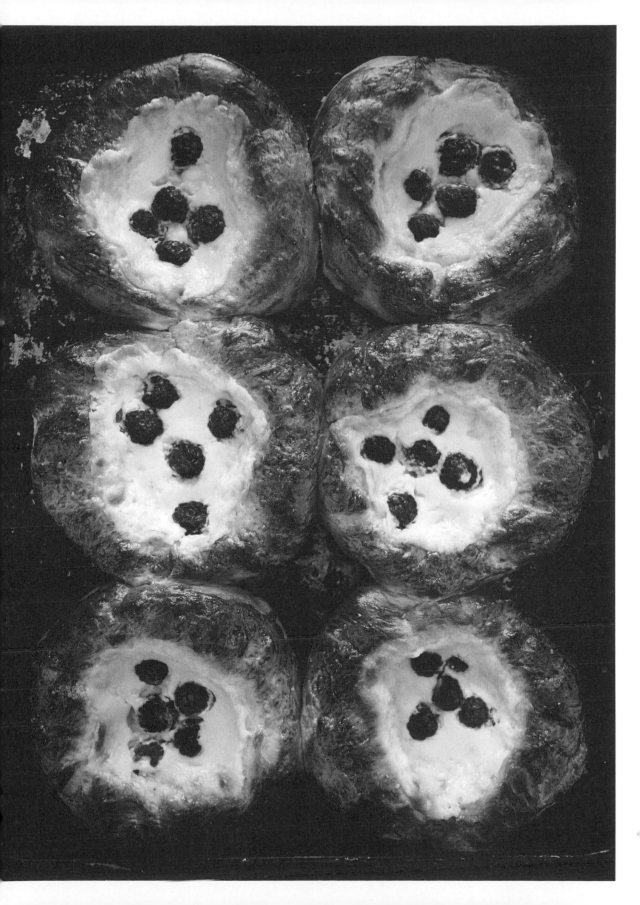

DOUGHNUTS

I don't imagine that it will come as a surprise to anyone to learn that doughnuts are bad for your health. These recipes are deep-fried, glazed, filled, frosted and sugared, but it's precisely these health hazards that make the doughnuts taste so sublimely good. There are some who suggest baking doughnuts for a healthier alternative, but I think that misses the point entirely: what makes a doughnut a doughnut — instead of a bun or a cake — is the frying process, yielding a uniquely crisp, deeply coloured crust and moist texture.

A FRYING START

Frying is a very different means of cooking to oven baking, and it's important to understand the process before you get started.

— Preparing the oil is something which you'll need to allow time for, as it can take up to 15 minutes to come up to temperature. This is particularly important with time-sensitive items such as yeasted doughnuts, which will need to be fried as soon as they're proved. Always use a large pan — one large enough to allow for at least 8cm of oil in the pan yet still with plenty of room to spare. An over-filled pan could be incredibly dangerous, should the oil foam up, splash or spatter. And I wouldn't recommend a non-stick pan for deep-frying: steel or cast iron is better. I usually use sunflower oil, which has a neutral flavour and is safe to very high temperatures. Corn oil and groundnut oil make suitable alternatives.

— Monitoring the temperature of the oil is crucial. When dough hits the intense heat of the oil, the moisture near its surface rapidly heats and evaporates and is released as tiny bubbles of steam — hence the sizzling when a doughnut first enters the pan. Importantly, the outward rush of steam bars an inward rush of oil, preventing the doughnut from absorbing too much fat. As a result, if the temperature is too low, the doughnut will soak up the oil, leaving it greasy and heavy. High temperatures present their own problems, browning the exterior of the doughnut too quickly while leaving the inside uncooked.

    The ideal temperature for deep-frying doughnuts is 180°C. There's no need to worry about a few degrees either side of this, but it's important to be in the 170–190°C range. There is only one failsafe method of measuring this, and that is with a sugar thermometer. It's a small, inexpensive piece of kitchen equipment but will prove invaluable when frying dough. The other option is to test the oil's temperature using a cube of bread: if the bread browns all over in 60 seconds, the oil is approximately the right temperature. But this second method is unreliable and difficult to judge — my loyalties lie with the sugar thermometer.

— It's important to continue checking the temperature of the oil throughout the frying process, especially before frying each new batch. With a sugar thermometer, this is as simple as keeping it hooked onto the side of the pan as you work. Although you'll need a high heat to bring the oil up to 180°C in the first place, you won't need to continue with such a fierce flame once you start frying.

Turn down to a medium-low heat, increasing only if the oil's temperature begins to drop.

— Frying the doughnuts is the exciting part. Drop one in: the oil, until now deceptively placid, will suddenly fizz, bubble and hiss around the dough. The doughnut will sink slightly then rise back through the amber oil, bobbing on the surface. It will begin to swell and bronze. You'll then flip it over, leaving it belly-up for another minute or two before fishing it out, patting it dry and letting it cool.

I've given frying times for each of the following recipes: do stick to these, and use a timer rather than just guessing as the minutes roll by. A doughnut cooked too long will grow greasy, while one not cooked long enough will remain raw at its centre, even if the outside looks a promising hue.

A NOTE ON SAFETY

Hot oil is dangerous: please be careful, focused and organised when frying.

— Children and pets should be kept well clear of the kitchen.

— Don't leave hot oil unattended, even for an instant.

— Keep a close eye on the oil's temperature: if it exceeds 190°C, turn down the heat; if it begins to foam, spit or smoke, turn the heat off immediately.

— Tempting as it will be, don't eat the doughnuts straight from the hot oil, as their interiors will still be very hot.

— Have a sink of cold water ready to plunge your hand into in case of burns.

— As long as you're vigilant, it's highly unlikely that the oil will catch fire, but in the event that it does happen, do not use water on the burning oil. Put a heavy metal lid over the pan to 'suffocate' the flame and use a Class B fire extinguisher.

CUSTARD DOUGHNUTS

This is a recipe for those who must always have the biggest, most indulgent, least modest thing on the menu: a sugar-crusted doughnut — soft-textured, plump with custard and as big as your fist.

Prepare the pastry cream for this filling in advance: it will need a spell in the fridge before it's thick enough to use. If you're nervous about making custard you can buy a good ready-made one, although it will be slacker than homemade so may ooze out of the doughnuts. Whatever you do, don't debase these doughnuts with the canary-yellow, custard powder kind.

Makes 12
500g strong white flour
7g instant dried yeast
1 teaspoon salt
2 tablespoons caster sugar
215ml milk
2 large eggs
50g unsalted butter, softened

1.5 litres sunflower or corn oil
75g caster sugar, to coat

For the filling:
1 quantity of pastry cream (see page 312)

📷 p146

1   Combine the flour, yeast, salt and sugar in a large bowl, taking care to ensure that the yeast and salt don't come into direct contact prior to mixing. Heat the milk gently on the hob until just lukewarm, then whisk in the eggs. Add this mixture to the dry ingredients along with the softened butter then work with your hands to combine. Knead for 10 minutes. The dough will become smoother and elastic. Set aside the dough to prove in a large, covered bowl at room temperature for 1-1½ hours, or until doubled in size.

2   Divide the risen dough into 12 roughly equal pieces (my inner pedant likes to weigh the pieces to make sure that they're even, but I won't advocate that sort of painstaking accuracy here). On a surface dusted with flour, roll each piece into a ball, gathering any excess underneath and rolling under a cupped palm to give a smooth surface. Pat down slightly to give each a flattened shape. There's more information on shaping on pages 80-82, if you need it.

3   Cut 12 squares of baking parchment or foil, approximately 12x12cm, although the specific dimensions aren't important so don't worry about getting the ruler out. Lightly flour each of these squares and lay a doughnut on each. This is to allow for easy transfer of the fragile, risen doughnuts to the oil a bit later. Leave the doughnuts to prove for 45-60 minutes at room temperature, or until they're at least 1½ times their original size.

4   It should take the oil around 10-15 minutes to reach the required temperature, so start heating well before the end of the proving period. Pour the oil into a large pan (the oil needs to be at least 8cm deep, but nowhere near the top of the pan) and heat fiercely until it reaches 180°C. Then turn the heat down to medium-low while cooking to maintain the oil at this temperature. See page 142 for more guidance on frying temperatures and method.

5   Transfer the doughnuts over to the pan using their squares of parchment as gurneys before very carefully sliding them off into the oil, watching out for any splashes. You should be able to fit in 3-4 doughnuts at once. Fry for 2 minutes on each side then lift out using a slotted spoon. Pat dry with a few sheets of kitchen paper then roll in the caster sugar and let cool. Repeat the frying process with the remaining doughnuts.

You should notice a pale ring around their middles now, a few shades lighter than their tops and bottoms. This characteristic 'tan line' could be mistaken for a flaw, but it's actually the mark of a perfectly proved and carefully fried doughnut.

6   Once completely cooled, use a butter knife to poke a hole deep into the centre of each doughnut. Wiggle the knife around to create a hollow to accommodate the pastry cream. Using a pastry syringe or a piping bag with a wide nozzle, pipe some pastry cream into each doughnut. Don't just perch the nozzle at the edge of the doughnut when you do this, otherwise you'll end up with a tiny pocket of custard to one side of the doughnut. Press the nozzle right into the hollow you created and pipe generously. Repeat with the remaining doughnuts.

If you don't have a piping bag or nozzle, just make a small incision in the doughnut's side, prise open with your fingers and spoon the filling in.

7   Leave the doughnuts to settle for 10 minutes or so, propping them with the piping hole upwards if the custard is leaking. Eat soon after, with napkins at the ready for cleaning up custard-smothered lips, chins and fingers.

Variations

A chocolate glaze on top might just tip these from hedonism to lethality, but that's a risk I'm happy to take. The result is a sort of Boston Cream Doughnut, a riff on the Boston Cream Pie's (incongruously, not an actual pie) trademark clever combination of custard and dark chocolate ganache. Forgo the stage where you roll the doughnuts in sugar, instead dipping their tops in warm chocolate ganache (see page 321 for a recipe) after filling them.

If you're not keen on custard, jam makes a fine substitution — particularly a vibrant one such as rhubarb. I once even used lemon curd and crème fraîche — an unexpected triumph, cutting cleanly through the sweetness.

BATTER DOUGHS

Some enriched doughs have such a high ratio of water to flour that they cease to be a recognisable dough at all, resembling a batter instead. When the liquid content is this high, it's impossible to knead the dough on the work surface as you might usually do. Instead, gluten needs to be developed by beating the mixture in its bowl.

Although it's hard work doing this by hand (you can of course use a mixer with dough hooks, if you have one), it's well worth attempting it at least once to get a feel for the dough. Roll up your sleeves, put on some music and, cradling the bowl in one arm, beat rapidly with the other hand. The motion you use doesn't particularly matter: a circular movement will work well, as will repeatedly stretching the dough up then slapping it back down into the bowl — whatever works for you.

At first, the dough will be very wet and heavy, but as you continue to beat you will notice strands of gluten forming, helping the dough to come away from the sides of the bowl. The lifeless mass will transform into something more elastic, stronger, and (sorry!) progressively more difficult to mix. After about five minutes (and these may feel like the longest five minutes of your life), you'll notice that the dough feels very different. It will be firm rather than flabby, more alive and more resistant. It's a workout for both you and the dough.

However, this hard work is not for nothing. When beating the batter, you're not only strengthening the gluten, which gives the bread its structure, but also incorporating countless tiny air bubbles into the batter. These air bubbles will expand as the yeast gets to work, creating light, airy bread.

OLIEBOLLEN

These little Dutch doughnuts are traditionally New Year's Eve treats but I see no harm in bringing the date forward and making them whenever you please. Because they need only one rise, you can whip up a batch quickly, whenever the craving takes hold. I make these far smaller than a conventional-sized doughnut, which not only means they are easier to cook, but also eases the guilt of having eaten one, two, or a bowlful.

Makes 20-25
350g strong white flour
7g instant dried yeast
¾ teaspoon salt
40g caster sugar
350ml milk
Zest of 1 lemon

1 apple, peeled and cored
100g currants
100g mixed peel
1.5 litres sunflower or corn oil
60g icing sugar, to dust

📷 p149

1   Combine the flour, yeast, salt and sugar. Heat the milk over a low heat until tepid and then stir in the lemon zest. Add this to the flour mixture and stir to combine. Let the dough sit for 10 minutes. Meanwhile, chop the peeled apple into small cubes (really no bigger than about 5mm across).

2   If you have a mixer with dough hook attachments, now is the time to feel smug. Roll your sleeves up if not. This very wet dough needs to be vigorously beaten for

at least 5 minutes in its bowl to build up the gluten's strength. It's ready when it's more elastic, stringy and resistant.

3 Incorporate the chopped apple, currants and mixed peel then cover the bowl with cling film and let the dough rise at room temperature for about an hour. Once the hour is up, start heating the oil in a large pan, taking care not to fill the pan more than two-thirds full. The oil needs to reach 180°C, which is best gauged using a sugar thermometer, otherwise test by dropping a cube of bread in the hot oil — if it turns golden brown in 60 seconds, the oil is hot enough.

4 Using two tablespoons, scoop smallish balls of the batter into the oil, three or four at a time. Let fry for 1½ minutes on each side and carefully remove using a slotted spoon. Pour the icing sugar onto a wide, lipped plate or shallow bowl. Roll each doughnut in the icing sugar. Repeat in batches, checking the temperature of the oil between each lot. I did entertain the idea of eating these, still warm, with some lemon gelato. It might be an indulgence too far for some, but I'll leave you to make up your own mind on that count.

THE DOUGHNUT STALL

The best bit of the summer holidays was always doughnuts. Not jam doughnuts, but cinnamon-coated cake doughnuts, fresh from the fryer — six for £3, or 12 for a fiver — at the fair, the seaside and the festival. On tiptoes, you might just be able to see the doughnuts plop into the oil and inch along the long conveyor, sizzling and spitting all the way, before being thrown headlong into a bucket of cinnamon sugar and heaped into grease-stained paper bags. Much of my childhood was spent like this, forehead pressed to the perspex of the doughnut stall, while the funfair clamoured on without me.

GLAZED CAKE DOUGHNUTS

All the fun of the fair, in a mouthful.

If malt is in vogue at the moment, I can only wonder why it hasn't always been so. It's a fantastic flavour, particularly good at adding depth to vanilla and to chocolate. Here the malt comes in powdered form — by which I mean Horlicks and the like. This is easier to come by and less full-bodied than the dark, treacle malt extract syrups such as the one used in the Date Malt Loaf (page 38).

Because they're leavened with baking powder, which works instantly upon contact with the hot oil, these doughnuts are far quicker to make than the other doughnuts in this chapter. They have a very different feel, too: a fine-textured, soft inside and crisp, terracotta-coloured crust.

Makes 10–12
40g unsalted butter
4 tablespoons full-fat milk
3 tablespoons caster sugar
60g malted drink powder
2 large eggs
1½ teaspoons vanilla extract
2 teaspoons baking powder
¼ teaspoon salt
Pinch of ground cinnamon

300g plain flour
1.5 litres sunflower or corn oil

For the icing:
200g icing sugar
40g malted drink powder
40–45ml water
1 teaspoon vanilla extract

📷 p151

1   In a small pan, melt the butter over a low heat then add the milk. In a large bowl, combine the sugar and malted drink powder, before gradually adding the milk and butter liquid, whisking constantly to prevent any lumps from forming. Add the eggs and vanilla extract and stir to combine.

2   Mix the baking powder, salt, cinnamon and the flour in a separate bowl then add this to the wet mixture, stirring the sticky ingredients together into a cohesive mass. Cover the bowl with cling film and refrigerate for an hour.

3   Once chilled, the dough should be just firm enough to roll out but add a little more flour if not. Lightly flour the work surface and roll to a thickness of around 5mm. Stamp out ring shapes using an 8–10cm diameter circle cutter for the outside, and a smaller cutter for the 2–4cm holes. If you don't have the right size cutters,

freeform using a sharp knife or improvise using some other circle-shaped kitchen utensil — I use the bottom of a spice jar as a guide. Re-roll any offcuts and stamp out more shapes.

4   Cut 10-12 squares of baking parchment or foil, lightly grease them with some of the oil and place one doughnut on each. This might seem like a fussy step but it really does help when it comes to transferring the doughnuts to the hot oil safely.

5   Heat the oil in a large, deep pan (not non-stick) over a high heat — the oil needs to reach 180°C. See page 142 for information on the correct technique when frying.

6   Once the oil is hot, pick a doughnut up by its parchment/foil cradle and slide it into the oil. Be very careful not to let the doughnut drop from too great a height, or the oil may splash. You should be able to fit 3-4 doughnuts in the pan at once. Fry for 60 seconds then turn the doughnuts over in the oil and fry for a further 60 seconds. Remove with a slotted spoon and pat with kitchen paper to remove any excess oil. Repeat in batches until all of the doughnuts have been cooked, making sure that the oil is still around 180°C between each batch.

7   Once the doughnuts are cool, they can be iced. Combine the icing sugar and malted drink powder in a bowl then slowly add the water and vanilla extract, stirring continuously. You should be left with a smooth, thick icing. It's important to make it thicker than you might expect: even a few drops too much water will create an icing that runs straight off the doughnut rather than sitting proudly on top of it.

8   Dip the tops of the doughnuts in the icing then leave to set on a wire rack. These are best eaten soon after baking.

TO SHARE

COCONUT LIME LOAF

After the excesses of doughnuts, this gentle loaf might be a relief. It's a mild, coconut-flavoured dough flecked with lime zest and baked in a tin. Because coconut milk is relatively high in fat, no extra butter or eggs are necessary to make it soft and tender.

Makes one large loaf, enough for
  12–14 thick slices
400g strong white flour
7g instant dried yeast
1 teaspoon salt
3 tablespoons caster sugar

300ml full-fat coconut milk
Zest of 2 limes
Milk or beaten egg, to glaze (optional)

900g loaf tin

1   In a large bowl, combine the flour and yeast. Stir in the salt and sugar. Heat the coconut milk over a low heat until tepid, stirring well until smooth (coconut milk can tend to separate in the can, with the fat forming a thick layer on top). Add most of the coconut milk and zest to the dry ingredients and mix to combine. If the dough feels dry and rubbery, add the remaining coconut milk (better that the dough is slightly too sticky than too stiff). Knead for 10 minutes until stretchy and smooth. Set aside in a large, covered bowl to rise at room temperature for about 1½ hours, or until it has doubled in size.

2   Shape the risen dough into a rough rugby-ball shape, approximately the size of the loaf tin, folding it over on itself to collect any 'loose' dough underneath and leave a tight 'skin' on top. This careful shaping will help to ensure an even rise. Line the base of the loaf tin with a strip of baking parchment and place the dough in there to prove for a further hour. Meanwhile, preheat the oven to 180°C/fan 160°C/gas mark 4.

3   Brush the top of the loaf with milk or egg, if using, and score deeply along the length of the dough with a sharp knife. Bake for 40 minutes. The bread should sound hollow when tapped underneath if properly cooked. Let cool completely on a wire rack before serving with lime curd (adapt from the lemon curd on page 324) or, if you fancy it, chocolate spread.

Variations
I've deliberately left this loaf very plain — I like the reassuring simplicity of it. If you want a more bells-and-whistles type of bread, however, it can certainly be adapted. Packed with chopped dried pineapple, mango and apple, candied peel and sultanas it will become a sort of tropical tea loaf.

MONKEY BREAD

The origins of the name of this tear-and-share bread are anybody's guess. There's been plenty of speculation: perhaps it's a reference to the free-for-all serving style, or the 'monkeying around' involved in piecing it together. One person, perhaps hallucinating, suggested that it's because the bread resembles 'a bunch of monkeys jumbled together'. Forget the name, though: despite the whimsy, this really is a very good bread, cinnamon-spiced and stickily caramelised all over.

Makes one loaf, serving 8–10
400g strong white flour
7g instant dried yeast
1 teaspoon salt
250ml full-fat milk
30g unsalted butter, softened

For the coating:
75g unsalted butter

2 teaspoons ground cinnamon
100g soft light brown sugar

23–27cm diameter bundt tin or deep 20cm round cake tin

p155

1   Mix the flour and yeast in a large bowl before stirring in the salt. Warm the milk over a very low heat until just tepid then add to the dry ingredients along with the 30g butter. Combine, then knead for 10 minutes — you know the drill by now: the dough ought to be elastic, smooth and with a light sheen to it by the time you've finished. Leave the dough to rise in a large, covered bowl at room temperature until roughly twice its original size. This will take approximately an hour, but the yeast may act more slowly if your kitchen is particularly cold.

2   Melt the 75g butter for the coating in a small pan over a low heat. Brush the inside of the tin liberally with some of it then set the rest aside. In a separate bowl, combine the cinnamon and sugar.

3   Break the risen dough into small chunks — each no bigger than a ping-pong ball — and roll into rough spheres. Dip each ball in the melted butter and then in the sugar and cinnamon mixture to coat. Pile the sugar-coated dough balls into the greased tin (there's no need to overthink the arrangement. Just stack the balls in messy layers until you've used all of the dough). Don't press them down to neatly tessellate: they'll expand to fit snugly as they prove and bake. Leave to prove at room temperature for around an hour, preheating the oven to 180°C/fan 160°C/ gas mark 4 in the meantime.

4   When the dough has risen, bake for 30 minutes then turn the bread out of the tin as soon as it's out of the oven. It should slide out easily as long as the tin was well greased. Once it's been inverted onto a plate you'll be able to see the pattern of interlocking buns held together with a buttery, caramel glaze. Pick off a bun with your fingers and enjoy while still warm.

Variation
Sprinkle a small handful of chopped nuts (any will do) between the layers as you stack the dough balls in their tin.

CRUMBLE-TOPPED PEAR & ALMOND SLICE

This bread combines succulent pears with honey, almonds and a crumble topping. Best eaten at breakfast time, with a strong coffee.

Makes enough for 8
300g strong white flour
1½ teaspoons instant dried yeast
½ teaspoon salt
2 tablespoons honey
190ml milk

For the pear topping:
4 firm dessert pears, such as Williams, Comice or Bosc
30g unsalted butter

4 tablespoons honey
¼ teaspoon ground allspice
70g flaked almonds

For the crumble topping:
50g unsalted butter, at room temperature
50g white flour (preferably plain, but strong will do)
40g soft light brown sugar
30g flaked almonds, finely chopped

1   Combine the 300g flour, yeast and salt in a large bowl, watching that the salt and yeast don't come into direct contact before mixing. Dissolve the 2 tablespoons of honey in the milk in a small pan, heating until tepid, then add this mixture to the dry ingredients. Combine and knead for 5-10 minutes, until less sticky and more elastic, and then set aside in a large bowl, covered loosely with cling film. Leave to rise at room temperature for an hour, during which time it should approximately double in size.

2   While the dough rises, prepare the pear topping. Peel, core and slice the pears. Melt the 30g butter with the 4 tablespoons of honey and allspice in a large pan over a low heat then add the pears. Increase to a medium heat and cook, stirring regularly, for 5 minutes. The pears should slightly soften and caramelise, but take off the heat if the slices begin to disintegrate. Add the flaked almonds and stir to combine. Leave to cool.

3   Prepare the crumble by rubbing the 50g butter into the 50g flour and sugar with your fingertips until the mixture comes together in small clumps. Add the chopped flaked almonds and stir to combine. Chill in the refrigerator until ready to use.

4   Turn the risen dough out onto a lightly floured surface and roll to around 20x30cm, pausing after rolling to allow the dough to shrink back a little, then re-rolling until it stays at the desired size. Transfer to a large baking tray lined with baking parchment and leave to prove for 30-45 minutes. Preheat the oven to 200°C/fan 180°C/gas mark 6.

5   Arrange the honey-coated, almond-encrusted pear slices over the risen dough, leaving a border of a centimetre or two around the outside. Sprinkle over the crumble mixture. Brush the dough border with any remaining butter and honey liquid from the pear mixture. Bake for 10 minutes, then reduce the temperature to 180°C/fan 160°C/gas mark 4 and bake for a further 20 minutes.

BRIOCHE

The amount of butter used in this brioche looks heinous on paper but it's really important not to skimp: a low-fat brioche is no brioche at all. And as long as you're thorough when kneading and patient during the rise, the bread will emerge from the oven airily light in spite of the richness. This isn't a quick recipe — the bread needs a couple of long rises, and an overnight spell in the fridge — but it's this slow fermentation that will give the brioche a soft texture and help this heavily enriched dough rise.

Makes 1 large brioche
450g strong white flour
3 teaspoons instant dried yeast
1 teaspoon salt
3 tablespoons sugar
130ml milk
4 large eggs
250g unsalted butter, softened

1 large egg, lightly beaten, to glaze

Deep 20cm round cake tin or, if you're lucky enough to own one, a large brioche mould

📷 p158

1   Combine the flour and yeast in a large bowl, before stirring in the salt and sugar. Very slightly heat the milk over a low heat until barely lukewarm. This is particularly important if the milk is fridge-cold: the yeast already has to battle with a block of butter before it can get to work — it needs a little warmth to help it along. Whisk the slightly warmed milk together with the eggs and add this all to the dry ingredients. Mix well.

2   Knead the dough for 10 minutes until smooth and elastic. The aim here is to develop the gluten and strengthen the dough before the butter is added. Once the butter is incorporated, fat will coat the flour and inhibit gluten formation — so this period of kneading gives the gluten a head start.

3   Once the dough has been kneaded, work in the butter. This won't be a case of just stirring it in, as the butter and dough have very different consistencies. Put the dough back into the mixing bowl and add the butter a third at a time, squeezing it in with your hands. It will feel like trying to mix oil and water at first, but after some mixing (which, with the slippery, supple dough, is surprisingly therapeutic) you'll soon find that the dough comes smoothly together. Once all the butter has been worked in, you'll be able to tip the dough back out of its bowl and knead for a further 5 minutes. By this point the dough will feel unlike any other: cool, satiny, elastic — it's a pleasure to work with.

4   Place the dough in a large, covered bowl to rise at room temperature for 2 hours or so — long enough to double in size. Now gently press down the risen dough to deflate, re-cover the bowl and leave to rest in the fridge for at least 6 hours, or as long as 18 hours. During this time the dough will rise slightly due to the residual warmth from its initial rise, but as soon as it reaches fridge temperature the yeast will effectively become dormant and the rising will cease. This spell in the fridge is therefore more about flavour and practicality than about the rise itself: at cooler temperatures, more nuanced flavours will develop in the dough, whilst the cooling

will set the butter and allow for far easier shaping. One thing to bear in mind is that the fridge will have a drying effect on the dough if the bowl isn't securely covered, so do give it a couple of layers of cling film or foil.

5   When ready, prise the chilled dough from its bowl. By now it should be almost putty-like in its plasticity. Shape into a large ball and press down so that it's wide enough to fill the 20cm round tin. Grease the base and sides of the tin and, if the tin isn't loose-bottomed or spring-form, line the base with a circle of baking parchment. Place the dough in the tin. You could also shape it more intricately if you'd prefer, as in the cheese brioche recipe on page 117.

6   Cover the tin loosely with cling film and leave the dough to prove at room temperature for up to 2½ hours, or until almost doubled in size. This proving period is a good deal lengthier than for most other breads because the dough is both highly enriched and still cool from the fridge. Towards the end of the proving time, preheat the oven to 200°C/fan 180°/gas mark 6.

7   Brush the top of the brioche with egg to glaze and bake for 15 minutes, then reduce the temperature to 180°C/fan 160°C/gas mark 4 and bake for a further 25 minutes. The crust should be a deep colour thanks to the browning effect of the egg glaze, and the loaf should be well risen. Let it cool for a short while in the tin before unmoulding and cooling completely on a wire rack.

MARZIPAN

I love marzipan. I like to painstakingly peel it from battenberg cake and eat it in one long strip, or to uncover, with joy, a log of the stuff nestled inside the buttery dough of a stollen. Every year, great slabs of Christmas cake are left, marzipan-less, around the house. There are even finger-shaped gouges in the block in the kitchen cupboard. For all its sweetness and lurid yellow colouring, I'm very fond of the shop-bought variety, although if you prefer your marzipan with a little more delicacy of flavour, making your own is very easy to do. The pistachio marzipan below is a more grown-up version of the traditional type. Feel free to add a couple of drops of vanilla extract or even rosewater to taste. A little orange zest can work well, too. This is one for even the most stubborn of marzipan-phobes.

CHERRY STOLLEN WITH PISTACHIO MARZIPAN

Sour cherries partner with citrussy cardamom and pistachio in this stollen variation. Unlike cheap supermarket versions, which have a heavy, cakey feel and a taste that lies somewhere between cloves and cardboard, homemade stollen is a joy to eat. This is not the time to scrimp and save — generosity is key: stud with as much fruit and peel as it will hold, brush liberally with melted butter and dust with a thick crust of icing sugar. More really is more here.

250g strong white flour
5 cardamom pods, seeds only, crushed
½ teaspoon ground cinnamon
2 cloves, crushed, or 2 large pinches of
   ground cloves
7g instant dried yeast
20g caster sugar
½ teaspoon salt
150g unsalted butter
115ml milk
1 large egg
1 teaspoon vanilla extract
Zest of 1 orange

125g dried cherries, roughly chopped
75g mixed peel
30g icing sugar, to dust

For the pistachio marzipan:
150g pistachio kernels
130g icing sugar
Pinch of salt
30g egg white
A couple of drops of vanilla extract
   or rosewater, to taste

📷 p161

1   Combine the flour, ground spices, yeast, sugar and salt in a large bowl.

2   Melt half the butter in a small pan. Once melted, stir in the milk, egg, vanilla extract and orange zest. The mixture should be lukewarm from the residual heat in the pan, but if it's not quite tepid, heat it very, very gently over a low heat, just enough to make it slightly warm to the touch. Take care not to heat it too much — if it feels very warm, let it cool a bit.

3   Add the milk mixture to the dry ingredients. Once everything's thoroughly combined in the bowl, tip it out onto a clean work surface and knead. Prepare to get your hands dirty: the mixture needs to be kneaded for a good 10 minutes now. The mixture may start out a little wet, but due to the high butter content you'll find that it's less annoyingly sticky than some doughs. It will soon begin to feel smoother and more elastic (although it'll never reach the sort of silkiness you might expect in a basic bread dough), and after 10 minutes you can add the dried cherries and the peel.

4   Hard graft over, pop the dough back in a large bowl, cover with cling film and leave it for 1½-2 hours to double in size. It rises quite slowly, but don't be tempted to put it in too warm a spot to speed it up — normal room temperature is perfect for the yeast to get going.

5   While the dough is rising, make the pistachio marzipan. Grind the pistachios in a coffee grinder, in batches, or in a food processor. Alternatively, you could finely chop them then pound using a pestle and mortar. Transfer to a mixing bowl, add the icing sugar and salt and stir to combine. Sift the mixture into another bowl. Add the egg white (30g equates to around two-thirds of the white of one large egg — this may seem fiddly, but adding even slightly too much risks making the mixture wet and sticky, so do weigh it if possible). Combine the egg with the pistachio mixture by stirring and mashing it under the back of a fork. It might look too dry to start with, but it will come together. Once integrated you can use your hands to very lightly work the paste into a smooth mixture. If it's too dry to come together add a few more drops of egg, or even some vanilla extract if you'd prefer.

6 Turn the risen dough out onto a work surface dusted with flour, and roll it out to a rectangle approximately 30x20cm. It doesn't matter if the dough is still slightly sticky — just flour the surface with extra flour as necessary. Roll the marzipan to a rough 30cm long log shape and lay it along the middle of the dough. Roll the dough around the marzipan with the seam downwards, and fold the ends of the log underneath. Gently pat into a more squat, slightly flattened shape. Let it rise for about 1 hour, or until the bread has increased in size by half. Preheat the oven to 180°C/fan 160°C/gas mark 4 towards the end of the rising time.

7 Bake for 40 minutes. Towards the end of the bake, melt the remaining 75g of butter over a low heat. As soon as the stollen is ready, brush it all over (even underneath) with the melted butter. It seems like an extravagance, but this is what will create a meltingly soft crust and the sort of richness that really makes you think twice before going in for a second slice. Once cool, dust generously with icing sugar.

Because it's almost mummified in butter and sugar, this bread keeps surprisingly well. Wrap in greaseproof paper or foil and continue to indulge, at your leisure, over the Christmas period.

Variations
Stollen is archetypal Christmas fodder, but it's too good to have just once a year. Swap the cloves for a pinch of nutmeg or perhaps ginger for a less Christmassy-tasting bread. Even better, add a handful of dark chocolate chips to the dough and use a traditional almond marzipan.

WHITE CHOCOLATE HAZELNUT COURONNE

Why go for the jewel in the crown when you can have the crown itself? This couronne, or crown, is rolled, layered, swirled, cut, woven, twisted and sealed to create a bread fit for a queen. The shaping might look difficult at first glance but it helps to skim through the basic steps before starting and to look at the photos to give yourself an idea of the end goal.

Makes one large couronne, serving 8-10
300g strong white flour
1½ teaspoons instant dried yeast
½ teaspoon salt
2 tablespoons caster sugar
200ml milk
¼ teaspoon almond extract
30g unsalted butter, softened
Zest of 1 lemon

For the filling:
60g unsalted butter, softened
40g soft light brown sugar
1 teaspoon vanilla extract
100g blanched hazelnuts
100g white chocolate, coarsely chopped
1 large egg, lightly beaten, to glaze

📷 p163 / p164

1 Combine the flour and yeast in a large bowl before stirring in the salt and sugar. Warm the milk and almond extract over a low heat until tepid then add this to the flour mixture along with the butter and lemon zest. Mix well to combine then knead for 5 minutes or so to develop the gluten in the dough. Leave the dough to

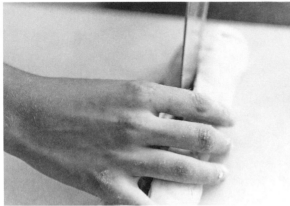

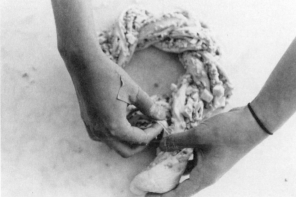

double in size at room temperature in a large, covered bowl. This should take 1–1½ hours.

2   Prepare the filling components: beat together the butter, sugar and vanilla extract until smooth and spreadable; roast the hazelnuts at 180°C/fan 160°C/gas mark 4 (if the ones you've bought aren't ready-roasted) before finely chopping them.

3   Roll the risen dough out to a rectangle that is approximately 45x20cm. You'll need to lightly flour the work surface and the dough. It will keep shrinking back as you roll it, but you should find that with some perseverance and a firm hand the dough will eventually reach the desired size and stay there.

4   Spread the butter and sugar mixture thinly over the dough then scatter over the chopped hazelnuts and white chocolate. Roll up tightly from long edge to long edge, to create a roll of dough approximately 45cm long. Tack the remaining long edge to the work surface using a slightly dampened finger and smear it outwards so that when the log is rolled onto it, it will stick to itself (see top-right picture, opposite).

5   This next stage is tricky, and it can be invaluable to have another pair of helping hands ready at this point to support the dough as you twist it. Line a large baking tray with baking parchment and transfer the dough to this. It's far easier to put it in place now than after it has been woven into a fragile ring shape.
    Using a sharp knife, cut right through the dough along the length of the roll, almost completely halving it but stopping just before one end, to leave the two halves barely attached. Now, keeping the cut sides of the dough strands facing upwards at all times, cross the strands over each other, starting at the end where they join. Now cross them over each other again — the strand that went underneath the first time, will this time go over the top. Repeat until the two strands are twisted together along their entire length. Curve this plait round into a circle shape. Don't worry if the strands splay open a little as you work — just keep pressing them back into shape.
    Cut through the final piece of dough where the two strands were still joined and attach to the other end of the loop, pressing gently to secure the dough into one continuous circle. If there are any chunks of white chocolate protruding from the surface of the circle, lightly press these back down into the layers of dough to prevent them from burning as the bread bakes.

6   Leave to prove at room temperature for 45–60 minutes, or until around 1½ times its original size. Preheat the oven to 180°C/fan 160°C/gas mark 4 while you wait.

7   Brush the risen couronne with the egg wash and bake for 30 minutes. It should be well risen, with intertwined layers of rich, golden brown dough.

Variation
For a festive couronne, swap the filling for a tin of sweetened chestnut spread with some currants, a couple of tablespoons of cornflour, a capful of brandy and some orange zest mixed in.

BISCUITS

CRUNCH

GINGER BISCUITS

DARK CHOCOLATE ORANGE BOURBONS

BISCOTTI

CHEW

ROSE & BURNT HONEY FLORENTINES

ORANGE LEMON COCONUT BISCUITS • PECAN COOKIES

HAZELNUT DARK CHOCOLATE COOKIES • SPICED OAT THINS

CRUMBLE

SHORTBREAD • RYE OAT DIGESTIVES

TAHINI LEMON BISCUITS

SNAP

CINNAMON ORANGE TUILES • FENNEL SEED & CHILLI SNAPS

STILTON & POPPY SEED CRACKERS

I used to think that baking biscuits was more hassle than it was worth. The pleasures of the biscuit tin, full of worthy rich teas, custard creams and hobnob after hobnob after hobnob (because one is never enough) weren't to be complicated or tampered with. But one day, I made a buttery shortbread and finally realised what I'd been missing. You can prepare a batch of florentines, chocolate hazelnut cookies or fennel seed crackers in about the time it takes to trudge to the shop for a packet of digestives, and the taste is incomparable. If you want your biscuits neatly dimpled, crimped and stamped, rippled with chocolate or jammily grinning back at you — buy them. But if you want biscuits with oomph — heavily spiced, packed with chunks of chocolate and nut or bursting with citrus — you'd better turn the oven on.

SHAPING BISCUITS

In this chapter you'll find biscuits of every shape and size. Some are neatly rolled and stamped into shapes as simple or as artful as you like. One is thinly spread with a spatula and a steady hand — a hair's breadth between success and broken shards. Another is piped into elegant fingers. But for others, the magic doesn't happen until after the biscuits are in the oven and out of your hands: cookies which, at first dolloped haphazardly onto the tray, emerge from the oven as fat, craggy, chewy discs.

How a biscuit ought to be shaped depends entirely on the type of dough in question. Both the initial consistency of the dough and the way in which it behaves when heated will have a bearing on the shaping methods suitable. The former is easy enough to gauge, but the latter is less straightforward. Chilled cookie dough, for instance, can be rolled thin and cut into neat circles but spreads a great deal as it bakes, so if you start off with just a thin layer of the stuff, you'll end up with a crisp. Don't worry too much, though: I've tried to be clear in these recipes regarding shaping, and the more biscuits you make, the more you'll get a feel for the dough.

RAISING DOUGH

Many biscuits use baking powder or bicarbonate of soda to give them a little lift in the oven. Even if the rise itself is only marginal, it has a significant impact on the texture: the tiny air pockets expanded by raising agents lighten the biscuit, giving a better crunch. Plus the more a biscuit grows vertically, the less it'll spread outwards. This honeycomb structure isn't the only benefit of using a raising agent, though. Bicarbonate of soda brings with it a whole set of benefits for flavour and colour, too, which I've explained on page 178. Some crackers even use yeast for a rounder flavour and good snap.

CHILLING OUT

Not all biscuit doughs need to be chilled, but a spell in the refrigerator can be useful for those particularly high in fat, firming the dough and helping the biscuits to retain their shape while baking. Whether this chilling period should happen before or after shaping depends on the biscuit: a very rich, piped dough will need to be chilled *after* shaping, or else it will be impossible to pipe; a rolled-and-cut-out biscuit will benefit from being briefly chilled *before* being shaped, making the dough easier to handle. A balance does need to be struck, though: if dough is allowed to chill completely prior to being rolled, it will tend to crumble and crack, so give it 10 minutes or so at room temperature to very slightly soften before shaping.

You can also freeze most doughs. Wrap in baking parchment and then seal in a freezer bag, defrosting the dough overnight in the fridge when you're ready to use it.

A NOTE ON BAKING

Because biscuits are small, and have high sugar content and low hydration, they bake very quickly, with only a few minutes separating raw dough from burnt biscuits. To avoid blowing it all at this last hurdle, time the biscuits accurately in the oven and keep a close eye on them. Most are ready when their edges have deepened to a golden brown colour.

The type of baking tray you use will have a greater impact on biscuits than with other baking. A heavy-duty one will conduct heat more slowly than a thin one, so you might find that biscuits cooked on the latter will spread less and cook faster.

A common error is to bake biscuits for too long, mistaking their softness when they first come out of the oven for rawness. Most biscuits will be chewy when freshly baked, firming only as they cool. Even the crunchiest biscuit will be a little limp while it's still hot. The cooling period here is therefore every bit as important as the oven time. Remember that you can always return a batch of slightly underdone biscuits to the oven for a few minutes if they're still soft after cooling, but there's no salvaging over-baked, rock-hard ones.

TEXTURE

I've arranged the biscuits in this chapter by texture: crunch, chew, crumble and snap. It's not a rigorous categorising scheme, but it does a fair job of dividing biscuits by fancy, I think. A biscuit with crunch is fine with tea, but a chewy cookie provides a comfort all of its own. A crumbly, butter-rich biscuit is an exercise in indulgence, while a crisp cracker is a simpler pleasure.

CRUNCH

GINGER BISCUITS

There are always ginger biscuits left in the tin once the more exciting ones have long since been pilfered. Not even the lengthiest soak in a mug of tea can soften them. I'm convinced that they would be the last biscuits standing after a nuclear apocalypse.

This version, however, bears little resemblance to those bright orange rusks. These are spicily gingery and dark with treacle. With a little luck you'll bake them just right, leaving the centres densely chewy while the edges set to a crunch.

Makes 28-32
250g plain flour
125g unsalted butter, cubed
5 teaspoons ground ginger

½ teaspoon bicarbonate of soda
200g caster or granulated sugar
1 large egg
100g black treacle

1   In a large mixing bowl, rub the butter into the flour using your fingertips until only very small visible flakes of butter remain. Stir in the ginger, bicarbonate of soda and sugar. Whisk together the egg and treacle and add to the dry mixture. Use the back of a fork to mash the ingredients until the dough comes smoothly together.

2   Refrigerate the dough for 30 minutes, meanwhile preheating the oven to 180°C/ fan 160°C/gas mark 4. Line two baking trays with baking parchment.

3   Break off pieces of the chilled dough, each about the size of a Brussels sprout, and roll into balls, spacing them widely apart across the baking trays. You should be able to fit 8-12 on each tray. Whatever dough is left over can be placed back in the fridge until ready to be baked in a second batch.

4   Bake for 15-17 minutes, swapping the baking trays on their shelves halfway through cooking if you're not using a fan oven. The biscuits will seem very soft when they first come out of the oven, but please don't be tempted to bake them longer as they set firmer as they cool. Leave them on a wire rack until completely set.

5   Repeat shaping and baking in batches until all the dough has been used.

Variations
Try adding a teaspoon of cinnamon and ¼ teaspoon of ground cloves for a more Christmassy biscuit, similar to continental *lebkuchen*. Alternatively, you could add the bright zest of an orange to kick the biscuit out of its languid toffee sweetness and into life.

GINGER LIME SANDWICHES

A slick of buttercream can transform a biscuit. Make your ginger biscuits (see page 171) and prepare this buttercream while they cool.

60g unsalted butter
Zest and juice of 2 limes

160g icing sugar

Beat the butter until smooth then add the lime zest. Beat in the icing sugar a little at a time and add a splash of lime juice, to taste. Sandwich pairs of cooled ginger biscuits together with a dollop of buttercream.

DARK CHOCOLATE ORANGE BOURBONS

The key to a good bourbon is the contrast between the mild cocoa biscuit and the chocolate kick inside. These ones stir things up with a peppering of orange zest, too.

The biscuits will lose some of their crispness after several hours, so if you won't be eating them all at once (although I can't imagine why anyone wouldn't) reserve some of the biscuit halves and buttercream to fill them when you're ready. The buttercream should be kept in the fridge in the meantime, but bring it up to room temperature before using.

Makes 16-20 sandwich biscuits
240g plain flour
4 tablespoons cocoa powder
140g unsalted butter, cubed
100g caster sugar
Zest of 1 orange
30ml milk or water

For the buttercream:
100g unsalted butter, softened
2 tablespoons cocoa powder
Zest of 1 orange
150g icing sugar

📷 p172

1   Sift the flour and 4 tablespoons of cocoa powder together into a large bowl. (I rarely advocate sifting but here it helps to incorporate the cocoa powder, which has a tendency to clump.) Rub in the 140g butter using your fingertips, working lightly and speedily until no visible flakes of butter remain. Stir in the caster sugar and orange zest then sprinkle on the milk or water. Use a butter knife or similar to 'cut' through the mixture, blending the liquid with the dry ingredients until the whole lot has begun to come together in small clusters.

2   Press the dough into one piece, wrap in cling film and refrigerate for 30 minutes or more. Meanwhile, preheat the oven to 180°C/fan 160°C/gas mark 4 and line a large baking tray with baking parchment.

3   Depending on how chilled the dough is after its time in the fridge, you may need to let it soften just slightly before rolling. If the dough is too hard, it'll crack as you roll; if it's too soft, it'll stick. It should feel cool to the touch and just firm. Roll out on a lightly floured work surface to around 25x30cm. Cut into rectangles approximately 8x3cm, although the precise dimensions don't matter as long as

all of the shapes are more or less the same size. You can stack and re-roll any offcuts, but doing this more than once could result in the dough toughening.

4   Transfer the shapes to the lined baking tray and bake for 12 minutes. Leave to cool completely on a wire rack.

5   While the biscuits are cooking and cooling, prepare the buttercream. Beat the 100g butter, 2 tablespoons of cocoa powder and orange zest until smooth then add the icing sugar a little at a time. The mixture should be smooth and soft enough to spread or pipe.

6   Spread or pipe a generous layer of buttercream onto half of the cooled biscuits, sandwiching with the remaining biscuits. Chill in the fridge for 10 minutes if they need any extra help setting.

BISCOTTI

Considering that the word 'biscuit' (and so 'biscotti') has etymological roots in old French for 'twice cooked', it could be said that these are some of the few biscuits that live up to their name. Biscotti are cooked first as a 'log' of dough, and again later in slices to dry the biscuits, taking them to their trademark state of desiccation.

These keep well when stored in an airtight container, meaning that you can double or even treble the quantities given here to make a larger batch.

Makes 12-16
125g plain flour
1 teaspoon baking powder
Pinch of salt
¼ teaspoon ground cinnamon
85g caster sugar
Zest of ½ lemon

50g blanched almonds or pistachio
   kernels, roughly chopped
50g currants
1 large egg, lightly beaten
1 tablespoon milk

p175

1   Preheat the oven to 180°C/fan 160°C/gas mark 4 and line a baking tray with baking parchment.

2   In a large bowl, combine the flour, baking powder, salt, cinnamon and sugar. Add the lemon zest and toss through the almonds or pistachios and currants. Add the egg and milk, first stirring then cutting through the mixture to combine. You should be left with a reasonably sticky, heavy dough.

3   Lightly flour the dough and your hands and shape into a rough log, 20-25cm long. It doesn't matter if it's not completely even. Position it in the middle of the lined baking tray.

4   Bake for 35 minutes then, while it's still hot, cut the baked dough into slices 1½-2cm thick using a sharp, serrated knife and a gentle sawing motion.

5   Reduce the oven temperature to 150°C/fan 130°C/gas mark 2. Lay the slices

across a large baking tray (or two, if necessary) and bake for a further 10 minutes before turning the slices over and baking for another 10 minutes. Leave to cool completely before serving with — of course — a strong coffee for dunking.

Variations
This is a versatile recipe, so feel free to adapt it to your tastes. The flavours I've used are simply cinnamon, lemon and almond but you could also add a teaspoon of ground ginger, some sour cherries or a handful of chocolate chips. One particularly good variation includes ground fennel seeds, added to taste.

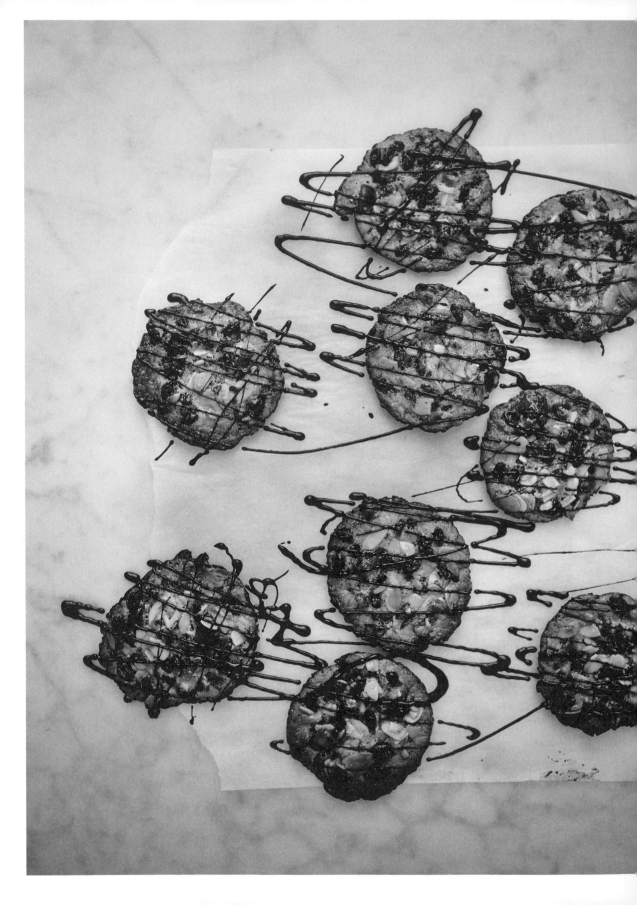

CHEW

ROSE & BURNT HONEY FLORENTINES

I'd usually cringe at the thought of using something as twee as rose petals but they're actually lovely to eat as well as to look at. You can find them online, in specialist cake decorating shops and in some of the more expensive supermarkets. Just make sure you buy the kind sold as edible rose petals — nobody wants potpourri florentines. But if you can't find (or be bothered to find) rose petals it's really no tragedy.

Cooked for a few minutes until it darkens and sizzles, honey takes on a far mellower flavour. The intense sweetness is subdued and toasted, toffee notes come to the fore. It's an easy way of making a little honey go a long way.

Makes 8-10 florentines
50g honey
50g caster sugar
50g unsalted butter
1 tablespoon single cream
1 teaspoon rosewater
2 tablespoons plain flour

50g flaked almonds
50g sultanas or raisins
50g glacé cherries, roughly chopped
4 tablespoons dried rose petals
150g dark chocolate

 p176

1   Preheat the oven to 180°C/fan 160°C/gas mark 4 and line a large baking tray with a sheet of baking parchment.

2   Place the honey in a medium pan over a low heat. After a couple of minutes it'll begin to bubble: let it simmer, stirring regularly, for 1-2 minutes, or until the honey is fragrant and has darkened by a couple of shades.

3   Add the sugar, butter, cream and rosewater to the pan, stir to combine and then bring back to a simmer. As soon as it reaches the boil, turn off the heat and add the flour, beating to combine. Add the flaked almonds, dried fruit, cherries and rose petals.

4   Spoon into small mounds spaced well apart on the lined baking tray (they'll spread a lot while baking — don't underestimate them). You may need to spread the batch over two baking trays to lessen the likelihood of a conjoined monster florentine emerging from the oven later.

5   Bake for 15-17 minutes. The florentines will spread to wide discs and their edges will become lacy and golden brown. Once baked, but while they're still hot, gently nudge their outer edges inwards using a spoon, pushing them back into a neatly circular shape. Leave to cool in the tray until firm, then transfer to a wire rack.

6   Melt the chocolate in a heatproof bowl suspended over a pan of simmering water or, very carefully and in short bursts, in the microwave. Using a pastry brush, spread the underside of each florentine with a layer of chocolate and leave to set, in the fridge if necessary.

ORANGE LEMON COCONUT BISCUITS

Coconut has a tendency to be blandly sweet but lifted by orange, lemon and cardamom these biscuits are a far cry from the terminally beige biscuits we've grown used to. They're bright, light and chewy.

Makes 20
110g butter
175g caster sugar
1 large egg
Zest of 1 orange
Zest of 1 lemon
150g plain flour
½ teaspoon bicarbonate of soda

¼ teaspoon salt
8 cardamom pods, seeds only, ground
   or crushed*
100g desiccated coconut

* I grind the seeds in a coffee grinder, although crushing in a pestle and mortar will work just as well

1   Preheat the oven to 180°C/fan 160°C/gas mark 4 and line a couple of baking trays with baking parchment.

2   Cream the butter and sugar together in a large bowl, beat in the egg and then add the orange and lemon zest.

3   In a separate bowl, combine the flour, bicarbonate of soda, salt and ground cardamom. Stir this into the wet ingredients then fold in the desiccated coconut.

4   Use two teaspoons to heap little mounds of batter onto the lined trays, spacing them well apart as they'll spread as they cook. You may have to bake in a couple of batches if they won't all fit in at once.

5   Bake for 12-14 minutes, or until barely golden. Let firm slightly on their tray before transferring to a wire rack to cool completely.

GOLDEN BROWN: BICARB OF SODA & THE MAILLARD REACTION

There's more to bicarbonate of soda than rising power. In the next two recipes, it helps to give the cookies their hallmark golden brown colour and lightly caramelised flavour. The chemistry at work here is complex and comprises many individual reactions, but to sum up: when sugar is strongly heated in the presence of certain proteins, the Maillard reaction occurs. This involves the browning of the outside of the food and the development of a set of unique flavours. It's what happens to the outside of a steak as it sears on the griddle, to the crust of a baking loaf, to deep amber *dulce de leche* and to sizzling chips.

The Maillard reaction works best in quite alkaline environments, and this is where bicarbonate of soda, which is an alkali itself, comes in. When a food that contains proteins, sugar and bicarbonate of soda is cooked at a high heat, the Maillard reaction will occur particularly quickly. For this reason, when cookies are leavened with bicarbonate of soda, the result is a golden, caramel-flavoured biscuit — despite their short baking time. It's an exciting bit of kitchen chemistry. It's also what gives bagels (see page 109) their perfectly browned crust.

PECAN COOKIES

Walnuts are bitter, almonds sweet, hazelnuts stridently autumnal and fat macadamia nuts buttery. Pecans, however, perch somewhere in between: sweet, nutty, delicate, rich and woody all at once. It's this balance which, in my opinion, makes pecans the finest and most versatile of the lot.

Makes 14-16
150g pecans, roughly chopped
140g unsalted butter
60g soft light brown sugar
100g caster or granulated sugar

1 large egg
1½ teaspoons vanilla extract
200g plain flour
¼ teaspoon bicarbonate of soda
¼ teaspoon salt

1   Preheat the oven to 180°C/fan 160°C/gas mark 4. Line a large baking tray with baking parchment.

2   Toast the pecans for 8-10 minutes on a baking tray in the preheated oven, or until they just begin to darken. They should by now smell sweet and nutty. Set aside to cool, leaving the oven on ready for the cookies.

3   Melt the butter either in the microwave or in a pan over a low heat. Set aside to cool slightly before adding the sugars to it, beating vigorously for a minute. Stir in the egg and vanilla extract. In a separate bowl, combine the flour, bicarbonate of soda and salt. Add this to the wet ingredients, mixing only until just combined. Add the chopped pecans.

4   Using a couple of tablespoons, scoop out walnut-sized balls of dough and space well apart on the baking tray, reserving some for a second batch if they won't all fit. Bake for 13-15 minutes — they should be just turning golden brown at the edges. They'll firm as they cool, so don't worry if they feel soft straight after baking. As for the eating, there's no need for preciousness: dunk unceremoniously in a glass of cold milk.

LET IT REST

If you can bear to wait, try wrapping your next batch of raw cookie dough tightly in cling film and refrigerating for 24-48 hours before baking. During this time some of the starches in the flour will begin to break down into sugars. The result: cookies that are chewier, more deeply coloured and with a toffee taste.

HAZELNUT DARK CHOCOLATE COOKIES

These cookies are vegan, but you could be forgiven for not realising it. They're laden with chocolate and nuts, densely chewy at their centre, with caramelised, gold-brown edges. There's nothing about them that feels lacking. I made these regularly when I was living in university halls of residence and they were always stolen from my cupboard. I would have been annoyed but it was a bittersweet victory, seeing the biscuit-pilferers — vocally, obnoxiously anti-vegetarian and anti-vegan — unwittingly eating their words.

Where most biscuits use butter for tenderness and taste, these use nut oils. I like to use hazelnut oil to complement the hazelnut in the dough, but almond oil also works very well (and is far cheaper) for a gentler, sweeter flavour. You ought to be able to find both almond and hazelnut oils in most large supermarkets. You could swap the nut oil for corn oil or groundnut oil at a push — the texture will still be good, but the flavour will be compromised, so add a tad more vanilla extract if you do so.

You can buy specialist vegan chocolate for these cookies if you want, but you'll find that most good-quality dark chocolate is vegan anyway, especially those with high-percentage cocoa solids. But do check the ingredients first: all sorts of dairy-derived products, amongst them butterfat and milk powder, can be smuggled into cheaper brands. If you're not fussed about making these cookies vegan, it won't matter what dark chocolate you use, and you can use dairy milk in place of the specified soya milk.

Makes 14-16
100g soft light brown sugar
100g caster sugar
100ml hazelnut or almond oil
60ml soya milk
1 teaspoon vanilla extract
200g plain flour

¼ teaspoon bicarbonate of soda
¼ teaspoon salt
75g dark chocolate, chopped into small chunks
75g hazelnuts, roughly chopped

p181

1   Preheat the oven to 180°C/fan 160°C/gas mark 4 and line a large baking tray with baking parchment.

2   In a large bowl, beat the sugars, oil and milk vigorously for one minute — this helps to incorporate air and to emulsify the mixture — before stirring in the vanilla extract. In a separate bowl, combine the flour, bicarbonate of soda and salt. Stir the dry ingredients into the wet mixture, mixing for only as long as is necessary to achieve a smooth mixture. Fold in the chocolate chunks and hazelnuts.

3   Using a couple of teaspoons, space heaped spoonfuls of the cookie dough well apart on the baking tray. The cookies probably won't all fit on one baking tray, so bake in batches if necessary.

4   Bake for around 15-17 minutes in the preheated oven, cooking for as long as it takes for their edges to just begin to lightly brown. Steal a couple while they're still soft and warm, sandwich a scoop of ice cream between them and eat without shame or restraint.

SPICED OAT THINS

These oat biscuits might boast an ingredient list as long as your arm, but it's comprised mostly of spices that you'll have in your cupboards already. Some of the flavours here are baking regulars, others are less commonplace — fiery black pepper and earthy celery salt, for instance, lift these biscuits out of the generic Christmas-spice-mix rut and push them in a different direction altogether.

Makes 18
100g unsalted butter
100g dark muscovado or soft dark
  brown sugar
2 tablespoons golden syrup
Pinch of ground cloves
½ teaspoon ground cinnamon

¼ teaspoon ground allspice
½ teaspoon ground ginger
½ teaspoon ground black pepper
¼ teaspoon celery salt (or normal
  table salt)
120g regular rolled oats
90g plain flour

1   Preheat the oven to 180°C/fan 160°C/gas mark 4 and line a large baking tray with baking parchment.

2   Gently heat the butter, sugar and golden syrup together until the butter has melted. Take off the heat and stir in the spices and salt followed by the rolled oats and flour.

3   Using two teaspoons, spoon small mounds of the mixture well apart on the baking tray (they'll spread quite substantially during baking). I managed to fit only six on my baking tray, so you will probably have to bake in batches. Bake for 10 minutes and let cool completely before peeling off the parchment. As these are so robustly flavoured, I find it best not to serve them with anything else that might vie for attention: complement them simply with a pot of black tea.

CRUMBLE

A SHORT STORY

In baking, 'short' refers to a dough or pastry that is rich, crumbly and tender. That is exactly what these next biscuits are. The following recipes all differ slightly in their means for achieving this shortness, but the aim is the same: minimise gluten formation. Gluten in flour is responsible for elasticity and a strong structure. Such properties play a crucial role in other areas of baking (most notably in bread, where gluten is positively courted) but they're antithetical to a crumbly biscuit.

And bad news for the health-conscious: fat is the key to subduing this gluten — the more butter, the better. Gluten cannot work without first being hydrated. Coating the flour generously with fat before adding the water therefore hinders gluten development. As such, you'll notice that the following recipes use a reasonably high proportion of fat and as little water as possible.

Gluten is also encouraged to form by handling of the dough, which is why we knead bread so vigorously. For short biscuits, however, it's important to manipulate the dough as little as possible. The shortbread dough below, for instance, is simply pressed into its tin. For rolled biscuits, roll lightly and sympathetically, teasing the dough into shape and taking care not to stretch it. The biscuits will usually survive one rerolling of the dough, to use up any offcuts — any further rolls will yield progressively tougher biscuits. Resting the dough in the fridge prior to baking can help to remedy this, though.

Another option for a crumblier biscuit is to use flour that is low in, or even free from, gluten. The Rye Oat Digestives (page 184) are an example of this; the use of rye flour leaves them so delicate that they crumble under the slightest pressure.

SHORTBREAD

It would be wrong to talk about crumbly biscuits without mentioning shortbread. It's all in the name, of course: shortbread, with a ratio of near equal parts butter and flour, is superlatively short. A bad one will be tough as a ship's biscuit and approximately as tasty, but good shortbread is delicate, light and sweet. The key is a heavy hand with the butter and a light touch when handling the dough. Be sure to chill the mixture thoroughly, and bake slowly.

Ground rice is crucial for achieving a slight grittiness and crunch, as shortbread made with flour alone tends to feel almost claggy. You can use semolina instead of the ground rice if you prefer.

Makes 8–10 wedges
140g unsalted butter, softened
75g caster or granulated sugar
70g ground rice or semolina
Generous pinch of salt

130g plain flour

20cm round cake tin, preferably loose-bottomed or spring-form

1   Beat the butter in a large bowl for a minute until completely smooth before adding 60g of the sugar and stirring to combine. Mix in the ground rice or semolina and the salt. Add the flour to this paste, combining lightly but firmly. It'll likely seem quite dry and lumpy, but with a little perseverance you'll soon see the mixture come together — try mashing it gently under the back of the spoon. Just take care not to over-mix, as this will toughen the dough and leave the biscuits chewy rather than with the desired delicacy.

2   Line the base of the tin with baking parchment. Pat the dough down into the tin, moulding it to the tin's shape without too much rough handling. Refrigerate for an hour, preheating the oven to 160°C/fan 140°C/gas mark 3 during the tail end of this chilling period.

3   Sprinkle the remaining sugar on top of the chilled shortbread round and lightly pat down. Bake in the preheated oven for 50–60 minutes, or until it's just the palest golden colour and sandy on top. Let cool completely before cutting into fat wedges.

RYE OAT DIGESTIVES

The perennial favourite, but here made with dark rye flour for a rounder wholemeal taste. You might question the point of making these at home when you can buy a packet for £1 from the corner shop. To that I say (almost sacrilegiously), homemade digestives are immeasurably better. They're packed with oats, soothingly sweet, rubbly and faintly nutty. I'm not advocating any biscuit puritanism here and I firmly believe that for most tea breaks, mid-morning pick-me-ups and furtive snacks, a shop-bought biscuit will do just fine. But when a real treat is in order, try a batch of these.

Makes 16–20
80g regular rolled oats
100g dark rye flour
1 teaspoon baking powder
Generous pinch of salt

80g unsalted butter, cubed
40g soft light brown sugar
1–2 tablespoons milk

p185

1   Preheat the oven to 180°C/fan 160°C/gas mark 4 and line a large baking tray with baking parchment.

2   Blitz the oats in a food processor or coffee grinder until no whole oats remain, but stop before it becomes powdery — the oats should just be broken down into smaller fragments. If you don't have a food processor or grinder, just buy cheap porridge oats instead. Unlike the good-quality whole rolled oats, cheaper versions tend to be composed of broken or partly powdered oats in the first place.

3   In a large bowl, combine the rye flour, baking powder and salt. Using your fingertips, rub the butter into the flour mixture until no visible flakes of butter remain. Toss through the blitzed oats and sugar then drizzle over the milk. 'Cut' through the mixture using a butter knife to incorporate the milk. It will

begin to clump and will soon be moist enough that it can be squeezed together into one mass.

4   There's no need to chill this dough before baking, although you can of course do so if you want to prepare it in advance. I roll the dough out straight away on a well-floured work surface to a thickness of about 5mm. Thanks to the wholemeal, low-gluten rye flour and the high proportion of oatmeal, it's a crumbly, difficult dough to roll, but you should find that it holds its shape a little better once compacted under the weight of the rolling pin. If the dough does crack as it's rolled, don't worry: just piece together the broken bits and pinch to seal.

5   Cut into whatever shape you want — I go for simple squares so that I don't have to bother with re-rolling the offcuts — and carefully transfer to the lined baking tray. Bake for 15 minutes, until the edges are beginning to brown. Leave the biscuits to cool and firm for a few minutes before moving to a wire rack to finish cooling. Serve them in the only way a digestive ought to be served: with a mug of no-frills, perfectly brewed English Breakfast tea.

Variations
If you can't get hold of dark rye flour, a more storecupboard-friendly version of these biscuits can be made using wholemeal wheat flour instead. You could even dip the tops in melted chocolate, although whether it should be milk or dark chocolate is a surprisingly divisive issue, and a choice that only you can make.

TAHINI LEMON BISCUITS

Tahini, a paste made from sesame seeds, has a powerful flavour — reminiscent of peanut butter but far more bitter. Yet, lightened with lemon zest and well sweetened, it mellows to a gentler nuttiness. The result is a delicate biscuit, as tender as shortbread but without the heaviness. You'll find tahini in the vaguely named 'World Foods' section of most supermarkets, and in many North African, Turkish and Middle Eastern grocery stores.

Makes about 24
120g unsalted butter, softened
120g tahini
120g caster or granulated sugar
Zest of 2 lemons

240g plain flour
1 teaspoon baking powder

📷 p187

1   Preheat the oven to 180°C/fan 160°C/gas mark 4 and line a large baking tray with a sheet of baking parchment.

2   Cream the butter, tahini and sugar together until pale and fluffy, then mix in the lemon zest. In a separate bowl, combine the flour and baking powder. Stir the flour mixture into the wet ingredients, mashing gently under the back of a spoon to combine.

3   Roll out 24 conker-sized balls from the mixture and space them apart on the baking tray. Pat each ball down to a flattish disc, about 1cm thick. It doesn't matter in the slightest if the biscuits have little cracks around the edge. You can use a fork at this point to make lines or a crosshatch pattern on the top of the biscuits.

4   Bake for 12–15 minutes; the edges should be golden brown. The biscuits will be very crumbly when first baked but leave them on the tray and they will become firmer as they cool. Once cold, transfer them to a wire rack.

SNAP

SNAP JUDGEMENTS

The next three recipes are for very thin, crisp biscuits and crackers. With these, it's not so much the mixing that's important but rather the baking. Timing is everything: for wafers barely a millimetre thick, an extra 30 seconds can mean the difference between doughy and perfectly cooked; a further minute could leave them bitter and burnt. A biscuit that snaps cleanly and crisply needs to be watched, carefully timed and impeccably judged. Use a timer rather than guesstimating and have oven gloves at the ready.

CINNAMON ORANGE TUILES

Whether these are strictly biscuits is open to debate. They certainly don't fall into line with the very British idea of a biscuit: something comforting, butter-rich and robust enough to be dunked with impunity into a mug of tea. Instead, they are wafer-thin and — with some careful baking — perfectly crisp.

Why, then, include them here amongst the heavyweight shortbreads, digestives and cookies? Firstly, they look very much at home in a biscuit tin. Secondly, there's something very moreish about them at any time of day — with coffee, after dinner, at snack times and huddled in bed — which means they rarely stay safe in that biscuit tin for very long at all. It's hardly the comprehensive criteria of biscuithood, but it's enough to make these tuiles honorary biscuits, at least in my eyes.

Makes about 16
30g unsalted butter
30g plain flour
½ teaspoon ground cinnamon
30g icing sugar

Zest of ½ orange
1 large egg white, lightly beaten
50g dark chocolate, roughly chopped

📷 p188

1   Preheat the oven to 180°C/fan 160°C/gas mark 4 and line a large baking tray with baking parchment.

2   Melt the butter over a low heat then set aside to cool a little. In a separate bowl, combine the flour, cinnamon, sugar and orange zest. Whisk in the egg white and melted butter to form a smooth, thick batter.

3   There's a neat way of doing this next step... and then there's the way I do it. The proper way is to cut a circle out of an old ice cream tub lid, or similar, and use this as a tuile template. Lay the template over the baking parchment-lined tray, then dollop a small amount of batter into the centre of the circle. Using a palette knife or spatula, spread the batter very thinly across the template. Peel the template away to reveal a crisp-edged, neat circle of batter. Repeat until there's no space left on the baking tray (these will have to be baked in batches). My easier, though less polished, tuiles are shaped as follows: place about a teaspoonful of batter

onto the baking parchment — a blob about the size of a £2 coin — and spread it thinly using a spatula until you've got a uniform smear of batter around 5x10cm in size. The resulting ragged-edged biscuits aren't the most professional, but they are very quick. The most important thing is to spread thinly and evenly: varying thicknesses will yield a biscuit that's alternately chewy and burnt. Don't worry if the first ones aren't perfect — there's enough batter here that you'll need to bake in batches, so you can improve your spreading technique as you go.

4   Bake for 6-7 minutes in the preheated oven. The biscuits should be golden, just beginning to brown at the edges. In the meantime, have a rolling pin on hand to mould the baked tuiles.

5   This next step must be done quickly while the tuiles are still malleable, fresh from the oven. They will of course be hot, so do be careful. If the duck-bill curve of a moulded tuile isn't, to your mind, worth the risk of burnt fingers: no problem. It's only aesthetic, after all. If you do decide to mould them, lay each tuile across the rolling pin and gently wrap it to the curve. You should be able to fit a row of them along the length of the pin. After a minute or so they'll cool and harden. Those gifted with asbestos fingers may be able to go one further, rolling the tuiles into delicate cigar shapes, cones and other biscuit origami. It's up to you.

6   Repeat the spreading and baking in batches until all the batter has been used.

7   Melt the chocolate either in short bursts in the microwave or in a heatproof bowl suspended over a pan of simmering water. Dip the ends or rims of the tuiles into the chocolate and set aside to cool. These are good enough to eat by themselves but they excel as a crisp, smart counterpoint to a bowl of chocolate ice cream.

FENNEL SEED & CHILLI SNAPS

Good cheese deserves a good cracker. These very thin, crisp ones are flavoured with fennel and laced with chilli. If you're not keen on spice use just ¼ teaspoon of the chilli flakes, but these snaps aren't excessively hot as they are.

Makes 20-25
200g plain flour
¼ teaspoon salt
1 teaspoon caster sugar
1 teaspoon fennel seeds
½ teaspoon dried chilli flakes

Generous grind of black pepper
2 tablespoons olive oil
70ml water
Sea salt flakes (optional)

📷 p191

1   Preheat the oven to 200°C/fan 180°C/gas mark 6. Lightly grease a large baking tray or line it with baking parchment.

2   In a large bowl, combine all of the dry ingredients then add the oil and water, kneading lightly for a minute just to bring the dough together. If it's too dry to come together, sprinkle over a little extra water — barely a teaspoon at a time — until no surplus flour remains.

3   Let the dough rest for 15 minutes or so to allow the gluten in the flour to relax, then roll out, on a lightly floured work surface, as thin as you can. It should stretch to around 35-45cm in diameter and 2-3mm thick.

4   Cut into whatever shapes you want. I cut freeform with a sharp knife into rectangles, around 5x8cm. The only thing to bear in mind is that very small shapes will take less time to cook. Sprinkle with sea salt flakes, if using.

5   Bake for 10 minutes in the preheated oven and serve with a good, soft cheese — perhaps Camembert. Alternatively, these go surprisingly well with a curry in place of traditional poppadums.

STILTON & POPPY SEED CRACKERS

I was put off cheese snacks for a long time by the only kind that I knew: the sort that leaves you with bright orange fingertips and contains (probably) no real cheese. But these crackers are a different story altogether: crisp, salty-sharp biscuits quite good enough to eat by themselves.

You can replace the Stilton if you're not keen on blue cheese, but I would first reassure you that the Stilton flavour here is quite mellow. If you do swap cheeses, be sure to choose a strongly flavoured, hard cheese as a softer cheese will add too much water to the mix, resulting in unacceptably chewy crackers.

Makes 24-32
100g unsalted butter, cubed
200g wholemeal flour
Pinch of salt
100g Stilton

30g poppy seeds
1-2 tablespoons cold water

📷 p192

1   In a large bowl, rub the butter into the flour and salt. Crumble in the cheese and lightly rub this in, too, stopping when there are no longer any large chunks. Stir in the poppy seeds then drizzle over the water. Using a small knife, 'cut' through the mixture repeatedly to incorporate the water. The flour should all be moistened, coming together in clumps. If there's still dry flour, add a drop more water.

2   Press the dough into one lump, wrap in cling film and refrigerate for around 15 minutes, until firmer but not rock solid. If chilling for longer, give the dough a little time at room temperature afterwards to make it slightly more manageable to roll. Meanwhile, preheat the oven to 200°C/fan 180°C/gas mark 6 and line a large baking tray with baking parchment.

3   On a lightly floured work surface, roll the dough to a thickness of about 3mm. It'll be slightly crumbly thanks to the wholemeal flour and the poppy seeds, but just patch any breakages with more dough. Cut into slim rectangles (mine were about 2.5x10cm) and arrange on the prepared baking tray.

4   Bake for 10-12 minutes or until the crackers are just beginning to deepen to a golden brown at the edges.

PUDDINGS & DESSERTS

CHEESECAKE

INDIVIDUAL PASSION FRUIT CHEESECAKES

RASPBERRY, WHISKY & OAT CHEESECAKE

BLACKBERRY RICOTTA CHEESECAKE

MERINGUES & CUSTARDS

AUTUMN BERRY PAVLOVA • LEMON MERINGUE ROULADE

BAY & BLACKCURRANT CRÈME BRÛLÉE • BLUEBERRY CLAFOUTIS

SPONGE PUDDINGS

RASPBERRY CHOCOLATE FONDANTS

MAPLE PECAN SPONGE PUDDINGS • STICKY TOFFEE PUDDING

STEAMED ORANGE & GINGER PUDDING

LIGHTER CHRISTMAS PUDDING • ORANGE & SAFFRON SPOTTED DICK

RHUBARB JAM ROLY-POLY

Talk about saving the best till last. I can't help but be suspicious of those who are happy to leave their meal on a savoury note: for me, there has to be a pudding or dessert of sorts, even if it's as simple as a plate of perfectly ripe figs, otherwise the dinner just isn't complete.

I'm not advocating some rigorous taxonomy of baking, but I do think that there's a difference between puddings and desserts, here in the UK at least. Desserts — by which I mean slivers of cheesecake, fruit-laden pavlovas and snowy lemon roulades — are about lightness, brightness and elegance. They're designed to sate a sweet tooth without being inelegantly hearty or rich. Puddings lumber at the opposite end of the spectrum with the sort of food served in school canteens and on cold winter nights. Think Christmas pudding, spotted dick and jam roly-poly — the sorts of food that don't seduce you as much as challenge you to take them on and finish them right up. Even the word 'pudding' has a heavy, clumsy quality to it. I love it.

CHEESECAKE

There is a cheesecake for just about everyone: New York-style baked cheesecake with the tang of soured cream; unbaked ones so tremulously soft that they melt in the mouth; fruit-topped versions; imported adaptations using ricotta, quark or mascarpone. I prefer to keep things simple — perhaps some fruit or zest, even a swirl of chocolate. Anything else is just gilding the lily.

In terms of method, there are three basic types of cheesecake. The first is baked, adding eggs to the mixture to set in the heat of the oven. The next is gelatine-set. I'm loath to mess around with setting agents like gelatine unless it's absolutely necessary and, as it happens, it's not: the third type of cheesecake — unbaked, with firmly whipped cream folded through it — will set perfectly well in the fridge without any gelatine at all. The type you choose will depend on your personal tastes, the flavours to be included and the time available to you. Baked cheesecakes tend to be slightly firmer, with a mellower flavour. Set cheesecakes have a brighter taste but, especially when set with whipped cream, can verge on cloying: they need fruit or zest to cut through the creaminess.

There's no mystery to set cheesecakes, as you'll see in the recipe for Passion Fruit Cheesecakes on page 199. But baked cheesecakes require a little more care if they're to be excellent rather than merely good. It is attention to detail that will make all the difference...

THE BASE

It is possible to make it with pastry, but for me much of the joy of cheesecake lies in the crumbly biscuit base. The type of biscuit is an open question: ginger biscuits go well with lemon, lime or passion fruit; digestives are a good all-rounder; I've used oatcakes in the Raspberry, Whisky & Oat Cheesecake on page 201, while the more adventurous will use Oreos, shortbread rounds or amaretti. But regardless of which biscuit you use, it's important to pre-bake or chill the base. This will give it a chance to set before the wet filling goes in, preventing (or at least minimising) any sogginess.

MIXING

It really does help to have all of the filling ingredients at room temperature before you start mixing. Mix eggs straight into a block of cold cream cheese and you'll end up with an infuriatingly lumpy mixture that you'll then have to strain. Always beat the cheese until smooth before adding the other ingredients, and then do so gradually. Take care not to beat too much air into the mix, however: this is one of the rare instances in baking where density is a virtue.

BAKING

It's this stage that is the most crucial. Bake too quickly at too high a temperature and the cheesecake will puff up, brown on top and develop a grainy, almost chalky, texture. Patience pays off here, and I say that as a chronically impatient person. Cheesecake bakes best at very low temperatures: the slower it cooks, the smoother it sets. For most baked cheesecakes 110–130°C is about right.

WATER BATHS

Some insist that cheesecake must be cooked in a water bath for a perfectly smooth set. Because water (in its liquid state, at least) can't reach temperatures higher than 100°C, it protects the dessert from the fierce heat of the oven. This helps the cheesecake to cook evenly (reducing the appearance of puffy edges and a sunken middle) and gives a creamy finish. But, although I concede that it does make for a velvety texture, I'm not convinced that it's really necessary. You can achieve the same result by baking the cheesecake at a lower temperature for a longer time. Half-submerging a cheesecake in a pan of sloshing water is a fraught kitchen experience, and even the most carefully foil-swaddled tin can leak, leaving the cheesecake curdled and with a sodden base: avoid it if you can.

COOLING

Sometimes a cheesecake will develop a great crack down its centre as it cools — usually just as you proudly usher everyone into the kitchen to show them how fabulous it looks. You can't always predict or prevent this, but it'll certainly be less likely to happen if you bake at a low temperature. Another solution is to gently loosen the edges of the cheesecake from the tin after baking: the cheesecake will shrink slightly as it cools, but if the sides as free to fold inwards a little, it'll be less likely to tear. And importantly: cool the cheesecake slowly. You could turn off the oven slightly before the cheesecake is set and let it cool in the oven; otherwise, cool completely to room temperature before transferring to the fridge to chill.

INDIVIDUAL PASSION FRUIT CHEESECAKES

You could make this as one large cheesecake, but I think it's best served in individual ramekins: it's far quicker than making a 'real' cheesecake, you don't have to worry about it setting perfectly firm, and you get the selfish pleasure of having something to eat that is all yours — no need to share with anyone else.

Because this cheesecake isn't baked, it has a softer set than the others in this chapter. It uses double cream, whipped to firm peaks, for its structure. The result is a creamy texture and rich flavour, offset by the brightness of the fruit.

Makes 6

6 passion fruits, plus 1 for the topping (optional)

200g full-fat cream cheese

80g caster sugar

150ml double cream

120g ginger biscuits

6 small glasses or ramekins

1   Halve the 6 passion fruits, scoop out their pulp and seeds and strain through a sieve. Spend a bit of time pressing the pulp into the sieve to extract as much juice as possible.

2   Beat the cream cheese in a bowl until smooth. Add the passion fruit juice and stir to combine. In a separate bowl whisk the sugar with the cream until the mixture is firm and just about holds stiff peaks. Fold the whisked cream through the cheese and passion fruit mixture, cutting through with the spoon or spatula to gently combine the two. The cheesecake mixture should be unctuous and smooth. Taste it: if it needs a touch more passion fruit juice or sugar, add it now.

3   Crush the ginger biscuits in a large bowl with the end of a heavy wooden rolling pin or, more efficiently, in a food processor, if you have one. Divide the crushed biscuits between the glasses or ramekins to give an even layer across the base of each, and press down firmly. Spoon in the cheese mixture, level with the back of the spoon and refrigerate the cheesecakes for at least 2 hours to allow them to firm up.

4   Just before serving, scoop a little passion fruit pulp over the top of each cheesecake. The black seeds and bright orange juice will look striking against the creamy cheesecake, but it's not an essential addition.

RASPBERRY, WHISKY & OAT CHEESECAKE

Here the building blocks of Scottish cranachan are brought together in a different guise, layered into an alternately crisp, creamy and fruity cheesecake. It's not as rustically simple as the dessert that inspired it, but it does — I think — stay true to cranachan's ingredient-centric ethos: just honey, raspberries, whisky and oats, in perfect balance.

Serves 8, generously
For the base:
150g oatcakes
25g rolled oats
25g caster sugar
100g unsalted butter

For the filling:
400g full-fat cream cheese
150ml sour cream
4 tablespoons honey

100g caster sugar
1 teaspoon vanilla extract
2–3 tablespoons whisky
3 large eggs
200–300g fresh raspberries

20cm round loose-bottomed or spring-form tin

📷 p200

1   Preheat the oven to 180°C/fan 160°C/gas mark 4.

2   Crush the oatcakes with a rolling pin or blitz them in a food processor until sandy and no chunks remain. Stir through the rolled oats and sugar. Melt the butter over a low heat in a small pan then add this to the crushed biscuits, stirring to combine. Add a bit of extra butter if the mixture feels dry: it needs to be moist enough to hold together in small clumps. Spoon it into the tin and press down firmly using the back of a spoon. Bake in the preheated oven for 10–15 minutes, or until just set (it will firm as it cools). Set aside while you prepare the filling ingredients. Turn the oven temperature down to 120°C/fan 100°C/gas mark ½.

3   In a large bowl, beat the cream cheese until smooth. Add the sour cream and stir to combine before adding the honey, sugar and vanilla extract. Stir in the whisky to taste. (You can add a little extra, or none at all, if you'd prefer.) Lightly whisk the eggs together in a separate bowl then gradually add this to the cheese mixture, stirring continuously as you go to prevent lumps from forming. You should be left with a thick, smooth cream.

4   Pour the filling over the pre-baked base. Bake for around 1½ hours, or until the cheesecake is set with just the slightest wobble still at its centre. Because it's been baked at such a low temperature, it should have barely coloured, just deepening to a light gold. Let it cool to room temperature in its tin before unmoulding and chilling.

5   Shortly before serving, arrange the raspberries on top of the cheesecake, fat ends down and tapered bottoms upwards. You can cover with the raspberries earlier but there's a risk that, if they're particularly ripe, they'll 'bleed' into the creamy cheesecake.

BLACKBERRY RICOTTA CHEESECAKE

I love the swirls of deep purple berries against this creamy cheesecake. Ricotta gives a less smooth texture than the heavier cream cheese, but the taste is cleaner, allowing the fruit to really shine.

Serves 8-10

For the base:
150g digestive biscuits
75g unsalted butter

For the blackberry swirl:
150g blackberries
2 tablespoons caster sugar
Juice of ½ lemon
1 teaspoon cornflour (optional)

For the filling:
500g ricotta cheese

2 tablespoons cornflour
150ml double cream
125g caster sugar
2 large eggs, plus 1 large yolk
Zest of 1 lemon
1½ teaspoons vanilla extract

20cm round loose-bottomed or spring-form tin

📷 p203

1   Preheat the oven to 180°C/fan 160°C/gas mark 4.

2   Crush the biscuits with a rolling pin or blitz them in a food processor, until sandy. Melt the butter over a low heat then mix with the biscuit rubble in a large bowl. The crumbs need to be moist enough that they'll hold in clumps if squeezed together, so add extra butter at this point if necessary.

3   Spread the biscuit mixture over the base of the tin and press down firmly all over. Bake in the preheated oven for 10 minutes, then take out, leave to cool slightly and reduce the oven temperature to 120°C/fan 100°C/gas mark ½.

4   In a small pan, heat the blackberries, sugar and lemon juice over a low heat until the blackberries soften. Crush with the back of a fork until no whole berries remain, then set aside to cool. If the blackberries release a lot of juice, add one teaspoon of cornflour while the pan's still on the heat and stir for a further minute or two, until thickened.

5   Beat the ricotta and cornflour together in a large bowl until smooth, then stir in the cream. Once combined, incorporate the sugar, followed by the eggs and yolk (one at a time), lemon zest and vanilla extract.

6   Pour the filling onto the baked biscuit base. Dollop spoonfuls of the blackberries into the cheesecake and gently swirl through using a spoon. Bake for 1¾-2 hours, or until the cheesecake has no more than a slight wobble at its centre. The cooked cheesecake should be quite firm all over, except for the blackberry swirls, by now slightly sunken, jammy and a deep purple colour.

7   Leave the cheesecake to cool completely in its tin before attempting to unmould it. Then, for a firmer texture, chill in the fridge before serving.

MERINGUES & CUSTARDS

Like a lot of home cooks, I'm both intrigued and terrified by meringue. It's the building block of some of the most impressively extravagant desserts in the baker's repertoire, but it can seem intimidatingly tricky. It doesn't deserve this reputation, though. Once you've become familiar with a few basic dos and don'ts, you'll find a billowing meringue every bit as simple to whip up as a Victoria sponge.

There are three main types of meringue: French, Italian and Swiss. Each has slightly different characteristics and methods, but the one I use in these next recipes is the most basic — a French meringue.

GETTING STARTED WITH MERINGUE

First things first: use a very, very clean bowl and whisk. Even the slightest residue of grease will interfere with the meringue's development as it's whisked, leaving it flat and flabby. Plastic bowls are unsuitable for meringues for that very reason, often retaining a film of dirt and oil after even the most thorough of scrubs. Glass or stainless steel bowls are the best options, and make sure that you use a large one: the meringue will expand a lot as it's whisked.

THE INGREDIENTS

Meringue is, quite simply, egg white and sugar. That something so strange and delicious can come from two such unremarkable ingredients is part of its charm.

Reasonably fresh eggs make the best meringues. You'll notice that older eggs have runnier whites — a sign that their proteins, responsible for structure in the meringue, are breaking down, so the resulting dessert will be less voluminous. If your eggs are a little older, you can add a pinch of cream of tartar or a drop of lemon juice (roughly ¼ teaspoon per 2 large whites) to the egg before you begin to whisk. This touch of acidity will help to strengthen the meringue. The temperature matters, too: fridge-cold eggs will whip up more slowly than those at room temperature.

As for the sugar, use caster. Granulated sugar will take far longer to dissolve and could lead to 'weeping' in the finished meringue, when tiny droplets appear on the surface of the meringue after it's been baked. The amount of sugar depends on the sort of meringue you're aiming for. A crisp, firm meringue will need up to 60g of sugar per egg white, whereas a softer version, such as that heaped on top of a meringue pie or Baked Alaska, can work with just a couple of tablespoons.

SEPARATING THE EGGS

Yolk is bad news for meringue — as little as a speck of golden yolk in the egg whites can stop a meringue from gaining the volume that it should. This leaves the whole process of separating the eggs quite fraught: the building blocks for your meringue are nestled snugly alongside its nemesis. Just work slowly and, if you're not a confident egg-breaker (I still get eggshell in my cakes), separate the whites over a small bowl one at a time, decanting each into the larger mixing bowl as you go.

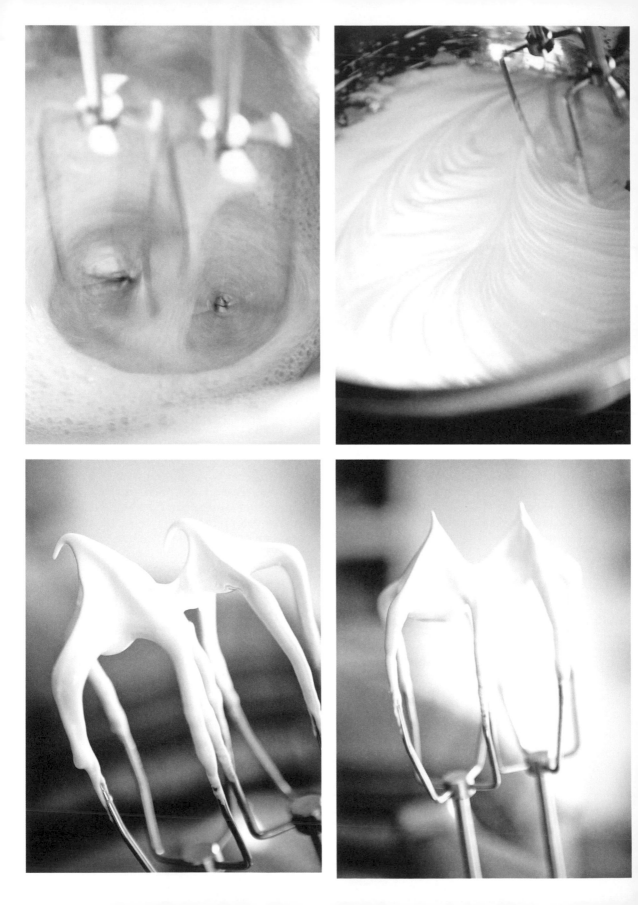

WHISKING

The first step is to whisk the egg whites (with the cream of tartar or lemon juice, if using) until they're completely foamy. This stage is crucial, but it's important not to overdo it: the eggs need a head start before the sugar is added, otherwise the meringue will be dense, but if they're over-whisked they could be weakened and collapse. Whisk only until the whites are thick enough that when a bit drops from the whisk, it sits happily on the foam's surface rather than sinking straight back in. The foamy whites should hold in crests and waves.

Next, add the sugar. This must be done slowly, as the sugar needs time to dissolve in the whites. Adding too much at once will leave the meringue deflated and can cause weeping (beads of moisture on the meringue's surface) after cooking. I usually pour the sugar in a quarter at a time, whisking well between each addition.

As you continue to whisk the eggs and sugar you'll see the mixture transform. Air is beaten into the whites and the vigorous whisking 'rearranges' their proteins to form a dense foam. The result is that the whites — at first slimy and heavy — become thick, voluminous and bright white. A well-whisked meringue should have moved from mere foaminess to become almost creamy, with a glossy finish to it.

Unless otherwise specified, you'll have to keep whisking the meringue until it reaches stiff peaks. This is the stage at which, when the whisk is lifted slowly from the meringue, it leaves a 'spike' of the mixture behind it — bolt upright, not curling at its tip (if it does droop, it's only a 'soft peak', and you've got another few minutes of whisking to go).

Another, more theatrical, test is to hold the bowl upside down. If the meringue is stiff enough, it won't budge. Unfortunately, this is a bit of an all-or-nothing approach — if the meringue isn't ready, you'll have a big mess to clear up.

It does take a while for the meringue to reach stiff peaks but, as long as the equipment is clean, the eggs aren't too old and the sugar is added slowly, you ought to be able to whisk the whites up to volume in 10–15 minutes — and even quicker if you have an electric whisk or stand mixer. My electric whisk at home makes a din so terrible that I'm always forced to make meringues by hand, and it really isn't too much of a chore.

BAKING

How you bake a meringue can determine whether it's crisp, chewy or soft. A long, very cool bake (sometimes for as long as overnight in a barely hot oven) will give very dry, crisp meringues — the sort that maintain a snowy white glow and break into thick sugar shards as you eat them. Baking for an hour or so in a medium oven, such as in the pavlova recipe (page 208), will give a meringue that's crisp outside and chewy inside: for me, by far the best type. A short time in a moderate oven will cause the meringue to brown slightly but won't allow it time to dry out, leaving it with a just-set exterior and mousse-like interior. You'll have to take the sugar content (see page 205) into account too, though, as this will also have a bearing on texture.

AUTUMN BERRY PAVLOVA

The only difficult thing about this pavlova is saying no to second and even third helpings. It's a good way to familiarise yourself with basic meringue, too, if you've never made it before.

You can use more or less any berry or soft fruit for a pavlova, but I like to choose something bold enough to stand its ground in the face of mountains of meringue and cream. Raspberries, with a hint of acidity, are perfect. So are sharp blackcurrants and redcurrants and inky blackberries. Morello cherries are fantastic but their easier-to-find sweet cousins are unfortunately less punchy. And then of course there are strawberries, for the classic summer pavlova.

Serves 8
For the meringue:
3 large egg whites
150g caster sugar

For the filling:
300ml double cream

50g caster sugar
1 teaspoon vanilla extract
300g fresh berries

📷 p209

1   Preheat the oven to 140°C/fan 120°C/gas mark 3 and line a large baking tray with baking parchment.

2   In a large, very clean (preferably glass or metal) bowl, whisk the egg whites for a couple of minutes until they're whipped up into a dense foam. Add the sugar gradually — a couple of tablespoons at a time — and whisk well between each addition to give the sugar time to dissolve. Once all of the sugar has been added, continue whisking for an extra 5 minutes or so, until the meringue mixture is very thick and glossy. It should hold in stiff peaks when you slowly lift the whisk out.

3   Spoon the meringue in a heap straight onto the baking parchment and gently spread it out, using the back of a spoon, to a circle 23–25cm across. Scoop out a slight hollow in the centre, pushing the extra meringue towards the edges to give a wide, gently sloping rim. This 'bowl' of meringue is what will hold the cream and fruit filling.

4   Bake in the preheated oven for 1 hour. The meringue should be barely a shade darker but shouldn't have browned. If, at any point during the cooking stage, it appears to be browning or burning, turn the oven temperature down a bit.

5   Leave the meringue on its baking tray to cool for 15–20 minutes, then carefully peel back the baking parchment underneath and transfer the meringue to a large serving plate or tray.

6   In a large bowl, whisk the cream, sugar and vanilla extract until firm, then spoon this into the 'bowl' of the meringue. Crush a few of the berries under the back of a fork (their bright juices will look amazing against the cream and meringue) and spoon all of the fruit over the cream. Enjoy soon after making, refrigerating the rest if you don't eat it all in one sitting.

LEMON MERINGUE ROULADE

The bare bones of a lemon meringue pie — sharp, sunny lemon curd, voluminous meringue — without having to mess around with a pastry crust.

Shop-bought lemon curd is ok in this filling, but homemade will have far more zing to it. There's a handily economical recipe for it on page 324, which uses all the yolks left over from making the meringue.

Serves 6-8
4 large egg whites
½ teaspoon lemon juice
200g caster sugar
30g icing sugar, to dust

For the filling:
300ml double cream

40g icing sugar
150-200g lemon curd, to taste

Roasting dish or Swiss roll tin, approximately 22x33cm

📷 p211

1   Preheat the oven to 160°C/fan 140°C/gas mark 3 and line the tin with baking parchment.

2   In a very clean, dry bowl, whisk the egg whites with the lemon juice just until they're completely foamy and hold in soft mounds as the whisk is lifted out. Add the caster sugar a little at a time, whisking thoroughly between each addition. Adding the caster sugar all at once or before the previous addition has been incorporated may cause the meringue to collapse, so do be patient here.

3   Once all the caster sugar has been added, keep whisking. You'll feel the meringue become thicker, you'll see it grow glossy and smooth, but don't stop until the point when, as you slowly lift your whisk away from the meringue, the mixture holds in a firm, well-defined, straight peak. Carefully spoon the meringue into the tin, level it and bake for 30 minutes.

4   Once the meringue is baked, dust another sheet of baking parchment with the 30g of icing sugar and turn the meringue out onto it so that it's upside-down. Peel the paper off the underside (now the top) of the meringue and let cool.

5   Whip the cream and the 40g of icing sugar until the cream holds in soft peaks. Gently fold the lemon curd into the cream. Spread this lemony mixture over the cooled meringue then, using the baking parchment as an aid, roll the meringue up into a log. Roll from long edge to long edge (creating a roll that is around 30cm long). Don't worry if the meringue cracks or if some of the cream oozes out — this is a beautiful dessert but not one to get precious about.

BLACKCURRANTS

Blackcurrants are an unrivalled joy when you can get them fresh, but even during their short season (primarily July and August) they can be difficult to find in the shops. A huge percentage of blackcurrants grown in the UK are, woefully, turned into syrupy squash, so they rarely grace our supermarket shelves. But do keep an eye out over the summer for the occasional, fortuitous punnet of the inky, jewel-like berries. They're mouth-puckeringly sharp when raw, but with the addition of heat and sugar they really come alive. If you can't get hold of blackcurrants for the crème brûlée below, try some blackberries or leave out the bay leaf and use redcurrants instead. Their flavour is shallower but they have the tartness required to cut through the creamy custard. They're far easier to get hold of, too.

BAY & BLACKCURRANT CRÈME BRÛLÉE

A whisper of liquorice left on the tongue by a velvety bay-infused custard, and the dark warmth of blackcurrants at the end of a spoonful. This is one of my favourite flavour combinations. Crème brûlée is an impressive way to end a meal, and if you have a blowtorch to caramelise the sugar on top: even better. People are rarely as thrilled as when their dessert comes with a side of pyrotechnics.

These desserts are a nutritionist's worst nightmare but there's really no point trying to devise a slimmed-down version of a recipe whose very essence is indulgence. Enjoy the crème brûlée in all its calorific glory; just don't make a habit of it.

Makes 2-4, depending on the size of your ramekins
3 large egg yolks
3 tablespoons caster sugar
300ml double cream
50-75g blackcurrants

2-4 fresh bay leaves
40-60g granulated sugar

2-4 individual ceramic or glass ramekins

📷 p212

1   Preheat the oven to 150°C/fan 130°C/gas mark 2.

2   In a mixing bowl, whisk the egg yolks and caster sugar together until the mixture begins to lighten in colour. Heat the cream in a small pan until almost boiling. Pour the cream slowly over the egg and sugar mixture, whisking all the while. Scatter a few blackcurrants into each ramekin.

3   Divide the hot custard between the ramekins, then stand a bay leaf in each (it doesn't have to be fully submerged — if you leave it propped against the side of the dish, it will be easier to pull out later).

4   Put the dishes into a small tin or oven dish deep enough to accommodate hot water reaching two-thirds of the way up the ramekins. Bake until barely wobbling in the centre — this should take 30-45 minutes, depending on their size, but do keep an eye on them and give them more or less time, as necessary. They're done when they're almost completely set, although there'll be little to indicate this except the slight ripple in the middle as they are jiggled. When they're ready,

gently tease out the bay leaves, leave the custards to cool to room temperature, then chill.

5   Sprinkle the granulated sugar generously over each custard. The caramelising can be done either using a blowtorch or under a hot grill — either way, be vigilant. If using a blowtorch, first make sure that the work surface is completely clear, then — giving it your full concentration — work the tip of the blue flame lightly over the sugar. The sugar will at first seem unmoved, but will soon melt, then bubble, brown and burn. If using the grill, allow the grill plenty of time to heat up before you put the custards underneath: they need to be caramelised quickly to allow the top to set without melting the underneath.

6   Leave to cool at room temperature for 10 minutes or so before serving. Take a spoon in your hand and bring it firmly down onto the surface of the crème brûlée with a crack. It's a feeling to be relished. Enjoy.

BLUEBERRY CLAFOUTIS

This is actually a batter — similar to a pancake mix — but enriched with plenty of sugar and butter and baked to a slight wobble, it feels more like a thick custard, hence its inclusion here. It's usually made with cherries but the floral fruitiness of blueberries works very well.

Serves 6
30g butter, melted
90g caster sugar
2 large eggs
40g plain flour
¼ teaspoon salt
Zest of 1 lemon
½ teaspoon vanilla extract

100ml milk
150ml single cream
400g blueberries, frozen or fresh
30g icing sugar, to dust

23-25cm pie dish or deep tin

📷 p215

1   Preheat the oven to 180°C/fan 160°C/gas mark 4. Use a little of the melted butter to grease the dish or tin. Sprinkle roughly a tablespoon of the caster sugar around the greased dish to coat.

2   Whisk the eggs with the remaining caster sugar then stir in the flour, salt, lemon zest and vanilla extract. Slowly add the milk, cream and the rest of the melted butter.

3   Arrange the blueberries in the bottom of the greased and sugared pie dish then slowly pour the batter over. (If using frozen blueberries, use straight from the freezer otherwise they'll dye the batter an unappetising shade of grey.) Bake for 30-40 minutes, or until just set. If you've used frozen blueberries, it may take a little longer. There should still be a bit of a wobble in the centre. The clafoutis will have risen, and turned a golden brown in parts, and the blueberries will have burst their papery skins and melted down to pockets of fragrant blueberry juice. Let cool until just warm, dust liberally with icing sugar and tuck in.

SPONGE PUDDINGS

These puddings are hearty, winter fare. They can be made in individual portions or baked in one large, domed pudding basin. The sponge can be fluffy or dense, baked or steamed, zesty or dark. Some, such as the maple pecan sponges on page 218, are soothingly sweet whereas others (the dark chocolate fondants below and ginger orange pudding on page 222) are bolder. What they have in common, though, is that they should all be served steaming hot with plenty of ice cream, custard, cream or sauce. A pudding served dry is no pudding at all, in my eyes.

RASPBERRY CHOCOLATE FONDANTS

As far as baked puddings go, these fondants sit at the more refined end of the spectrum. They're elegantly minimalist and, alongside a neat scoop of ice cream, nothing less than beautiful. It's not all about appearances, though: beneath the moist sponge exterior is (if you cook them just right) a molten chocolate core.

Chocolate fondants can sometimes be too rich, even for my taste, but the raspberry in the centre of these helps to lift that darkness. If you don't have individual pudding basins, you can use a muffin tin instead. The fondants will be smaller, but that may not necessarily be a bad thing, considering how decadent they are.

Makes 4 large or 8 small fondants
110g unsalted butter
100g dark chocolate, 70% cocoa solids
2 large eggs
110g caster sugar
60g plain flour

75g raspberries

4 individual pudding moulds or 12-bun muffin tin

📷 p216

1   Preheat the oven to 200°C/fan 180°C/gas mark 6. Melt 30g of the butter over a low heat and use to grease the pudding moulds or eight holes in the muffin tin: brush the base and sides with a coat of butter, freeze for a couple of minutes to set, brush again with a second coat and leave in the fridge to chill. This might seem fussy but it's important if you want to be able to turn the cooked fondants out easily. The last thing you want is to end up having to heavy-handedly prise the delicate pudding out of its mould later.

2   Roughly chop the chocolate and melt it in a large, heatproof bowl suspended over a pan of barely simmering water. Make sure that the bottom of the bowl doesn't touch the water. Once the chocolate has melted, turn off the heat, add the remaining 80g butter and stir until fully combined. Set aside to cool slightly.

3   Whisk the eggs and sugar together for at least 5 minutes, until very, very thick and creamy. When the whisk is lifted from it, the mixture ought to fall in a 'ribbon' that sits on the surface for a second or two before sinking back in.

4   Gently fold the chocolate mixture into the whisked eggs, cutting through the mixture to combine and digging right to the bottom of the bowl (the chocolate will tend to sink through). Sift in the flour and fold in.

5   Divide the mixture between the moulds or muffin holes: put a spoonful in the bottom of each, followed by three raspberries (use just 1 or 2 raspberries if making the smaller, muffin-sized fondants), and then more batter on top of the raspberries.

6   At this point, you can chill the fondants to be baked later. Otherwise, bake now for 10–12 minutes for the large fondants, or 8–9 minutes for the small ones. The baked fondants should be well-risen with a crust. The trick is to cook them just long enough that they're hot through, but briefly enough that the centres remain liquid. You might want to sacrifice one if you're really not sure — using an oven mitt, unmould the pudding straight from the oven, halve, check for readiness and eat, all in the name of testing. If you decide to chill the fondants to bake later, add a minute or two to the cooking time.

    The larger, individually moulded puddings should be easy enough to turn out, but if you've baked a batch of smaller ones in a muffin tin, it takes a little more care to turn them out safely. Just slide a clean baking tray over the top of the fondant-loaded tin and, using oven gloves, deftly flip the whole lot over, leaving the muffin tin bottom-up, and the baking tray underneath. When you tease up the muffin tin you should be faced with 8 fondants in neat rows. Serve with cream or ice cream.

Variation
A couple of cubes of white chocolate in the centre of each fondant can bring a welcome sweetness to an otherwise dark dessert.

MAPLE PECAN SPONGE PUDDINGS

This twist on traditional syrup sponge puddings uses maple syrup in place of the usual golden syrup. Once turned out of their tins, the puddings have sweet, maple-soaked tops and nutty cake underneath. If you don't have a coffee grinder or food processor for blitzing the pecans, omit the ground pecans and the milk, and add a full 100g chopped pecans to the batter instead.

Makes 4 large or 8 smaller puddings
4 tablespoons maple syrup
100g pecans
80g plain flour
1 teaspoon baking powder
Pinch of salt
80g unsalted butter, softened

80g soft light brown sugar
2 large eggs
1 teaspoon vanilla extract
1 tablespoon full-fat milk

**4 individual pudding moulds or
   12-bun muffin tin**

1   Preheat the oven to 180°C/fan 160°C/gas mark 4. Grease the pudding moulds and line the base of each one with a small circle of baking parchment. Spoon one tablespoon of maple syrup into the bottom of each basin.

2   Toast the pecans on a baking tray in the preheated oven for 8–10 minutes, keeping an eye on them to make sure they don't burn. They're done when they're barely a shade darker and becoming fragrant. Leave the oven on ready for the puddings.

3   Blitz half of the toasted nuts in a food processor or coffee grinder until coarsely ground. Be careful not to process too much, as this will release the pecans' oils and the mixture will clump. Coarsely chop the remaining pecans.

4   Combine the flour, ground pecans, baking powder and salt. In a separate large bowl, cream the butter and sugar together, then beat in the eggs and vanilla extract. Stir in the milk and a couple of tablespoons of the dry ingredients. Once mixed, add the remaining dry ingredients and the chopped pecans and stir lightly to combine.

5   Spoon the mixture into the pudding moulds until they're just over two-thirds full. Bake for around 25 minutes (or 15–20 minutes for the smaller puddings), or until a knife inserted into the middle comes out clean. When they're ready, loosen the puddings with a small knife and turn them out onto serving plates. If their tops are particularly domed you may want to slice them off before turning out to give the puddings an even base. Serve immediately, with plenty of maple syrup and custard.

STICKY TOFFEE PUDDING

Arguably the ultimate comfort food. Whenever I've been in need of something gratuitously indulgent to see me through a weepy film or a cold winter evening, I seek solace in caramel: cubes of tablet, butter toffees to weld my mouth shut, dark treacle sponges and even, at lower ebbs, caramelised condensed milk, spooned straight from the can. This pudding, however, has always been my favourite.

Dates have a natural toffee-like edge to them, and when added to this damp cake and flooded with caramel sauce, they become as stickily sweet and chewy as if they were chunks of fudge themselves.

Makes one large pudding, enough for 6
200g dates, coarsely chopped
1 teaspoon bicarbonate of soda
200ml boiling water
75g unsalted butter, softened
100g soft light brown sugar
1 large egg
1 teaspoon vanilla extract
150g plain flour
1½ teaspoons baking powder
2 teaspoons cocoa powder
100g walnuts or pecans, roughly
    chopped

For the sauce:
100g soft light brown sugar
150ml double cream
75g unsalted butter
1 tablespoon black treacle
Good pinch of salt

**Cake tin or oven dish, approximately
    22x15cm, although the precise
    dimensions aren't important**

📷 p220

1   Preheat the oven to 180°C/fan 160°C/gas mark 4 and grease and line the tin or dish with baking parchment.

2   Combine the dates and bicarbonate of soda in a bowl and pour over the boiling water. Put aside while you prepare the remaining ingredients. You'll find that the bicarbonate of soda quickly softens the fruit.

3   Cream together the butter and sugar, add the egg and vanilla extract and stir to combine. In a separate bowl, mix the flour, baking powder and cocoa powder. Add the dry ingredients and the date mixture (water and all) to the butter and sugar, whisking lightly to combine. Stir in the nuts.

4   Spoon the mixture into the prepared tin and bake for 30-35 minutes. It's done when a knife inserted into its centre emerges with only a crumb or two stuck to it.

5   While the cake bakes, prepare the sauce: in a small pan, heat the sugar, cream, butter, treacle and salt over a low heat until combined. Increase the heat slightly and let bubble for a minute or two. Serve the pudding cut into generous portions (how else?) with a ladleful of toffee sauce over each.

STEAMING

Steaming is a clever way of keeping a pudding moist. This is particularly useful for large puddings, which — if baked in the dry heat of the oven — become tough on the outside before they have time to cook through. It's also crucial for suet puddings, about which we'll hear a little more in a moment. This method of cooking is slightly more involved than plain baking, but the results are spectacular: the cakes end up spongy, soft and damp.

The first step is to prepare the steamer. Fill the bottom of a steamer pan with a few centimetres of water and perch the rack or steamer compartment over the top, ready to accommodate the pudding basin.

It's no tragedy if you don't have a specialist steamer, though: it's easy enough to create a makeshift one. Make a small stand or platform for the pudding inside a large, deep pan. For this, choose something that the pudding basin will rest on comfortably — perhaps a small can, a metal pastry cutter, a trivet or a ramekin. This is just to raise the pudding up away from the intense heat of the pan itself, leaving the boiling water and steam to do the cooking. Make sure that you can still fit the lid onto the pan once the basin has been lowered into it.

The pudding then needs to be wrapped or covered to shield it from the direct heat and moisture of the steam: it's one thing to have a slightly damp cake, it's quite another if it ends up sodden. Cover the pudding basin with two layers of baking parchment, making sure that you fold a wide pleat into the middle of each sheet to allow the pudding room to expand as it cooks. Tie each consecutive layer securely around the pudding basin with a length of string.

You can also make a string handle at this point if you're worried that it might be tricky to lift the hot pudding out of the steaming pan. Just tie a piece of string over the top of the basin, securing it at each end to the lengths already securing the baking parchment.

The steaming itself is easy: bring a few centimetres of water to the boil in the steamer, add the wrapped pudding (if using an improvised steamer, the water shouldn't reach any further than a few centimetres up the sides of the basin), put the lid on and steam. This takes longer than baking the pudding, but the advantage is that it's far harder to overcook and almost impossible to burn. Just keep the water topped up throughout the cooking time, test as you would for any other cake, inserting a knife into the centre and seeing that it emerges basically clean.

STEAMED ORANGE & GINGER PUDDING

There's a whole orange lurking inside this pudding. This is no gimmick, though: as it steams, the orange releases juice and flavour into the surrounding cake, leaving the pudding fantastically moist, zesty and tender. Serve with (lots of) ice cream.

Makes 1 medium pudding, serving 4-6
2 medium oranges
125g unsalted butter, softened
125g soft dark brown sugar
2 large eggs
5-7cm fresh ginger, peeled and grated
3 teaspoons ground ginger

75g stem ginger, roughly chopped
125g plain flour
1½ teaspoons baking powder

0.8-1.2 litre pudding basin

📷 p223

1   Prepare a steamer using the instructions on page 221. Get out your baking parchment and a length of string.

2   Bring a small pan of water to the boil. Zest both of the oranges, setting the zest aside until later. Boil one of the oranges in the water for 10 minutes then set aside to cool while you prepare the remaining ingredients.

3   Cream the butter and sugar together for a couple of minutes then add the eggs and all the ginger (fresh, ground and stem). In a separate bowl, combine the flour and baking powder before adding these to the wet ingredients. Now add the reserved orange zest and stir to combine.

4   Grease the pudding basin generously with butter then line the bottom with a circle of baking parchment (this will help with the unmoulding later). Cut one slice from the un-boiled orange and place in the bottom of the basin. This will look impressive when the pudding is turned out and also serves to hide the top of the orange that you're going to put inside the pudding.

5   Half-fill the basin with the cake batter. Pierce the boiled orange all over with a sharp knife or cocktail stick then press this into the mixture, placing it centrally. Spoon the remaining batter around the orange — if its top is still peeking above the level of the cake mix at this point, don't worry: the cake will rise to cover it as it bakes. You may not need all of the batter, depending on the precise size of your pudding bowl and of the orange inside it — just add enough to fill to 2-3 centimetres below the rim.

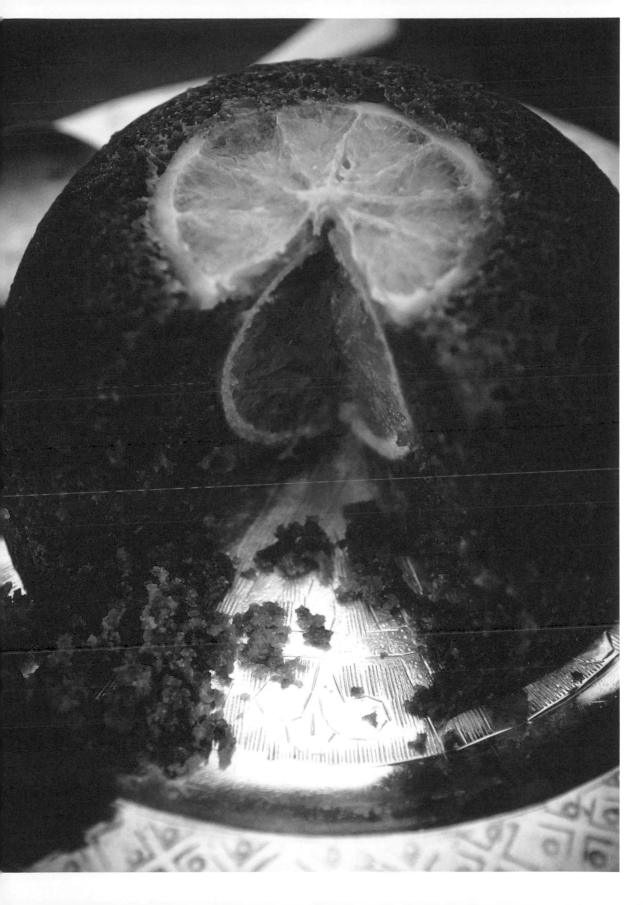

6   Cut two large squares of baking parchment, make a wide, crisply folded pleat down the middle of each and lay them over the top of the pudding basin. The pleat will allow plenty of room for the pudding to expand. Secure the paper using a length of string tied tightly around the basin rim.

7   Place the pudding onto the steamer rack (or makeshift steaming platform), make sure that there's plenty of water in the base of the pan, and put a lid on. Steam for 2 hours, topping up the water periodically.

8   When the pudding is ready, unwrap it, loosen the edges with a knife and turn out onto a plate. Peel back the circle of baking parchment on top and slice proudly down the middle to reveal the whole orange inside. This is a dish best served hot.

LIGHTER CHRISTMAS PUDDING

All the delicate flavours of panettone, in a steamed sponge pudding.

I know that Christmas is a good excuse for gluttony (and I always seize such opportunities with both hands), but having a traditional, dark Christmas pudding after a day of feasting is sometimes a bit too much. It is a spectacular pudding — especially booze-soaked, lit and brought to the table in a merry inferno — but I prefer something lighter to top off the Christmas meal.

This pudding strikes a fine balance between the sort of stodginess we've come to expect in a Christmas pudding and the lightness required if we're actually going to be able to stomach the thing. Because it's suet-free, it's far spongier than the old-fashioned types. It's not nearly as alcoholic either: just a splash of sweet white wine to soak the fruits (save the brandy for the post-dinner drinking).

This won't keep for nearly as long as a traditional pudding, but it will cook far more quickly, so there's no need to lose an entire day to its preparation. Just soak the fruit on Christmas Eve, make the batter in a jiffy in the morning and leave to quietly steam for two hours on the hob while dinner's in the oven.

Makes 1 medium pudding, serving 4-6
Zest of 2 lemons
100ml sweet white wine, such as Muscat
40g raisins
40g dried cranberries or cherries
40g dried apricots, coarsely chopped
40g prunes, coarsely chopped
40g stem ginger, coarsely chopped
2 tablespoons syrup from the stem ginger
40g candied peel
125g unsalted butter, softened

50g soft light brown sugar
75g caster sugar
2 large eggs
2 teaspoons vanilla extract
135g plain flour
1½ teaspoons baking powder
Pinch of salt

0.8-1.2 litre pudding basin

📷 p224

1   The day before you make the pudding, mix the lemon zest, wine and dried fruit in a bowl, cover with cling film and leave to soak overnight, at room temperature.

2   The following day, prepare the steamer, referring to the instructions on page 221. Prepare the pudding basin by lightly buttering all over and placing a circle of

baking parchment in the base, to help with unmoulding later. Have a couple of large pieces of baking parchment and some string to hand, ready to cover the pudding.

3   Add the stem ginger, syrup and candied peel to the soaked fruit mixture. In a large bowl, cream the butter and sugars until pale and fluffy, then add the eggs and vanilla extract. Mix the flour, baking powder and salt together in a separate bowl, then stir this into the butter mixture. Now add all of the fruit and ginger along with their soaking liquid. Stir lightly to combine.

4   Spoon the batter into the prepared pudding basin. Lay one sheet of the baking parchment over the top of the basin, fold a wide pleat into it (to allow the pudding to expand as it cooks) then use a length of string tied around it to secure. Repeat with the second sheet of baking parchment. The cover should be secure but loose enough that it won't constrict the rising pudding.

5   Bring the water in the steamer to the boil, put the pudding in and the lid on, and steam for around 2 hours, or until well risen, firm and a knife inserted into the centre comes out clean. It's important that you keep an eye on the water levels during this time, topping up regularly so that the pan doesn't boil dry.

6   When it's ready, carefully unmould the steamed pudding, loosen around the edges and invert onto a large plate. Serve with ice cream (homemade, spiked with a dash of sweet white wine, is particularly good) to finish the feast.

SUET

Suet is the last word in puddings, and in spite of the blight that is 'low-fat diets', it's still alive and well in our kitchens. It's actually had a resurgence lately, with the burgeoning national appetite for revival food, British culinary heritage and so on. I can only hope suet is here to stay, and not just a passing fad.

Traditionally you might have used beef suet (that's the fat scraped from around the animal's kidneys) but I've called for the vegetarian version for these sweet puddings. Beef suet gives a slightly richer flavour, but I feel uneasy about sullying a jam roly-poly with animal fat, and vegetarian suet gives a perfectly good texture. By all means use the old-fashioned variety if you'd rather for authenticity's sake, but it's really not a deal-breaker. You can still find fresh suet in some butchers, but by far the easiest way to get it is from the supermarket baking aisle: it's less messy and comes 'shredded' — in small pellets ready to be stirred straight into the flour.

Suet contains more fat and less water than butter. And unlike butter, which melts with the slightest warmth, suet doesn't become liquid until it reaches around 45°C. This gives the surrounding dough time to set first, so as the pieces of suet melt, they leave tiny gaps behind. The upshot is that puddings and pastry crusts made with suet tend to have a fine, open texture when freshly baked.

But the problem is that as suet cools, it re-solidifies to give a pastry that — no matter how tender and light it was when it left the steamer — becomes waxy, solid and dense. For this reason suet puddings are always best eaten hot.

ORANGE & SAFFRON SPOTTED DICK

It still brings chokes of laughter to our dinner table, but Spotted Dick is too perfect a pudding to forgo just because of the name. It's an old-fashioned pudding but has persisted for a reason, making something instantly comforting from just a handful of ingredients.

The saffron and orange blossom water included here are good counterpoints to the pudding's characteristic stodginess. They balance earthiness with floral lightness, and the orange zest follows through with a kick. If you'd rather omit the saffron, that's no problem — just add in some more zest or vanilla extract in its place.

The quantities here are slightly smaller than usual for a suet pudding, but I find that this amount fits comfortably in a medium steamer and is enough to satisfy the family in one sitting without leftovers. This really isn't something that should be left to cool once made — when fresh out of the steamer it's moist, light, delicate; once cool it gains the density and mouthfeel of a block of lead. Get it while it's hot.

This version of the pudding is steamed but you could also bake it in a steamy oven if you'd prefer — follow the cooking instructions for the jam roly-poly on page 229, but bake for around 1 hour.

Makes one medium pudding, serving 6
115ml milk, plus an extra splash, if necessary
Couple of pinches of saffron threads
Zest of 1 orange
1 teaspoon orange blossom water
½ teaspoon vanilla extract
150g plain flour

1½ teaspoons baking powder
75g vegetable suet
120g currants
75g caster sugar
¼ teaspoon salt
Butter, to grease

📷 p228

1   Heat the milk and saffron over a low heat until the milk is just scalding. Remove from the heat, add the zest, orange blossom water and vanilla extract, give it a stir and let it cool. The milk will turn a sunny yellow hue as the saffron infuses.

2   In a large bowl, combine the flour, baking powder, suet, currants, sugar and salt. Measure the cooled milk, and if there's any less than 115ml (some of it may have evaporated over the heat) top up with an extra splash, and stir in to combine with the dry ingredients. The dough will be sticky, making it difficult to handle at this point but producing a far lighter pudding in the end. Let it sit for a few minutes.

3   You'll need a medium/large steamer or pan with a steamer rack. Bring a kettle to the boil. Cut two large sheets (around 35x35cm) of baking parchment and grease one side of one of them with butter. Prepare four short lengths of string.

4   Scoop the wet dough neatly into the middle of the greased piece of baking parchment to form a sausage-shape around 20cm long (or approximately the diameter of the pan you're using). Fold the paper up around it, folding a wide pleat into the paper on top of the dough, to allow room for the pudding to expand as it cooks. Twist the ends of the paper and secure with string. Wrap this parcel in the other piece of baking parchment, pleating, twisting and tying as before. You will be left with a sort of giant Christmas cracker.

5 Pour the boiling water into the pan or steamer and place the pudding onto the steamer shelf or rack. Put a lid on and steam for 1¼-1½ hours, topping the water up regularly so that the pan doesn't boil dry. The pudding should be golden and firm but springy, and a knife inserted into the centre should come out clean.

6 Straight after cooking, cut into thick slices, serve with ice cream and loosen your belt a notch — what other way is there of eating a pudding like this?

RHUBARB JAM ROLY-POLY

Roly-poly is designed to be stodgy — the sort of pudding that could sustain you through a long, cold winter — but it doesn't have to be sickly sweet. Roly-polys made with jams such as strawberry, raspberry or (heaven forbid) apricot end up cloying and bland. It's crucial that there's some balance in the recipe: something acidic to balance the richness of the pastry and accompanying custard. This pudding uses rhubarb jam for that reason. You can make your own jam, following the recipe on page 323 if you have the time and if there are good, tender stalks of rhubarb in the shops. Otherwise, buy a good-quality rhubarb conserve.

Like all suet puddings, this is prone to drying as it cooks so should be baked over a pan of hot water in the oven and swaddled in baking parchment and foil to minimise the formation of a thick crust. You could also steam it on the hob for an even more tender result. Wrap and cook it as instructed for the Orange & Saffron Spotted Dick on page 227 if so, steaming for approximately 1 hour.

Serves 4 generously
150g plain flour
1½ teaspoons baking powder
75g vegetable suet
30g caster sugar

Zest of 1 orange
100ml full-fat milk
150g rhubarb jam
Butter, to grease

1   Preheat the oven to 180°C/fan 160°C/gas mark 4. Find a large roasting dish and set a steaming rack or basic wire cooling rack in it. There needs to be sufficient clearance between the rack and the base of the tray for a couple of centimetres of water, so prop the rack up on a couple of metal pastry cutters or little tins if necessary. Have a couple of large pieces of baking parchment and four lengths of string ready for wrapping the pudding. Boil a kettle full of water.

2   In a large bowl, combine the flour, baking powder, suet, caster sugar and orange zest. Add the milk and stir to bring together to a slightly sticky dough.

3   Dust a work surface with plenty of flour and roll the dough out to a rectangle approximately 20x30cm. Flour generously as you go, otherwise the dough will stick. Spread the jam over the rectangle, leaving a border of a centimetre or so around the outside. Roll up from short edge to short edge to give a roll roughly 20cm long.

4   Grease one of the sheets of baking parchment with butter, lay the roll down in the centre of the sheet and roll the paper around it, leaving a wide pleat on top to afford the pudding room to expand as it cooks. Tie the ends using two pieces of string. Wrap again with the second sheet, pleating and tying as before. Rest the pudding in the centre of the wire rack.

5   Transfer the roasting dish with the rack and pudding in it to the oven shelf then carefully pour a couple of centimetres of boiling water into the tray. Bake for around 45 minutes, after which time the pudding should be fat and cooked through. Serve as is only right for a rhubarb-swirled, suet pudding comfort food: with a jug of thick vanilla custard.

PIES & TARTS

SHORTCRUST PASTRY

SPICED AUBERGINE & SWISS CHARD PIE

BROCCOLI & GORGONZOLA QUICHE

BUTTERNUT SQUASH & MOZZARELLA TARTLETS WITH HERB PASTRY

HOT WATER CRUST PASTRY

SPICED PORK PIE • CAULIFLOWER GRUYÈRE PASTIES

QUICK PUFF PASTRY

CHICKEN, PALE ALE & CHICORY PIE • FISH PIE

BANANA THYME TART

SWEET SHORTCRUST PASTRY

PEAR, SESAME & CHOCOLATE TART • CHERRY PIE

LEMON & BASIL TART • ROSEMARY PECAN PIE

STEM GINGER TREACLE TART • SPICED CHOCOLATE TART

There aren't many foods that don't taste better encased in a pastry crust. What good would baked, crimson cherries be if not sandwiched between two layers of shortcrust? Or chicken baked in a creamy sauce, without flaky pastry draped on top? It's a shame, then, that pastry has such an unfair reputation for difficulty. We often reach unquestioningly for the ready-rolled stuff, concerned that homemade pastry will be too thick, crumbly, wet, tough, time-consuming or fiddly. The term 'soggy bottom' has given rise to a national neurosis, whereby a pie is declared a disaster if its pastry base isn't perfectly crisp. These impossible standards might be how success is calibrated in patisseries and TV shows, but they have no place in the home kitchen. I'd go so far as to say we should champion the soggy bottom: I can see nothing not to love about buttery pastry sodden with fruit juices, or custard, or rich gravy.

LINING A PIE DISH OR TART TIN

There's no great secret to lining a pie dish or tart tin with pastry, although it is something that grows easier with practice. I've outlined the basic steps below for those of you who want the pastry to be even, smart and symmetrical, but if you're not bothered about appearances, just get stuck in. The worst that can happen is that you'll end up with a slightly lopsided, rough-edged, undulating pie crust, bubbling through with syrup, or fruit juices, or gravy... and that really doesn't sound so bad.

1   Roll the pastry to a circle that is big enough to cover the base and sides of the dish or tin, making sure that you roll evenly and to a reasonable thickness — 3–5mm is about right. Too thick and the pastry will dominate; too thin and it risks tearing or leaking. I often roll on a sheet of lightly floured baking parchment. This not only prevents sticking, but also helps when transferring the pastry to the dish or tin.

2   To move the pastry into position, either slide it off its baking parchment into the dish or tin or use your rolling pin to pick it up — roll one edge over the pin and pick up from this edge, draping the rest behind the rolling pin, sliding the tin underneath and lowering the pastry into it. Don't worry if the pastry cracks a little — you can patch this up later.

3   Press the pastry into the dish or tin, and neatly into the grooves if you are using a fluted dish. You could use a small piece of pastry to do this, thus avoiding excessively touching and warming the dough, but I've never found it necessary. As long as you don't fiddle around for too long, the pastry will be fine. Take care not to stretch the pastry· let it fall back under its own weight, and only gently tease it into shape. It helps to press the pastry up a few millimetres proud of the rim of the dish or tin, too, to allow for any shrinkage as it cooks.

4   Chill the lined pie dish or tin for at least half an hour in the fridge before baking.

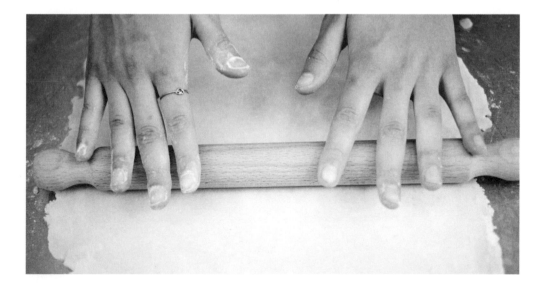

BLIND BAKING

This is not as scary as it sounds. Blind baking is simply cooking a pie or tart shell prior to filling it, to give the pastry a chance to set and crisp up. This is crucial when using liquid fillings such as those in custard tarts and quiches, although it's a trick that can be used on more or less any pie or tart when you want to have a perfectly crisp, dry base. Most of the time, the pastry is subsequently returned to the oven with the filling to continue cooking, but if you bake blind for an extra 5 minutes or so, you can completely cook the shell. A fully blind-baked pastry case can then be used as a vessel for pastry cream and fresh fruits, or even a chocolate ganache.

It's common to use baking weights to hold the pastry down while blind baking, otherwise it's liable to dome upwards at its centre and sink down at the sides. You'll find purpose-made baking weights or beans (little ceramic marbles) in the shops, but there's no need to shell out when uncooked rice or dried pulses make perfectly effective, and far cheaper, substitutes.

To bake blind, first line the pie dish or tart tin as described on page 233. Leave to chill for 30 minutes or so while you preheat the oven to 200°C/fan 180°C/gas mark 6. Scrunch up a large piece of baking parchment then roughly smooth it out again (this just makes it easier to fit the pastry contours) and lightly press it into the pastry-lined tin so that it covers the base and sides. Fill with a thick layer of baking beans, uncooked rice or dried pulses. Bake for 15 minutes, then carefully lift out the parchment parcel with its filling, and cook the pastry uncovered for a further 5-10 minutes, until firm and dry to the touch.

SHORTCRUST PASTRY

Despite so often being billed as a 'basic' pastry, for a long time I found shortcrust to be one of the trickiest of them all. There are only four ingredients — flour, butter, water and salt — leaving little margin for error and no place to hide. Too warm, cold, dry, wet, buttery or lean, and it'll lack that crucial shortness. It's the Goldilocks of pastry, but with a little care and patience, you should have no trouble getting it right.

BEFORE YOU START

The butter should be firm, but not fridge-cold. If it's too hard, it'll prove difficult to rub into the flour; too soft and it'll melt between your fingers, leaving the pastry greasy and tough. The water, however, should be chilled so if it's a particularly warm day, have a few ice cubes ready to chill the water before adding it to the pastry.

MIXING

This stage is a balancing act, but not an impossible feat: you'll need to mix thoroughly but avoid handling the pastry for too long. The key is keeping the mixture cool. Toss the cubes of butter through the flour then, using only your fingertips, work quickly and lightly to rub the butter into the flour, breaking it into smaller and smaller pieces until there are no visible chunks of butter remaining. In doing this, you coat the flour particles with fat. This layer of fat repels water and restricts the development of gluten (the protein responsible for making dough strong and elastic), so the resulting pastry is as crumbly and tender as possible.

Once the butter has been incorporated, mix in the salt (and sugar or spices, if using) followed by the water (some sweet shortcrust doughs use egg instead). Always use cold liquid and add it gradually — too much will leave the dough sticky and difficult to roll and, worse still, encourage the gluten development we're aiming to avoid. When mixing in the water, use a 'cutting' motion: draw a small, sharp knife through the mixture again and again, until the moisture is distributed evenly through the flour. This combines the dough without working the gluten. As soon as the flour is moistened and beginning to come together in small clumps, the mixing is done.

Use your hands to lightly but firmly press the pastry into a ball. If it won't hold, add a few more drops of water. Wrap the ball in cling film and refrigerate for at least 30 minutes to give the butter a chance to chill, and the dough time to relax.

ROLLING AND SHAPING

Roll gently, don't use excessive flour to dust the surface, and don't stretch the dough. After such careful mixing, it'd be a shame to overwork the pastry now. If the pastry begins to stick, let it chill a little more; if it's crumbly, let it warm for a few minutes at room temperature. As for re-rolling any offcuts, you can do it, but don't do so more than once, otherwise the dough risks becoming elastic.

RESTING

Once you've rolled the pastry and lined your dish or tin (see page 233), it's crucial to let it rest before baking. This should be done in the fridge for at least 30 minutes, or 15 minutes in the freezer if you're short on time. During this resting period, the gluten in the pastry will relax, minimising shrinkage during baking. It also affords you time to prepare any filling ingredients and preheat the oven.

BAKING

Depending on the type of pie or tart, you may have to blind bake your shortcrust pastry shell separately before filling (see page 234). A well-baked shortcrust should be firm to the touch, sandy-textured (a French version of sweet shortcrust pastry is called *pâte sablée*, or 'sandy pastry') and no darker than a light golden brown. And in terms of texture — the crumblier, the better.

WHY IS MY SHORTCRUST PASTRY...

Because its method is straightforward and its ingredient list short, it's usually easy to figure out where your shortcrust went wrong. Here are a few of the most common problems, and some suggestions for avoiding them in future.

... SHRUNKEN ONCE BAKED?

— Too much water. This encourages troublesome gluten to form, leaving the pastry elastic and prone to shrinking in the oven. Add the water gradually next time, and use only as much as is necessary to bring the pastry together.

— When shortcrust is handled too much or re-rolled too many times, it'll lose that important fragility and become rubbery.

— If the pastry is stretched when lining the tin, it will spring back as it's cooking.

— Patience is a virtue. Shortcrust that has not rested for long enough after being rolled won't have had time to relax, and so will shrink.

— Too much flour used when rolling can also be a cause. Dust your work surface with just enough flour to stop the pastry sticking.

... TOUGH?

— Again, this may be a case of too much water or excessive handling or re-rolling.

— It may also be that you used too much flour when rolling.

... TOO HARD AND CRUMBLY TO ROLL?

— Your pastry may actually be too cold. Let it rest at room temperature for a few minutes, then give rolling another shot.

— Your pastry may also be too dry. Roll slowly and carefully, patching up any cracks as you go, and remember to add a little more water to the dough next time.

— Too much wholemeal flour or sugar can also create a crumbly pastry.

... TOO STICKY TO ROLL?

— The dough might be too warm. Let it chill for another 10 minutes before attempting to roll it.

— If the pastry is tacky even after chilling, you might have used too much water.

... RAW UNDERNEATH?

— Sometimes pastry needs a head start if it's going to play host to a particularly wet filling, such as a custard or cream. On such occasions, the pastry needs to be blind baked (see page 234) before being filled.

— If the pie filling can tolerate a little extra time in the oven, it might just be that the pastry hasn't been baked for long enough. From raw, most shortcrusts will need at least 20 minutes to become crisp, and this could take much longer depending on the topping or filling.

— Try baking in a slightly hotter oven next time. If the oven is too cool, the pastry will end up greasy and soft. The temperature shouldn't be any lower than 180°C/fan 160°C/gas mark 4 for shortcrust.

SPICED AUBERGINE & SWISS CHARD PIE

There's little to be gained in trying to make a vegetarian pie into an ersatz steak-and-kidney or second-rate 'mince' and potato version. Meat-free pies should be exciting and different, not apologetic. They're all the more interesting for not relying on the usual meat-and-gravy formula. This one's all about showcasing the vegetables: aubergine, carrot and Swiss chard, seasoned, spiced and layered.

You could make this pie vegan by swapping the butter for vegetable shortening, such as Trex, in which case you might need an extra tablespoon or so of water to bring the dough together. The problem with vegetable shortening, however, is that it doesn't taste of much. Consider adding a couple of teaspoons of spice — perhaps ground coriander or toasted cumin seeds — to make the pastry more interesting.

Makes 1 large pie, serving 8
For the shortcrust pastry:
400g plain flour
200g unsalted butter, firm but not
  fridge-cold, cubed
¼ teaspoon salt
4 tablespoons cold water
1 large egg, lightly beaten with a pinch
  of salt, to glaze (optional)

For the filling:
4 large carrots, peeled and thickly sliced
3 cloves garlic, peeled
Juice of ½ lemon

50g sesame seeds
8 tablespoons olive oil
2 large onions, sliced
2 teaspoons ground coriander
2 teaspoons ground ginger
1 teaspoon paprika
200g Swiss chard, roughly sliced
1 aubergine
Salt and black pepper, to taste

**Deep 20cm round spring-form or
  loose-bottomed cake tin**

📷 p241

1   First make the pastry. Rub the flour and butter together in a large bowl, working quickly and lightly to fully combine without melting the butter. Add the salt then the water, cutting through the pastry with a small knife until all of the flour is moistened and beginning to come together in clumps. Add an extra couple of teaspoons of water if the dough is too dry to hold together. Press into a disc, wrap in cling film then chill for at least 30 minutes.

2   Bring a large pan of water to the boil, then add the carrots and garlic cloves. Boil until the carrots are tender. Drain, then use a hand-held blender or food processor to purée the carrots and garlic together until smooth. Stir in the lemon juice and sesame seeds. Season, then put aside to cool.

3   Heat half the oil in a large frying pan then gently cook the onions with a pinch of salt for 10 minutes or so, until soft and translucent. Add the spices and fry for a further minute or two, so that the mixture grows fragrant. Add half of this to the carrot mixture and stir well to combine. Return the other half to a low heat with the Swiss chard, stirring gently for a couple of minutes until the leaves have wilted. Season again then leave to cool.

4   By this point the pastry should be well rested. On a lightly floured surface, roll out just over two-thirds of it to a circle roughly 25cm in diameter. Forget what you might've heard about thinness and delicacy being the keys to a good pastry case: this is a deep, hearty pie and needs a reasonably robust pastry to hold it all together. Line the tin with this circle, pressing neatly into the corners, then put it in the fridge to chill for half an hour. Alternatively, freeze for just 15 minutes if you're in a rush. Re-wrap and chill the remaining third of the pastry.

5   While the pastry shell chills, preheat the oven to 200°C/fan 180°C/gas mark 6. Prepare the aubergine by first cutting it in half across its width, to give two fat chunks, then thinly slicing these two pieces lengthways. They ought to be delicate, floppy slivers. If the slices hold rigid when held up by one corner, they've been sliced too thickly.

6   Now assemble the pie. Lay one third of the aubergine strips over the base of
    the pie, drizzle lightly with olive oil and season. Top with half of the carrot
    mixture. Repeat the aubergine layer, followed by all of the chard, the final third of
    aubergine and then the remaining carrot mixture. If you have any aubergine strips
    left, you can top it off with these. Roll the rest of the pastry to a circle roughly
    20cm in diameter, lay this over the pie and crimp the edges to seal. Brush with
    beaten egg, if you want a deeper colour to the top, and make an incision in the top
    (so that steam can escape as the pie filling cooks). Bake for 15 minutes then turn
    the oven down to 180°C/fan 160°C/gas mark 4 and bake for a further 45 minutes.

You can eat this pie while it's still hot, but I think it's best cold — even better the
following day. Just leave it to cool in its tin before carefully unmoulding. It holds its
shape better once cold, too: perfect for cutting into fat wedges for picnics.

BROCCOLI & GORGONZOLA QUICHE

A savoury wholemeal pastry lends a welcome nuttiness to this quiche, chiming well
with the blue cheese within. You can make this marginally healthier if you like, by
replacing the cream with more milk, but I'm not sure that shaving those few extra
calories off is worth the trouble. Just enjoy with a peppery green salad, and rest
assured that it's a good deal less fattening than the more common, bacon-laden
Quiche Lorraine.

Makes 1 family-sized quiche, serving 6
For the pastry:
125g plain flour
75g wholemeal flour
100g unsalted butter, firm but not
    fridge-cold, cubed
Large pinch of salt
2 tablespoons water

For the filling:
150–200g broccoli florets

100ml full-fat milk
150ml single cream
3 large eggs
150g Gorgonzola
50g walnuts, roughly chopped
Salt and black pepper, to taste

23–27cm flan tin or dish

📷 p242

1   In a large bowl, combine the flours then rub in the butter until fully combined.
    Stir in the salt followed by the water, using a cutting motion through the mixture
    to distribute the water until all of the flour comes together in small clumps. Add
    a few drops more water if necessary. Press the pastry into a ball, flatten it slightly,
    then wrap in cling film and chill for at least 30 minutes.

2   Once chilled, roll out the pastry into a circle large enough to line the base and
    sides of the tin or dish. Because of the proportion of bran-rich, wholemeal flour
    in this dough, it's more crumbly than a standard white-flour pastry. Roll out on
    a sheet of lightly floured baking parchment and don't fret if it cracks or breaks as
    you slide it into the tin: just use scraps and offcuts to patch up any holes to stop
    the filling from leaking. Leave the lined tin to rest in the fridge for 30 minutes, or
    the freezer for 15 minutes, and pre-heat the oven to 200°C/fan 180°C/gas mark 6.

3   Bake blind (see page 234 for more information): line the chilled pastry case with baking parchment, then fill with baking beans, dried pulses or rice and bake for 15 minutes. Remove the parcel of baking beans and return the pastry to the oven, uncovered, to cook for a further 5 minutes or so, until sandy and firm.

4   While the pastry is in the oven, boil or steam the broccoli florets for a few minutes — just long enough to rid them of their crispness while leaving them firm. Drain and leave to cool slightly while you prepare the filling liquid.

5   Whisk together the milk, cream and eggs, then crumble in the Gorgonzola followed by the walnuts. Season the mixture well. Cut any large pieces of broccoli into more manageable chunks and arrange over the base of the cooked pastry case. Pour over the filling liquid (you may not need all of it depending on the size of your tin or dish).

6   Reduce the oven temperature to 180°C/fan 160°/gas mark 4 and bake for around 30 minutes, or until set and barely firm to the touch. Leave the quiche to cool for at least 15 minutes in its tin, on a wire rack, before serving.

BUTTERNUT SQUASH & MOZZARELLA TARTLETS WITH HERB PASTRY

It's not difficult to make pastry interesting. A scattering of herbs, a spoonful of mustard powder, some chilli or perhaps even a fistful of Parmesan is all it takes to elevate a pastry shell from a cursory vessel to a feature in its own right. The pastry for these tartlets has fresh herbs in the dough but for a stronger flavour you could use dried herbs instead, decreasing the amount by half.

If you don't have a set of small tart tins (I got mine only very recently), use a single, larger tin instead.

Makes 8 individual tartlets or 1 large tart
For the pastry:
125g unsalted butter, firm but not
    fridge-cold, cubed
250g plain flour
¼ teaspoon salt
2 tablespoons fresh oregano or sage,
    finely chopped
3 tablespoons cold water

For the filling:
1 medium butternut squash, peeled and
    cut into medium-sized chunks

2 cloves garlic, unpeeled
3 tablespoons fresh oregano or sage,
    roughly chopped
¼ teaspoon chilli powder
2 tablespoons olive oil
250g mozzarella
50g flaked almonds, plus extra for
    scattering

8 x 10-12.5cm tart tins or 1 x 20-23cm round cake tin, pie dish or tart tin

📷 p245

1   Preheat the oven to 200°C/fan 180°C/gas mark 6.

2   In a large bowl, rub the butter into the flour until completely integrated, with no chunks of butter remaining. Stir in the salt and 2 tablespoons of herbs, then add the water, cutting it in with a small knife until all of the flour has been moistened,

and begins to come together in clumps (see page 235 for more information on making shortcrust pastry). If lots of dry flour remains, add a little extra water, a few drops at a time. Take care not to use more water than is absolutely necessary: too much will leave the dough sticky, and tough once baked. Press the clumps together to form one large disc of pastry, wrap in cling film and leave to chill in the fridge for at least 30 minutes (although it can be rested for up to a couple of days as long as it's tightly wrapped).

3   Combine the butternut squash, garlic, herbs and chilli powder in a roasting dish. Toss through the olive oil and roast in the preheated oven for 30 minutes or so — as long as it takes for the squash to become tender. (If your oven takes a while to preheat, leave it on at this point. If it heats up quickly, however, save energy by turning it off until you've finished preparing the filling and the pastry shells.)

4   Once cooked, squeeze the soft garlic cloves between your thumb and index finger to pop them from their skins, then mash them together with the squash and herbs in a large bowl. Once the mixture is reasonably smooth, roughly tear three-quarters of the mozzarella into pieces and add to the mixture with the flaked almonds and stir in to roughly combine. Set aside to cool while you prepare the pastry shells.

5   If using small tins, roll the pastry out until it's 3–5mm thick, then use a pastry cutter to cut eight circles — at least 3cm wider than the diameters of the tins. If you can't get eight circles from the pastry at the first roll, re-roll the offcuts and cut the remaining circles from this. Don't re-roll a second time, however: the pastry may become tough if handled too much and will shrink when baked. If using a single, large tin, just roll out the pastry until it's large enough to line the base and sides of the tin, but no thicker than 5mm. (If you have any excess pastry, you could try cutting it into fingers, scattering with grated Cheddar or crumbled mozzarella and baking for 15 minutes for an easy nibble.)

6   Chill the pastry case(s) in the fridge for 30 minutes, or in the freezer for around 15 minutes. Once cooled, fill with the butternut squash mixture, top with the remaining mozzarella and extra flaked almonds and bake at 200°C/fan 180°C/ gas mark 6 for 25–30 minutes. When the cheese is bubbling and golden, the tartlets are ready.

HOT WATER CRUST PASTRY

This robust, traditionally lard-based pastry is the sort used for pork pies. It's a no-nonsense dough that will neatly overturn everything you thought you knew about pastry making. Oblivious to standard pastry etiquette, it calls for boiling water and melted fat, prefers to be kept warm and is all the happier for being handled. It couldn't be less like the fragile, standoffishly cold pastry dough we've met so far. It doesn't bake to quite the same crispness as shortcrust pastry, but it is far sturdier and easier to work with, which is why it's so well suited to heavy-duty picnic pies and high-sided gala pies.

Because it can be held and handled, hot water pastry is a good dough to start with if you're not yet confident with making pastry. Have the filling more or less ready before you start on the pastry, though: you'll need to roll and shape the dough while it's still supple — if it cools too much, it will become dry and stiff. Although usually made with lard, hot water crust pastry can be made with butter, too. The pork pie below uses a little butter for flavour's sake (the lard itself, although nicely savoury, isn't particularly flavourful), while the Cauliflower Gruyère Pasties (see page 248) use an all-butter, vegetarian version.

SPICED PORK PIE

A good pork pie is hard to find. There's something quite Sweeney Todd about the ones in the supermarkets: tough pastry, salty jelly and a sad block of (ostensibly) pork, greying and bland. Unless you're lucky enough to live in Melton Mowbray, you're probably better off making your own. You'll know exactly what's gone into it, and it's really not difficult to make. You can forget about the gelatinous gunk, too: it's there to fill the cavity between the meat (which shrinks during cooking) and the pastry, and to keep the meat moist, but as long as you're not planning to send the slices much further than the dinner table or the lunch box, there's no need for it.

This is a reasonably shallow pie compared to the tall wedges of pork pie we're used to, but I think that the smaller slices are a welcome relief, when the filling is so meaty, spiced and rich.

Makes 1 large pie, serving 8–10
For the pastry:
75g unsalted butter, firm but not
  fridge-cold, cubed
300g plain flour
¼ teaspoon salt
½ teaspoon smoked paprika
135ml water
75g lard
1 egg, lightly beaten with a pinch
  of salt, to glaze

For the filling:
400g pork shoulder, finely diced
150g unsmoked back bacon
2 teaspoons smoked paprika
½ teaspoon cayenne pepper
Salt, to taste

**20cm round spring-form or
  loose-bottomed cake tin**

1   Preheat the oven to 200°C/fan 180°C/gas mark 6. In a large bowl, rub the butter into the flour using your fingertips, until the mixture resembles breadcrumbs. Stir in the salt and smoked paprika. In a small pan, heat the water with the lard over a low heat, until the water is steaming and the lard has melted. (I'm not a fan of the smell of melted lard, so I keep the pan at arm's length at this point.) Pour the hot liquid over the butter and flour mixture and stir to combine. Use your hands to bring the pastry together into a ball, and knead just a couple of times under the heel of your palm to help strengthen it. Leave to cool, uncovered, at room temperature while you assemble the filling ingredients.

2   In another large bowl, thoroughly mix the pork shoulder, bacon and spices. The bacon should impart sufficient saltiness, but if you're in any doubt about the seasoning, break off a small ball of the filling, fry for a few minutes separately and taste it. If it needs any extra salt or spice, add this to the remaining mixture now.

3   Check the slightly cooled pastry — it needs to feel just cool to the touch. The temperature of the pastry is important in order to neatly line the tin: warm pastry will be limp, greasy and soft; cold pastry will harden and crack. Just keep an eye on it, and as soon as it's cool and firm enough to be rolled and moulded without collapsing or sticking, line the tin.
    Roll out two-thirds of the dough on a piece of lightly floured baking parchment into a circle large enough to line the base and sides of the tin. Slide the dough into the tin and use your fingers to press it neatly into the corners and sides. Don't be shy about handling the pastry: this is a rare instance where you can hold, re-roll and press the pastry with impunity.

4   Firmly pack the filling into the lined tin, then roll out the remaining third of pastry on a lightly floured surface and transfer this to the top of the pie. Press the edges of the sides and lid together to seal them and make a hole in the top with a small knife (to allow steam to escape during baking). Brush the top with the beaten egg to glaze and bake the pie in the preheated oven for 15 minutes. Then reduce the oven temperature to 180°C/fan 160°C/gas mark 4 and bake for a further 45–60 minutes. When done, the pie should be a rich golden brown and you'll be able to see it bubbling merrily through the hole on top.

5   Leave to cool completely in its tin, on a wire rack. If you try to serve this while it's still warm, it'll fall apart and leak its paprika-stained juices across the plate: you need to wait until it's cooled and set. Once cool, refrigerate until ready to serve, ideally with some crisp lettuce, ripe tomatoes and plenty of pickle.

CAULIFLOWER GRUYÈRE PASTIES

Cauliflower gets a bad press, but it's a far more exciting ingredient than it gets credit for. It's particularly good when baked, deepening to a nutty, toasted flavour and golden brown colour — a far cry from the anaemic, sulphurous slop that it becomes when unsympathetically boiled. It's a good match for musky, full-bodied Gruyère.

These pasties are vegetarian, eschewing the standard lard-based hot water crust pastry in favour of an all-butter version. Most Gruyère is vegetarian, but do check the packaging to be sure.

Makes 8
For the filling:
1 cauliflower head, broken into florets
3 cloves garlic, unpeeled
1 red onion, peeled and quartered
2 tablespoons olive oil
1 large egg
150g Gruyère, grated
Salt and black pepper, to taste

For the pastry:
150g butter, firm but not fridge-cold,
    cubed

250g plain flour
Large pinch of salt
55ml boiling water
1 large egg, lightly beaten with a pinch
    of salt, to seal and glaze

📷 p249

1   Preheat the oven to 200°C/fan 180°C/gas mark 6 and line a large baking tray with
    baking parchment.

2   In a roasting dish, toss the cauliflower florets, garlic cloves, red onion and oil
    together. Roast for 25 minutes, or until patches of brown are creeping across the
    cauliflower, and the garlic is soft and aromatic.

3   Once cooked, roughly chop the cauliflower florets into quarters and pull apart
    the onion segments to thin crescents. Remove the garlic cloves, squeeze the soft
    insides from the skins into a separate bowl and mash them. Stir in the egg and
    then add the grated cheese, cauliflower and onion. Toss through to combine.
    Season the mixture, then set it aside while you prepare the pastry.

4   In a large bowl, rub the butter into the flour and salt until no visible pieces of
    butter remain. Pour in the boiling water and stir to combine, then use your hands
    to gather the mixture together. It should feel soft, pliable and slightly greasy.
    Knead very lightly for a few seconds, then leave it to cool and firm up, uncovered
    in its bowl, at room temperature. It's ready when it's no longer warm to the touch,
    and is stiff enough to be rolled and shaped without sticking or collapsing.

5   Divide the cooled dough into eight pieces. On a floured work surface, roll one of
    the pieces to a circle roughly 15cm in diameter. Place a heaped tablespoon of the
    filling mixture onto one half of the circle, leaving a border of a centimetre or so.
    Paint around the edge of the circle with a little of the beaten egg (this will help to
    seal the join), then fold the other half over the top to give a semicircular parcel.
    Glaze the top with more egg wash, then set aside on the lined baking tray while
    you prepare the remaining pasties.

6   When you have made all eight pasties, bake for 25 minutes in the preheated oven,
    until golden, fragrant and firm. These are best served while they're still warm, but
    they're good cold, too — the stuff that midnight feasts are made of.

QUICK PUFF PASTRY

'Real' puff pastry — triple-folded six times, layered with an entire block of pounded butter — is an incredible thing, but not possible unless you have the luxury of spare time. Here's a quicker alternative, using chunks of butter and fewer folds to give a marginally less decadent but far less time-consuming pastry. If you want to challenge yourself, the full puff pastry recipe can be found on page 291, but this easy version is more than adequate for the typical pie, especially those rougher, pointedly rustic ones such as the Chicken, Pale Ale & Chicory Pie that follows. It's still not as quick to make as shortcrust, and can't compete with the instant appeal of the ready-made stuff, but although it takes around 1½ hours to prepare, only a tiny fraction of that is hands-on. Most of the preparation time is spent chilling out — for both you and the pastry.

The most important thing here is to keep the butter cold and in large chunks. It's these chunks that, as they're rolled out and folded along with the dough, will form layers of butter in the pastry. When the pastry then heats in the oven, the butter melts and the steam forces the pastry layers apart. The pastry thus rises and sets into hundreds of flaky layers.

You won't need all of this pastry for the following recipes, but it does keep well — either in the fridge for a day or two, or in the freezer for a couple of weeks — so it's useful to set some aside, well wrapped in cling film, ready for another day.

Makes enough to cover 2-3 large pies
250g plain flour
Good pinch of salt

180g unsalted butter, chilled, in 1cm cubes
125ml ice-cold water

1 Combine the flour and salt in a large bowl. Add the cubes of butter and toss together. If you're used to making shortcrust pastry, check yourself now — this is usually the point at which I absentmindedly rub the butter into the flour, but it's important not to do this. Leave the chunks of butter as they are, coated in flour.

2 Add the water and quickly but lightly mix in using your hands. The dough will look a mess, but it's meant to look that way: a shaggy mass of flour dotted with cubes of butter. As soon as all of the water has been incorporated, gather the dough into a ball. It should hold its shape.

3 Lightly flour a work surface and roll out the dough to form a rectangle of around 45x15cm, or approximately three times as long as it is wide. Fold the top third down, then the bottom third up, as if folding a letter. Rotate the dough by 90 degrees so that the folds now run down along the dough's length, rather than across its width. Roll out to a large rectangle, again, around three times as long as it is wide. Fold the top third down, and then the bottom third up. Try to work quite quickly, so that the pastry doesn't warm. You've just completed two 'turns' of the dough. Wrap it in cling film and chill for at least 30 minutes.

4 Unwrap the chilled dough and complete another two 'turns' — rotating by 90 degrees, rolling and folding. It's important to remember to rotate each time so that each successive roll and fold is perpendicular to the preceding one, thus

building up criss-crossing layers. The dough has now had 4 turns. Wrap it again and chill in the fridge for another 30 minutes.

5   The pastry is now ready to be used in one of the recipes that follow. Just make sure that you keep it cool until the moment that it enters the oven — this includes keeping it away from hot fillings (if they need to be cooked before baking, give them a while to cool before laying the pastry on top) and not spending too long rolling and shaping it. Puff pastry should always enter a hot oven — at least 200°C/fan 180°/gas mark 6 — to give it the blast of heat it needs to rise. You can reduce the temperature mid-bake, but it needs to start out hot.

Variation

Using all wholemeal flour in puff pastry can be hit-and-miss, but if you blend 100g of wholemeal flour with 150g of white flour, you'll be left with a pastry that's still flaky, but with a rounded, savoury flavour. Whether the salutary benefits of wholemeal flour still stand when layered with butter is debatable, but it gives the illusion of being healthier, at least.

CHICKEN, PALE ALE & CHICORY PIE

There's no such thing as an 'ultimate' chicken pie, and you should be wary of anyone who claims to have the recipe for one. There are chicken pies for lazy days, the meat plucked from the bones of yesterday's roast, hearty ones packed with mush-rooms and more delicate versions with tender asparagus spears. There are as many chicken pies as there are dinners to be had, and with that in mind I present this one not as formula, dictum or brag, but as a humble suggestion, and my personal favourite.

Makes 1 large pie, serving 6
½ quantity of quick puff pastry
   (see page 251)
1 large egg, lightly beaten with a pinch
   of salt, to glaze

For the filling:
2 tablespoons butter
2 large onions, thinly sliced
150g unsmoked back bacon, diced
250ml pale ale
250ml chicken or vegetable stock

750-900g skinless chicken legs
   and/or thighs
3 tablespoons plain flour
150ml double cream
Leaves from 2 heads of chicory
Salt and black pepper, to taste

**Large pie dish, 25-28cm in diameter
   at its rim**

📷 p253

1   Having prepared the puff pastry as described on page 251, place it in the fridge to chill while you prepare the filling. On a low heat, melt the butter in a large pan then fry the onions until they begin to soften. Add the bacon, turn up the heat and cook for a further 2-3 minutes. Add the ale, stock and chicken pieces (still on the bone). The chicken needs to be just covered by the liquid, so top up with extra stock if necessary. Bring to a simmer then turn the heat down low enough that the surface of the liquid is just quivering, with only the occasional bubble breaking through. Poach the chicken for 30 minutes this way.

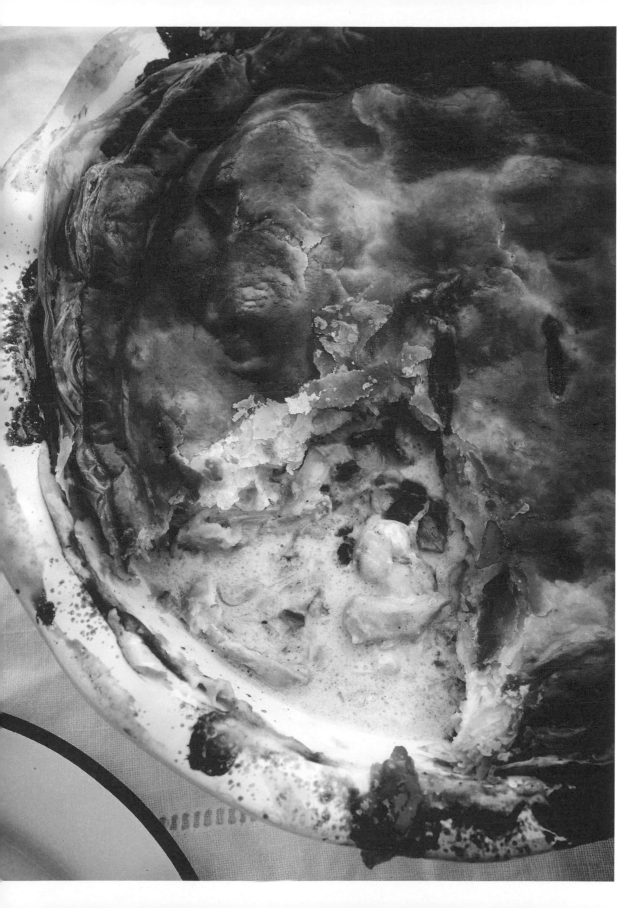

2   After half an hour, use a slotted spoon to remove the chicken from the pan, setting it down on a large chopping board. When cool enough to handle, remove the meat from the bones and set aside.

3   Add the flour to the stock mixture and whisk in until smooth. Increase the heat slightly and simmer, stirring, for a couple of minutes to thicken the sauce. Take off the heat, stir in the double cream and season to taste.

4   Transfer the chicken meat to the pie dish and toss through the whole chicory leaves (they will wilt as they cook). Pour over the sauce — you may not need all of it depending on the size of your pie dish, but do be generous. Leave to cool slightly while you preheat the oven to 200°C/fan 180°/gas mark 6.

5   Once the oven is hot and the filling has cooled a little (if the pastry goes straight onto the hot filling, the butter will melt and it will lack the crucial 'puff'), roll the pastry to a circle large enough to cover the pie and about 4mm thick. Lay it gently over the top, tucking it down slightly at the sides. Use a sharp knife to poke a hole or score a couple of incisions into the pastry in order to allow steam to escape during cooking. Glaze the top with egg wash if you want the pie to shine. Bake in the preheated oven for 25-30 minutes — or until the pastry is proudly puffed and flaky, and the filling is piping hot. Serve as is only right: with mashed potatoes and tender green beans.

FISH PIE

Dinnertimes would grow tiresome if every meal was an exercise in innovation. Here's a pie that salutes all things comforting, homely and simple. And in the spirit of back-to-basics food, don't feel restricted by the recipe: if you have only frozen fish fillets, use those; if the fishmonger near you has some good salmon or shrimp on offer, swap that in. The only non-negotiable point here is that you should look out for sustainably sourced fish and steer clear of overfished species such as cod.

Makes 1 large pie, serving 6
½ quantity of quick puff pastry
    (see page 251)

For the filling:
400ml full-fat milk
½ large onion, peeled but left whole
200-250g smoked fish, such as haddock
    or river cobbler

300g white fish, such as pollock or coley
30g butter
2 tablespoons plain flour
2-3 tablespoons tarragon leaves
200g prawns, cooked and peeled
Salt and white pepper, to taste

**Oven dish or medium pie dish, about
    15x22cm**

1   Having prepared the puff pastry as described on page 251, place it in the fridge to chill while you prepare the filling. In a large pan, warm the milk with the onion until it comes to a simmer, then take off the heat and let it steep for a few minutes while you prepare the fish. Chop both the smoked and white fish into large chunks, removing any skin or errant bones as you go. Remove and discard the onion from the pan of milk, replacing it with your pieces of fish. Return the pan

to a low heat and poach (just shy of a simmer) for 5 minutes, during which time the flavour of the fish should infuse the milk.

2   Strain the fish, collecting the milk in another bowl to be used in your white sauce. In another pan, melt the butter then whisk in the flour over a low heat. Let the butter and flour mixture (or roux) sizzle for a minute or two, stirring constantly, to cook out the taste of the flour. Now, very gradually, add the hot milk reserved from poaching the fish, whisking continuously. As long as you add the liquid slowly enough and beat well, you should be left with a smooth sauce. Heat this for a few minutes, stirring, until it has thickened to a custard-like consistency. Season to taste, although with the amount of fish in here, it really shouldn't need much salt. I'd steer clear of black pepper in a dish as creamily mild as this.

3   Place the poached fish into the oven dish and toss through the tarragon leaves and prawns with your hands. Pour over the sauce and jiggle the dish lightly to help settle the mixture. Leave to cool slightly while you preheat the oven to 200°C/fan 180°C/gas mark 6.

4   Roll out the pastry on a cool, lightly floured surface until it's big enough to cover the pie and about 4mm thick. Drape it on top of the filling, trim to fit and poke a couple of holes in the top to allow steam to escape. Bake in the preheated oven for 25 minutes. The pastry ought to be well risen and the filling bubbling.

Variation
As devoted as I am to all things pastry-crusted, I have to admit that fish pie is incredible the traditional way, too: topped with mounds of buttery mashed potato and, perhaps sacrilegiously, some grated Cheddar cheese.

BANANA THYME TART

This was initially an improvised dessert, scraped together from the leftovers in the fridge and half a dozen old bananas, but it has since become one of the recipes of which I am most proud. If you're in any doubt about pairing fruit and herb, just take a good sniff of ripe banana and a sprig of thyme side by side. The heady, Mediterranean aromatics of thyme sit as naturally with creamy banana as if they were made for one another. Like any great romance worth its salt, it's a perfectly odd, oddly perfect couple.

Whatever you do, don't use dried thyme, which will overpower even the ripest bananas.

Makes 1 tart, serving 4 generously
½ quantity of quick puff pastry
   (see page 251)

5-6 large, ripe bananas, but not
   overripe

4-5 tablespoons demerara sugar
Leaves from 2 sprigs of thyme (about
   1 tablespoon)

📷 p256

1 Having prepared the puff pastry as described on page 251, place it in the fridge to chill. Preheat the oven to 220°C/fan 200°C/gas mark 7 and line a large baking tray with baking parchment.

2 Cut the bananas into chunky slices, each around 2cm thick. In a large bowl toss the bananas together with the demerara and thyme until the fruit is encrusted with sugar crystals and little thyme leaves.

3 Roll your pastry into a rectangle around 20x25cm and lay it on the lined baking tray. Arrange the coated banana slices all over the pastry, leaving a border of a couple of centimetres around the outside. Bake for 20-25 minutes, until caramelised patches begin to creep across the tops of the bananas, and the pastry is flaky and crisp. Serve warm, with vanilla ice cream melting over the lot and, better still, drizzled with chocolate sauce (see page 322).

SWEET SHORTCRUST PASTRY

The sweet pies and tarts that follow all use a slightly enriched shortcrust pastry. Eggs often take the place of water, giving the dough a golden glow. A spoonful of sugar helps to sweeten the pastry, and gives it a deeper colour once baked. This pastry behaves in much the same way as the plainer shortcrust pastry earlier in the chapter, so refer to page 235 if you're unsure how best to handle the dough. The only difference you might find is that this variation is slightly more crumbly when rolling.

PEAR, SESAME & CHOCOLATE TART

For those bored with the traditional almond frangipane, here's a version made with ground sesame seeds instead. Despite their diminutive size, sesame seeds really pack a flavour punch, and their nuttiness sits well with the sweet pear and dark chocolate.

Makes 1 large tart, serving 6–8
90g unsalted butter, firm but not
   fridge-cold, cubed
175g plain flour
Pinch of salt
1 tablespoon caster sugar
1 tablespoon plus 1 teaspoon water

For the filling:
100g sesame seeds
100g unsalted butter, softened
100g soft light brown sugar
1½ teaspoons vanilla extract
¼ teaspoon almond extract
Zest of 1 lemon

Large pinch of salt
1 large egg
60g plain flour
1 teaspoon baking powder

For the topping:
2 ripe firm pears (such as Bosc or
   Comice)
50g dark chocolate

**22x15cm rectangular cake tin, or 20cm
round cake tin or pie dish**

📷 p258

1   Preheat the oven to 200°C/fan 180°C/gas mark 6. If your tin isn't loose-bottomed, line the cake tin with baking parchment, as this will help with unmoulding later.

2   In a large bowl, rub the 90g butter into the flour until the mixture resembles breadcrumbs, then stir in the salt and caster sugar. Add the water and use a butter knife to 'cut' it into the flour until it comes together in small clumps. If there's still dry flour left, gradually add a few more drops of water. The pastry should hold together in a ball when pressed between your hands. Wrap it tightly in cling film and chill in the fridge for at least 30 minutes.

3   On a baking tray or in a small roasting dish, toast the sesame seeds in the preheated oven for 12–15 minutes or until they're a couple of shades darker — a rich, golden colour. Leave to cool, but don't turn off the oven just yet. Once cooled, grind the seeds to a coarse powder in a coffee grinder or food processor. If you don't have either, but do have plenty of patience, use a pestle and mortar instead.

4 In a large bowl, beat the 100g butter and brown sugar together until completely smooth, then stir in the vanilla and almond extracts, lemon zest and salt. Now stir in the ground sesame seeds and the egg. In a separate bowl, combine the 60g flour and baking powder, then add these to the sesame mixture and stir until smooth.

5 On a lightly floured surface, roll out the pastry to a rectangle (or circle, depending on your tin) no thicker than 5mm, then carefully transfer to the tin. Press gently into the corners and trim off any excess. Chill in the fridge for another 30 minutes or the freezer for 15 minutes.

6 While the pastry chills, peel and core the pears and slice them into even segments, each wedge around 1cm thick at its widest point. Spoon the sesame filling into the pastry case and arrange the pears on top however you please: perhaps in lines, concentric circles or zigzags. Bake for 10 minutes in the preheated oven then turn the temperature down to 180°C/fan 160°C/gas mark 4 and bake for a further 20–30 minutes. The cooked tart should feel just firm to the touch in the middle. Leave to cool in its tin on a wire rack.

7 Melt the chocolate either in the microwave or in a small, heatproof bowl suspended over a pan of simmering water. Drizzle this over the cooled tart, leave to set and then serve. This is even better with an orange zest-flecked ice cream.

CHERRY PIE

This is *Twin Peaks* on a plate. Crisp golden pastry and sour-sweet crimson cherries. Enjoy with a 'damn fine' cup of black coffee.

Despite using primarily sweet cherries, what really makes this pie exciting is the comparatively small quantity of sour (or Morello) cherries mixed into the filling. You're more likely to find Morello cherries in a jar or dried than fresh so use whichever type you can get your hands on.

I'll admit that this isn't a cheap fruit pie — it's far from the frugal sort cobbled together from a few windfall apples and a sheet of ready-rolled pastry. To make it cheaper you can use frozen fruit, decrease the amount of sour cherries, or even swap in a couple of apples to bulk out the filling.

Makes 1 large pie, serving 8 generously
For the pastry:
400g plain flour
200g unsalted butter, firm but not
    fridge-cold, cubed
½ teaspoon salt
3 tablespoons caster sugar
4 tablespoons cold water
1 large egg beaten with a tablespoon of
    milk, to glaze

For the filling:
500–600g cherries, frozen or fresh,
    stoned

Juice of 1½ lemons
3 tablespoons cornflour
¼ teaspoon almond extract
75g caster or granulated sugar
200g sour/Morello cherries, either dried
    or from a jar

**Large pie dish, 25–28cm in diameter
    at its rim**

 p261

1   Measure the flour into a large bowl, then use your fingertips to rub the cubes
    of butter into it until completely combined. The mixture should resemble fine
    breadcrumbs. Stir in the salt and sugar, then drizzle in the water. Use a butter
    knife to 'cut' through the mixture repeatedly (as opposed to stirring) to break up
    any wet lumps of flour and evenly distribute the moisture. It should come together
    into small clumps before long. If it doesn't, add a splash more water. Quickly but
    firmly press the mixture together with your hands, form into a flattish disc and
    wrap it tightly in cling film. Refrigerate for at least 30 minutes.

2   Put the sweet cherries in a medium-sized pan over a low heat, and warm gently until they're beginning to release their juices. If using frozen cherries, there's no need to defrost first: use them straight from the freezer. Continue to heat the fruit for a couple more minutes, stirring all the while.

3   Add the lemon juice and cornflour to the now-juicy cherries. Cook for a few minutes until the juices begin to thicken with the cornflour. As soon as the juice has the consistency of double cream, take the pan off the heat. Stir in the almond extract, sugar and sour cherries then set aside to cool.

4   Divide the chilled pastry into two pieces, one of 400g and the other around 300g. Return the smaller piece to the fridge, again wrapped in cling film. Roll the larger piece into a circle big enough to line the base and sides of the pie dish (doing this on a lightly floured sheet of baking parchment will make it easier to transfer to the dish), then line the pie dish with the pastry and chill it for 30 minutes. Meanwhile, preheat the oven to 200°C/fan 180°C/gas mark 6.

5   Once the pastry case is chilled and the filling mixture has cooled, spoon the filling into the case. Now roll the smaller pastry piece to a circle big enough to form the lid of the pie. Lay the lid over the top of the filling and, brushing the edges with a little milk, press into the rim of the pastry sides to seal. You could crimp it with a fork, but it's not essential.

6   Brush the lid of the pastry with the egg and milk glaze, make a couple of incisions to allow steam to escape and bake in the preheated oven for 20 minutes. Reduce the oven temperature to 180°C/fan 160°C/gas mark 4 and cook for a further 25 minutes.

Variation
Fruit pie will take whatever you throw at it. Below is a recipe for a traditional apple pie, to which you could add a handful of blackberries, raspberries, currants, even grated marzipan. The only thing to bear in mind when playing around with fruit pie recipes is how wet the filling will be: cherries risk cooking down to mush if no cornflour is used to thicken the mixture; apples are far drier but still benefit from a couple of spoons of flour to soak up any juices.

1 quantity of shortcrust pastry, as in
   the Cherry Pie above
6 Cox or Braeburn apples
100g caster sugar

½ teaspoon ground cinnamon
3 tablespoons plain flour
Juice of ½ lemon

Prepare, chill and shape the pastry as above. Peel, core and slice the apples, toss them through a mixture of the sugar, cinnamon and flour and stir in the lemon juice. Fill, seal, glaze and bake following the recipe above.

LEMON & BASIL TART

Although lemon basil, with its distinctive citrus scent, would make sense in this lemon tart, I prefer the more common sweet basil. Because it's so deeply perfumed, just a few leaves are all that's needed to accent the sharpness of the lemon with notes of clove and spice. It's not always easy to balance two such robust flavours, but mellowed by the cream and sugar, they work beautifully here. Serve with perfectly ripe strawberries.

Serves 8
For the pastry:
175g plain flour
90g unsalted butter, firm but not
   fridge-cold, cubed
Pinch of salt
1 tablespoon caster sugar
1 large egg yolk
1 tablespoon milk

For the filling:
200ml double cream
Small handful of fresh basil leaves
4 large eggs
125g caster sugar
Zest and juice of 5 small lemons (you'll
   need 125ml juice)

20-23cm round flan dish or cake tin

1 In a large bowl, rub the flour and butter together using your fingertips, until the mixture resembles fine breadcrumbs and then stir in the salt and sugar. In a small bowl, beat the yolk with the milk then add this gradually to the flour mixture. Cut the liquid into the dry ingredients using a small knife, bringing the mixture together in small clumps. Once there's no dry flour left, press the dough together into a flat disc then wrap it in cling film and refrigerate for 30 minutes.

2 While the pastry is chilling, place the cream and whole basil leaves into a small pan and place over a medium heat. As soon as the cream comes to a gentle boil take the pan off the heat and leave the mixture to cool and infuse.

3 Once the pastry has chilled, roll it out on a floured surface to a circle large enough to line the base and sides of your tin and 3–5mm thick. Lower the pastry gently into the tin and, taking care not to stretch it, press it into the corners and against the sides. Trim off any excess and leave to chill for another 30 minutes in the fridge, or 15 minutes in the freezer. Meanwhile, preheat the oven to 200°C/ fan 180°C/gas mark 6.

4 Line the chilled pastry case with a sheet of baking parchment, fill with a layer of baking beans or dried pulses, and bake blind (see page 234) for 15 minutes. Remove the parchment parcel of beans and return the pastry case to the oven for a further 5 minutes, to crisp up. Once the case is baked, remove it from the oven and reduce the oven temperature to 150°C/fan 130°C/gas mark 2.

5 Lightly whisk the eggs together in a large bowl then beat in the 125g sugar. Pour the basil-infused cream into the bowl through a sieve, discarding the basil leaves. Add the lemon zest and juice and whisk gently to combine. Pour this into the baked pastry case and cook for around 25–30 minutes, until the edges are set but, when the tart is lightly shaken, the centre still wobbles slightly. If you wait until it's set at the centre, you'll have cooked the tart too long, and the filling will shrink and crack as it cools. Leave to cool on a wire rack before serving. Although it's best to store this in the fridge, the flavours will be brightest at room temperature, so factor in some time for it to warm slightly if preparing the tart in advance.

ROSEMARY

Rosemary is a herb replete with romance and symbolism: its heady scent, Mediterranean roots, even its etymology (it's said that the Virgin Mary herself turned the flowers blue). But even great love can turn bitter, and rosemary is no exception. Used with a heavy hand, it becomes astringent; when chopped or bruised its pungent oil is released, and it tends to overpower. The spiky leaves of a rosemary sprig look very similar to pine needles, and if not cooked with care they'll end up tasting like pine, too — forest floor, Christmas tree, toilet cleaner.

It's best to let rosemary's flavour permeate gradually. The Rosemary Pecan Pie recipe that follows works by this principle, steeping the rosemary in hot syrup to gently draw out its flavour. And because it is so aromatic, rosemary works well even in the dry heat of the oven: I've yet to find a better use for it than just studding little sprigs into the doughy dimples of a focaccia.

ROSEMARY PECAN PIE

The result of a childhood spent in thrall to US television was that those strange, distinctly American confections — key lime pie, pecan pie, peach cobbler, pumpkin pie — took on a mythical status in my mind. These fantastical pies conjured up fantasies of suburban bliss, shopping malls, yellow school buses and, crucially, huge portions. Even watching the film *American Pie* couldn't dispel these daydreams. In this version of pecan pie, rosemary adds a woody herbal note which complements the butteriness of the toasted pecans.

Makes 1 large pie, serving 8–10
For the pastry:
125g unsalted butter, firm but not
   fridge-cold, cubed
250g plain flour
2 tablespoons caster sugar
Generous pinch of salt
1 large egg, lightly beaten

For the filling:
200g soft dark brown sugar
150g golden syrup

100g unsalted butter
½ teaspoon vanilla extract
¼ teaspoon salt
3 whole sprigs of rosemary
3 large eggs
200g pecans

**Large pie or flan dish, 25–27cm in
   diameter at its rim**

📷 p266

1   In a large bowl, rub the butter into the flour using your fingertips until no large visible pieces of butter remain. Use swift motions and lift the flour and butter up from the bowl as you crumb them together so that the heat of your hands doesn't soften the butter. Stir in the sugar and salt. Pour in the beaten egg, a little at a time (you might not need all of it). Using a butter knife to cut through the mixture, combine the wet and dry ingredients. You'll notice the mixture beginning to come together in clumps. Once mixed, quickly and lightly use your hands to press the dough into a ball. Flatten slightly, wrap it in cling film and let it chill for 30 minutes or so.

2   Preheat the oven to 180°C/fan 160°C/gas mark 4. Combine the brown sugar, golden syrup, 100g butter, vanilla extract and salt in a pan over a low heat. Add two of the rosemary sprigs and bring to a very gentle boil. Simmer for 2 minutes, then turn off the heat and leave to cool. After 10 minutes, pull out the rosemary sprigs, beat in the eggs and leave to cool completely.

3   Place the pecans on a baking tray in a single layer and toast them in the preheated oven for around 10 minutes (check them after 6 or 7 minutes). Set aside to cool and leave the oven on.

4   Once the pastry is chilled, roll it out to a circle roughly 27–30cm in diameter — large enough to line the base and sides of your pie dish. Roll to a thickness of no greater than 5mm. It helps to roll on a piece of floured baking parchment to prevent the pastry sticking to the work surface and to make it easier to transfer the pastry disc into the tin. Line the tin with the pastry, patching up any holes or cracks with offcuts. (Any leftover pastry can be re-rolled, cut into shapes and

baked to make simple butter biscuits.) Gently press the pastry into the fluted sides and push it just above the edges of the tin, so that the pastry stands proud of the rim by a few millimetres. Chill for 30 minutes, or freeze for 15 minutes.

5   Roughly chop the toasted nuts, leaving a few whole to decorate the top of the pie. Add the chopped pecans to the filling mixture then pour into the pastry case. Pull the needles off the remaining sprig of rosemary and sprinkle these on top along with the whole pecans.

6   Bake for 30–45 minutes. The time will depend on the dimensions of your pie dish (wide and shallow will cook more quickly than small and deep), but you should be able to judge when it's ready by how set it feels: if, when jiggled, the pie filling ripples and sways, it needs longer; if there's barely a wobble, it's done.

STEM GINGER TREACLE TART

It was on holiday in Dorset, on the ketchup-stained back page of a tattered pub menu, that I first came across stem ginger treacle tart, and although I didn't have the appetite to try the dessert at the time, those four words repeated tauntingly in my mind for the rest of the week. I had barely been home from the holiday a few hours when I took to the kitchen to finally put my craving to rest. If I was hoping for some sort of closure, I failed miserably: I've been hankering for more of the sweet, ginger-spiced tart ever since.

Makes 1 large tart, serving 8
For the pastry:
90g unsalted butter, firm but not
   fridge-cold, cubed
175g plain flour
Pinch of salt
1 tablespoon caster sugar
1 large egg, lightly beaten

For the filling:
350g golden syrup
Zest of 2 lemons

125g fresh breadcrumbs
5cm root ginger, coarsely grated
75g stem ginger, finely chopped
1 egg
30g dark soft brown sugar
¼ teaspoon salt

**20–23cm round spring-form cake tin
   or flan/pie dish**

📷 p268

1   In a large bowl, rub the butter into the flour using your fingertips until the mixture resembles fine breadcrumbs. Stir in the salt and caster sugar. Add the beaten egg a little at a time to moisten the flour until it all comes together in small clumps (you won't need all the egg — half to three-quarters of it should suffice). Use a cutting motion through the mixture with a knife or a spoon handle to distribute the moisture. When it's well combined, quickly but firmly press the dough into a ball, wrap it in cling film and refrigerate for at least 30 minutes.

2   Once the pastry has chilled, roll it out on a piece of lightly floured baking parchment so that it is 3–5mm thick and large enough to line the base and sides of your tin. Line the tin with pastry, taking care not to stretch it or handle it too

long, and patch up any cracks in the dough. Refrigerate for at least 30 minutes, or freeze for 15 minutes if you're in a hurry. Meanwhile, preheat the oven to 200°C/ fan 180°C/gas mark 6.

3   Line the chilled pastry case with baking parchment, add a layer of baking beans or dried pulses, and bake blind (see page 234) for 15 minutes. Remove the parchment and beans and return to the oven, uncovered, for a further 5 minutes, or until the base feels reasonably dry and sandy.

4   While the tart case is blind baking, prepare the filling. Combine the golden syrup, lemon zest, breadcrumbs, root and stem ginger, egg, sugar and salt in a large bowl and lightly stir together.

5   Once the case is ready, reduce the oven temperature to 180°C/fan 160°C/gas mark 4 and pour in the filling. Bake for 40-50 minutes, or until the tart is set and barely firm to the touch. Leave to cool in its tin on a wire rack for 15 minutes.

SPICED CHOCOLATE TART

My first ever chocolate tart, and my favourite. I used to chew on aniseed balls every day on the way home from school — a tissue-thin, white paper bag full of the little purple sweets. At some point I discovered bubble gum — sweet, colourful, fun — and stopped buying the faintly medicinal, unfashionable aniseed balls, but the flavour is still one I love. The fennel seeds here impart that same warm, aromatic flavour.

There's often the temptation, with dark chocolate, to brighten and to lift. Forget that. This tart uses fennel to play to the liquorice notes in the chocolate, colouring its darkness with spiced warmth. The honey, too, is crucial: somehow just one tablespoon brings the whole thing into focus.

**Makes 1 tart, serving 8 small-but-
   rich slices**
For the pastry:
90g unsalted butter, firm but not
   fridge-cold, cubed
175g plain flour
Pinch of salt
1 tablespoon caster sugar
1 large egg yolk
1 tablespoon milk

For the filling:
90ml milk
150ml double cream

1 tablespoon fennel seeds
3 star anise
300g dark chocolate (70% cocoa solids),
   roughly chopped
1 large egg
50g caster or granulated sugar
¼ teaspoon chilli powder
1 teaspoon ground cinnamon
1 tablespoon honey

**20cm round spring-form or
   loose-bottomed cake tin**

📷 p271

1   In a large bowl, toss the butter cubes through the flour and — using only your fingertips — rub the two together until the mixture resembles breadcrumbs, and no visible chunks of butter are left. Try to work quickly and lightly, keeping the mixture cool so that the butter doesn't melt (this would leave the pastry greasy

and tough). Add the salt and sugar and combine. Lightly whisk the egg yolk and milk together, then add this to the dry ingredients. Use a small knife to cut through the mixture until all of the flour has been moistened. If a lot of dry flour remains, add a few more drops of milk. Once combined, use your hands to quickly but firmly press the pastry together into a ball. Flatten it into a disc, wrap it in cling film and refrigerate for at least 30 minutes, or as long as overnight.

2   Once the pastry has chilled, roll it out on a piece of lightly floured baking parchment. Don't go too heavy on the flour — just enough to stop the pastry sticking to the surface. Roll to a rough circle about 22–23cm in diameter and 3–5mm thick. Line the tin with the pastry, taking care not to stretch the pastry but gently pressing it into the corners, for sharp edges. Chill for 30 minutes, or freeze for 10 minutes. Meanwhile, preheat the oven to 200°C/180°C fan/gas mark 6.

3   Scrunch up a large piece of baking parchment into a ball and smooth it back out again (this makes it much easier to work with). Now line the pastry case with the baking parchment and fill with baking beans, dried pulses or similar. Push the beans up towards the sides a little to help to prevent the steep pastry walls from slipping. Bake in the preheated oven for 15 minutes then remove the parcel of beans and bake the pastry case for a further 5 minutes, uncovered.

4   While the pastry is blind baking, start preparing the filling. Combine the milk, cream, fennel seeds and star anise and slowly heat, either in a bowl in the microwave or in a small pan over a gentle heat. Remove from the heat just before it starts to boil — it should smell heavily aromatic and aniseedy.

5   Place the chopped chocolate in a bowl and strain the still-scalding cream mixture over it to remove the fennel seeds and star anise. Let it sit for just a minute, then gently stir together. The chocolate should melt smoothly into the hot cream. If chunks of unmelted chocolate remain you can heat the mixture very gently (either in the microwave or over a pan of simmering water) until it is smooth. In a separate bowl whisk the egg together with the sugar, chilli, cinnamon and honey, then fold this through the chocolate mixture.

6   Once the pastry case is baked, reduce the oven temperature to 160°C/fan 140°C/gas mark 3. Spoon the filling into the pastry, filling to a few millimetres below the rim. Bake for 20 minutes, or until just set with only a slight wobble at its centre. Leave to cool completely before serving, during which time it will firm up. Keep the tart chilled if not eating it the same day, but give it time to come back to room temperature again before eating, otherwise the filling will set too hard and become stodgy.

PASTRIES

THE BREAKFAST CLUB

DANISH PASTRY & CROISSANT DOUGH

CHERRY DIAMONDS · JAM PINWHEELS

CUSTARD ENVELOPES · PAIN AU CHOCOLAT

FRANZBRÖTCHEN · CROISSANTS

A BETTER LUNCHBOX

SALMON & CREAM CHEESE PARCELS

COURGETTE, STILTON & PECAN ROUNDS

PUFF PASTRY · FIG & WALNUT ECCLES CAKES

MARMALADE ALMOND GALETTE · MILLEFEUILLE

BEFORE MIDNIGHT

ÉCLAIRS · DILL & MUSTARD CHOUX BITES· BAKLAVA

Here are some of the most challenging recipes in this book, but if you can muster the courage to give them a go, you'll find them the most rewarding, too. They require patience and some planning ahead, but the processes themselves are not complicated and the finished pastries will taste all the better for the time that has gone into them. Once you've tasted homemade croissants, Danish pastries and choux buns you'll want to eat them all day, every day — and you can: I've divided this chapter into breakfast, lunch and dinner pastries. For those who, like me, cannot have too much of a good thing.

THE BREAKFAST CLUB

Breakfast should never be boring. There are the sensible options of porridge and muesli, the masochistic smoothies and meagre cereal bars. Hangover breakfasts thrown headlong into the frying pan, leftover feasts and bacon butties come in at the other end of the spectrum. And somewhere in between, for breakfasts where the aim is just pleasure — not nutrition, refuelling or belated sobering up — there are pastries. They roll leisurely onto the scene mid-morning, with coffee and orange juice, to set a good day quietly in motion.

Danish pastries and croissants use a laminated dough — a bread dough layered, or laminated, with fat. It's a hybrid of bread and pastry, straddling the two disciplines and yet more delicious than either of them. It has the complex flavours of bread (with even more depth, thanks to the long, cold rising periods) and the richness and flaking texture of puff pastry.

Pastries aren't quick: be prepared to set aside 6-7 hours from start to finish, or 4 hours if you have time to prepare the dough base the night before. The wait is well worth it, however, and only a fraction of this time is hands-on. Most of the preparation time is spent waiting for the butter to chill, the yeast to ferment or the dough to relax. I can't pretend that these are easy recipes, but they shouldn't be unmanageable as long as you take a moment to read through the method before you get started and get to grips with just how this particular dough works.

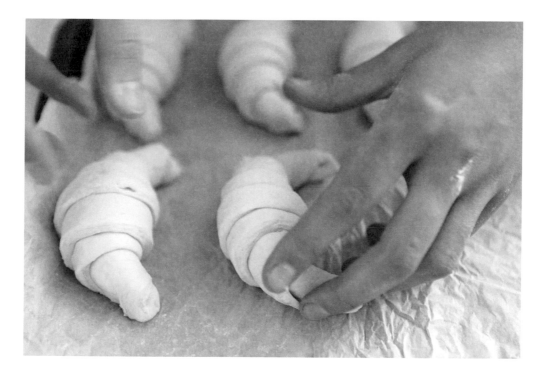

WHY IS MY DANISH PASTRY...

... SOFT AND STICKY WHEN ROLLING?

— The dough may be too warm. Return it to the fridge for an extra 15 minutes to help set the butter.

— It might be that the dough has ripped, leaving the butter at the surface. If this happens, try to fold the dough in a way that moves the tear to the inside.

— Dust the surface with flour as you roll to minimise sticking, but take care not to use too much.

... DIFFICULT TO ROLL OUT / SPRINGING BACK AS I ROLL IT?

Because it's quite dry and contains strong flour, Danish pastry dough tends to be difficult to roll out. And unfortunately, it becomes gradually more difficult to roll to size with each turn. There's no escaping this tug of war, but there are a few things you can do to avoid defeat.

— If the dough has too little resting time, it will be almost impossible to roll. That resting time is important not only for helping the butter to stay firm, but also for letting the gluten relax. Worked too hard and with too little rest, dough becomes uncooperative, inflexible and tired. Return it to the fridge for an extra 15 minutes to let it chill out, then try again.

— You might have dusted with too much flour. Although a small amount of flour helps to prevent sticking, too much can toughen the dough. Be sparing with it, and brush any excess off as you fold it.

... LEAKING BUTTER AS IT BAKES?

— When Danish pastry dough is under-proved, it won't have risen enough and the structure will be too tight when it first hits the oven. The result is that the butter layered inside is left with no place to go but out onto the baking tray, pooling at the feet of the pastries and leaving them greasy. Next time, prove the shaped pastries for slightly longer, until they're very puffy. When poked gently with your little finger, they shouldn't spring back into shape immediately — the indentation should slowly refill most of the way.

— It could be that the dough was too warm when proving, causing the butter to melt prematurely. Normal room temperature will suffice for proving — never leave the pastries to prove in an airing cupboard or boiler room.

See also the tips on page 85 for more common problems with yeast doughs.

DANISH PASTRY & CROISSANT DOUGH

The instructions below might look daunting, but they actually cover just a few basic steps. The dough is mixed and rested before being chilled for a few hours. Once chilled, it's wrapped around the butter (which has been pounded into a sheet) and left to rest in the fridge for 30-45 minutes. It is then given three turns — that's rolling, folding and rotating the dough three times — with a chilling period of around half an hour between each turn. The dough is then ready to be rolled and shaped however you please. The recipes for croissants, *franzbrötchen* and the sweet and savoury Danish pastries all use this dough.

A mixture of strong and plain flour in this dough gives a good balance between crispness, good rise and ease of rolling and shaping. For more information on strong flour, see page 73.

Makes just over 1kg dough
350g strong white flour
150g plain flour
50g unsalted butter, chilled and cubed
7g instant dried yeast

1½ teaspoons salt
2 tablespoons caster sugar
150ml cool water
150ml full-fat milk
200g block of unsalted butter, chilled

1   Combine the flours in a large bowl then rub in the cubed butter using your fingertips. Add the yeast and stir to combine, followed by the salt and sugar. Pour in the water and milk and use your hands to roughly combine everything, mopping up any dry flour to bring the ingredients together to form a dry, shaggy dough. Don't knead this: it needs to be only just mixed. If worked too vigorously at this early stage, the gluten will develop and make the dough incredibly difficult to roll out later on. Cover the bowl with cling film and leave the dough to rest for 30 minutes. Gently press the dough down if it has risen, then transfer to the fridge to chill for at least 3 hours, or as long as overnight. Make sure that the bowl is tightly covered with cling film otherwise the dough will dry out and form a skin.

2   Once the dough has thoroughly chilled, prepare the sheet of butter. Heavily dust the block of butter with flour then place it between two sheets of baking parchment and use a rolling pin to pound it to a square about 25x25cm. Return the slab of butter to the fridge for a few minutes while you prepare the dough. Remove the dough from the fridge, tip it out of its bowl and roll it to a large rectangle, roughly 50x30cm. Lay the butter sheet over one half of it then fold the other half over to completely cover the butter. Gently smooth this parcel to press out any air bubbles (which will burst and ruin the layers in the pastry if they get trapped) then seal the edges together by pressing down with either your fingers or the length of the rolling pin. You should be left with a completely sealed, dough-wrapped parcel of butter. Wrap this in cling film and return it to the fridge for 30 minutes, to allow the dough and butter to reach roughly the same temperature.

3   Gently roll the chilled dough out on a lightly floured surface to a large rectangle, at least twice as wide as it is long. The precise dimensions aren't important, but it ought to be rolled to a thickness no greater than 1cm. This first roll is a tricky one: work slowly to avoid squeezing the butter out of the sides or forcing it through the

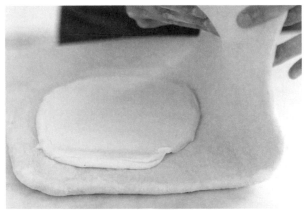

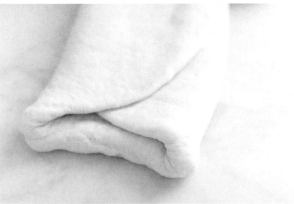

dough. Start by gently pressing down all over the dough with your rolling pin to slightly flatten it and evenly distribute the butter. Then roll carefully but firmly, making sure that it doesn't stick to the work surface. Lightly dust any excess flour off the surface of the dough then fold a third of the rectangle over and then the other third on top. Rotate the dough by 90 degrees, so that the fold lines now run across the width of the dough rather than towards you. Wrap this in cling film then leave it to rest in the fridge for 30-45 minutes. You've just completed one turn of the dough.

4   Give the dough two more turns, rolling, folding, rotating and chilling each time. It will become progressively more difficult to roll out as you go on, thanks to the gluten in the flour. You might have to put your weight behind the rolling pin by the time you come to the final turn, but do stick with it. If you find yourself in a stalemate with the dough, let it win: it doesn't need to reach exactly the same size each time, so just fold it as it is and then return it to the fridge. Better this than handle the dough for so long that the butter melts.

5   After the final turn and chill, the dough is ready to be rolled and shaped. It should be smooth and taut — neatly folded into a rectangle — very different from the rough mass of dry dough you started with. Whatever shapes you choose, remember that as these pastries are yeast-leavened, they need time to rise before baking — 1-2 hours, depending on the pastry. This second rise may be done overnight in the fridge, but it's far quicker to do it at room temperature. This might seem counter-intuitive, considering the lengths you've gone to in order to keep the dough cool all along, but as long as the pastries are left at normal room temperature (no higher than 20-22°C, preferably) they'll be fine. The butter will soften slightly during the proving period, but because there's yeast here to give the pastries their rise (unlike puff pastry, which relies only on steam from the butter), this isn't a problem.

The next few recipes all use Danish pastry dough as their base. Except for the croissants and the *franzbrötchen* (which are easiest to cut and shape in bigger amounts), I've given quantities for only small batches of each. This way, you can make several different types of pastry from one large batch of basic dough; having spent so long preparing the dough, it's good to be able to experiment with it. There are a couple of savoury Danish pastry recipes coming up in the next section, too.

   These pastries are always best eaten while fresh, but if you want to serve them any longer than a few hours after baking, they can be revived in a warm oven (180°C/fan 160°/gas mark 4) for 5-10 minutes.

CHERRY DIAMONDS

Cherry danishes are sour, fruity, buttery and sweet all at once, and in perfect balance. They're a classic for a reason.

Makes 4
¼ quantity of Danish pastry dough
(see page 277)

For the filling:
150g cherries, stoned
Juice of ½ lemon

2 tablespoons caster sugar
1-2 teaspoons cornflour
1 large egg, beaten with 1 tablespoon
milk, to glaze

📷 p281

1   Prepare the filling before rolling and shaping the dough, leaving time for it to cool before making the pastries. Combine the cherries, lemon juice and sugar in a small pan and heat until the cherries begin to soften and release their juices. Whisk in a teaspoon of cornflour and let the mixture simmer for a minute to thicken. Add an extra teaspoon of cornflour if necessary — the juices ought to be thick enough to coat the back of a spoon. Leave to cool completely.

2   Roll the prepared dough to a square about 20x20cm. Cut into four pieces, each 10x10cm. Using a very sharp knife, make four long incisions in each piece of dough: imagine that you're cutting a smaller square out of the piece of dough, 2cm shorter and narrower than the original, thus leaving a 1cm border around each side. But instead of completely cutting out this smaller square, you need to leave it attached to the larger one at two of its corners. You'll be left with two L-shaped cuts, each following the edges of the original square, and neither L-shape touching the other.

3   Fold one of the unattached corners of the larger square diagonally across and over, to align with the opposite corner of the small, interior square. Gently press into place. Now fold the opposite corner of the larger square over to align with the opposite corner of the small square. The pastry should now be a rough diamond shape, with a smaller diamond indent at its centre.

4   Place a spoonful of the cooled cherry mixture into the indent in the middle of each diamond. Leave the pastries to prove at room temperature, on a large parchment-lined baking tray and loosely covered with cling film, at room temperature. How long they take will depend on the room temperature and how much they've been handled, but 1 hour is about right. They're ready when they are puffy and spongy — rather than springy — to the touch. Preheat the oven to 220°C/fan 200°C/gas mark 7.

5   Brush the risen pastries with the egg wash then bake for 10 minutes before reducing the temperature to 180°C/fan 160°C/gas mark 4 and baking for a further 10-15 minutes. The finished pastries should be golden brown and crisp.

JAM PINWHEELS

I prefer a dark jam such as blackberry or damson for these, but anything will do. Even cheap strawberry jam works well against the richness of the pastry.

Makes 4

¼ quantity of Danish pastry dough (see page 277)

4 tablespoons jam

1 large egg, beaten with 1 tablespoon milk, to glaze

📷 p282

1   Roll the prepared dough to a 20cm square, then cut into four smaller 10cm squares. Use a sharp knife to make four incisions in each one: cut 4-5cm diagonally from each corner in towards the centre. You should have a square with four 'not-quite' triangles. Fold the corner of one of the four triangles over into the centre of the square. Repeat with the same corner of each of the remaining three triangles, until you're left with a pinwheel shape. Press the corners firmly down at the centre, then place a spoonful of jam over the join. Place the pastries on a large, lined baking tray, then loosely cover with cling film and leave to prove at room temperature for around 1 hour or until almost doubled in size. While you wait, preheat the oven to 220°C/fan 200°C/gas mark 7.

2   Brush the pastry of the pinwheels with egg wash then bake for 10 minutes. Turn the oven down to 180°C/fan 160°C/gas mark 4 and bake for a further 10-15 minutes, until crisp. Leave to cool on a wire rack before eating, and be careful of the dangerously hot jam.

CUSTARD ENVELOPES

More proof, should you need it, of the versatility of the humble pastry cream. This time it's wrapped in a square of flaky pastry. Tuck in a couple of raspberries or even a spoonful of rhubarb compote if you like.

Makes 4

¼ quantity of Danish pastry dough (see page 277)

½ quantity of pastry cream, chilled (see page 312)

1 large egg, beaten with 1 tablespoon milk, to glaze

1   Roll the prepared dough to a 20cm square, then cut into four smaller 10cm squares. Place a dollop of pastry cream into the centre of each square. Fold one corner of the square diagonally over towards the centre, over the pastry cream, then fold the opposite corner down over this. This should leave you with a flattened, open-ended tube of pastry, with the cream inside. Pinch the two layers of dough together on top to stop the tube from unfurling — lift the layers slightly and press only gently, otherwise the custard will squish out.

2   Leave the shapes to prove at room temperature on a parchment-lined baking tray, loosely covered with cling film. Prove for around 1 hour, or until the dough has almost doubled in thickness. Meanwhile preheat the oven to 220°C/fan 200°C/ gas mark 7.

3   Brush the risen pastries with egg wash and bake for 10 minutes in the preheated oven, then reduce the temperature to 180°C/fan 160°C/gas mark 4 and bake for a further 10-15 minutes. Leave to cool on a wire rack.

PAIN AU CHOCOLAT

Call these by their anglicised name — 'chocolate bread' — and that aura of French refinement falls quickly away. They are, after all, just chunks of chocolate wrapped in a butter-laden dough. They may be a dietician's nightmare, but I can't think of a better start to the day.

Makes 4
¼ quantity of Danish pastry dough
   (see page 277)

80g dark chocolate
1 large egg, beaten with 1 tablespoon
   milk, to glaze

1   Roll the prepared dough to a 20cm square then cut this into four smaller 10cm squares. Lay 2-3 chunks of chocolate along one half of each square, then fold over the other half and pinch shut to seal. Leave the pastries to prove at room temperature, loosely covered with cling film, on a baking tray lined with baking parchment for 1 hour. Preheat the oven to 220°C/fan 200°C/gas mark 7.

2   Brush the risen pastries with egg wash, then bake for 10 minutes before turning the oven down to 180°C/fan 160°C/gas mark 4 and baking for another 10-15 minutes. Let cool slightly on a wire rack before serving with a mug of milky coffee.

FRANZBRÖTCHEN

These German pastries have cinnamon and sugar swirled into them. What I like most about *franzbrötchen* is the shape: they're squashed down under the handle of a wooden spoon so that the spirals of dough ripple out either side.

Makes 12
1 quantity of Danish pastry dough
   (see page 277)
50g unsalted butter
150g caster sugar

2 teaspoons ground cinnamon
1 large egg, beaten with 1 tablespoon
   milk, to glaze

📷 p285

1   Melt the butter in a small pan, then let it cool slightly while you roll out the prepared dough. The butter shouldn't be too hot when it comes into contact with the dough — no more than slightly warm.

2 Roll the dough to a rectangle approximately 60x30cm. It can be a struggle to get it to this size, especially as it has already been handled so much, but a bit of firm rolling and re-rolling should do it. If it proves really difficult, let it rest for 5 minutes and then try again. Don't worry about reaching exactly those dimensions, though.

3 Brush the rolled dough with the melted butter. Stir together the sugar and cinnamon and sprinkle this all over the buttery dough. Now roll up the rectangle tightly from long edge to long edge, to give a roll roughly 60cm long. Trim off the uneven ends of the roll then cut it into 12 slices. Leave the slices sitting upright as they are, ready for shaping. To give the pastries their distinctive shape, lightly flour a wooden spoon handle and press it down onto the middle of each slice, parallel with the cut edges, almost as though cutting the slice into two, smaller slices. Press down firmly, pushing around three-quarters of the way through the dough, and see the swirls splay out either side. Take care not to push too far otherwise you'll accidentally halve it.

4 Arrange the shapes on a baking tray lined with baking parchment, leaving room around each for them to expand as they prove and bake. Cover the tray loosely with cling film and leave to prove for about 1 hour, preheating the oven to 200°C/ fan 180°C/gas mark 6 in the meantime.

5 Bake in the preheated oven for 15 minutes, then remove them from the oven, glaze with the egg wash and return to the heat for a further 5 minutes. (These pastries are glazed part way through the cooking time because the raw edges of the pastry layers face outwards — if you were to glaze right at the start, the egg would set, fusing the layers together.)

CROISSANTS

The original breakfast pastry. Don't rush these as they prove: it's during the rising period that they'll begin to develop the buttery honeycomb structure that makes croissants so good. If you cut short that time, the baked croissants will be heavy and chewy, and the butter will leak from them as they bake.

Makes 12   📷 p287 / p288

1 quantity of Danish pastry dough
  (see page 277)
1 large egg, beaten with 1 tablespoon
  milk, to glaze

1 Roll out the prepared dough to a rectangle 70cm long and 20cm wide. It will be difficult to roll the very elastic dough this thinly, so you'll need a little perseverance. As you go, gently lift the dough by one edge and flap it against the work surface to loosen it and give it a chance to relax. If you don't give it this opportunity to spring back a little now, the dough will shrink and deform later when you're cutting it into shape. Continue to gently roll and re-roll it, giving it a 5 minute rest if it's really not moving, until the dough stays at 70x20cm.

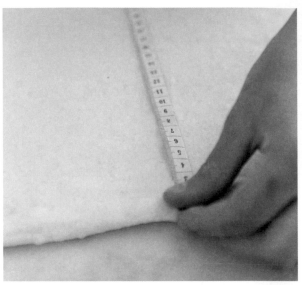

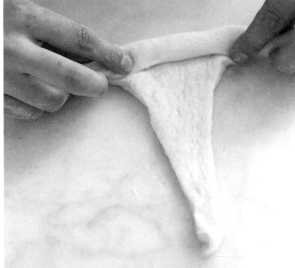
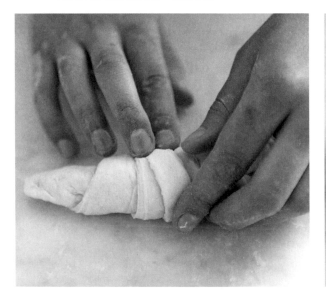

Throughout this rolling process, take care not to use too much flour on the work surface, which can toughen the pastry.

2   Cut the dough into triangles 10-12cm at their base and 20cm tall. It's worth using a ruler or tape measure at this point to get even shapes. The triangles should tessellate — imagine six of them lined up with their bases along the bottom edge of the dough, and six more upside-down in the gaps between them. When you've cut these triangles out, you'll also have a couple of half-triangle offcuts from either end of the dough, which you can fashion together into a thirteenth croissant for a full baker's dozen, if you want.

3   To shape each croissant, stretch the triangle by its bottom two corners, slightly elongating its 10cm base so that it flares out. Quite fittingly, it'll look a bit like an Eiffel tower. Now roll the triangle tightly up from base to tip, stretching the tip up slightly as you do so. It should now resemble the final croissant. Just curve the ends around slightly to give it a crescent shape, then leave to prove on a large baking tray lined with baking parchment. Cover the croissants loosely with cling film as they rise. Preheat the oven to 220°C/fan 200°C/gas mark 7.

    How long these take to rise will depend on the temperature of your kitchen, but I find that they usually need around 1½-2 hours. Check yours after an hour or so and then at intervals thereafter: they're ready when they've doubled in size and feel marshmallow soft. Gently poke one, and if it's springy rather than spongy, give it slightly longer.

4   Brush the risen croissants with the egg wash, trying to keep the egg only on the smooth tops of the swirls and not on the cut edges (otherwise it'll bind the flaky layers together). Bake in the preheated oven for 20 minutes then leave to cool slightly on a wire rack. Eat them while they're still a little warm: spread with salted butter, give it a moment to melt into the soft pastry then tuck in.

A BETTER LUNCHBOX

The pastries in this section are a change from the usual sad sandwiches and wilted salads. They're not as quick to make as just slapping a piece of ham between two slices of buttered bread, but they're around a thousand times more interesting. For quicker versions of these pastries, swap the Danish or puff pastry for quick puff pastry (see page 251) or even an all-butter shop-bought puff pastry (although it really won't taste the same).

SALMON & CREAM CHEESE PARCELS

Danish pastries don't have to be sweet. These encase smoked salmon and soft cheese in a neat pastry parcel. A sprinkling of chopped chives or a slick of mild mustard works nicely in them, too.

Makes 4
¼ quantity of Danish pastry dough (see page 277)
75g cream cheese

30g smoked salmon, cut in slivers
1 large egg, lightly beaten with 1 tablespoon milk to glaze

1   Roll out the prepared dough to a 20cm square and then cut into four smaller 10cm squares. Put a dollop of cream cheese in the centre of each then drape over some smoked salmon. Fold the four corners of the dough inwards to meet at the centre and press them very firmly together. Leave to prove for around 1 hour at room temperature, loosely covered with cling film on a baking tray lined with baking parchment. Preheat the oven to 200°C/fan 180°C/gas mark 6.

2   Brush the pastry with the egg wash and bake for 10 minutes in the preheated oven before reducing the temperature to 180°C/fan 160°C/gas mark 4 and baking for a further 10 minutes. Cool on a wire rack.

COURGETTE, STILTON & PECAN ROUNDS

Salty-sharp blue cheese, courgette and buttery pecans make these open tarts a lunch to savour. Use a mandolin (with extreme caution) or a vegetable peeler to get very thin slivers of courgette, so that it grows meltingly soft as it cooks.

Makes 4
¼ quantity of Danish pastry dough (see page 277)
½ courgette, sliced into ribbons
50g Stilton

50g pecans, roughly chopped
Black pepper, to taste
Olive oil, for drizzling
1 large egg, lightly beaten with 1 tablespoon milk, to glaze

1   Roll out the prepared dough to a 20cm square and cut into four smaller 10cm squares. Heap a large spoonful of the courgette ribbons in the centre of each square then sprinkle with crumbled Stilton and the chopped pecans. Grind black pepper over the top and drizzle with olive oil. Fold in the tips of the corners then roll the edges of the square in slightly to give a rounded shape with a raised border. Leave to prove at room temperature on a parchment-lined baking tray, lightly covered with cling film, for around 1 hour, or until very puffy and risen. Preheat the oven to 200°C/fan 180°C/gas mark 6.

2   Glaze the pastry edges with the egg wash then bake in the preheated oven for 20 minutes. Leave to cool on a wire rack.

PUFF PASTRY

Puff pastry undergoes perhaps the most impressive transformation of any of the doughs in this book. When first mixed, it is scraggy, dry and pale. Throughout the long process of rolling and folding, it remains anaemic and dull. But it's what's inside that counts: look closely at the cut edge of a thick block of raw puff pastry and you'll see faint yellow striations through the dough. These are streaks of butter, and the key to this pastry's success. When baked, the butter melts and the water in it evaporates, producing steam that provides the 'puff'. The dough then sets around these pockets of air, separating into (quite literally) hundreds of tissue-thin layers. It's so airily light that you'd be forgiven for not realising that it contains almost as much butter as it does flour. The crisp, golden pastry that emerges from the oven couldn't be further from the ugly duckling it was in the mixing bowl.

Puff pastry isn't a quick or an easy dough to make: it needs plenty of time in the fridge to rest and chill, a lot of rolling and at times some forcible pounding. If you're in a hurry, look at the slightly less buttery, but easier, quick puff pastry on page 251 instead. But, although it takes a while, the method here really isn't too taxing — it's very similar to the method for Danish pastry dough (see page 277): mixing, several 'turns' of the dough (six turns for proper puff pastry, rolling, folding and rotating each time), plenty of time in the fridge and then a quick bake at a high temperature.

Temperature is the secret to perfect puff pastry — everything needs to be kept cool until the moment the pastry is baked. The butter needs to be firm enough that it stays in distinct layers, but not so cold that it breaks, tearing the pastry as you roll. The temperature of the oven is crucial, too: it must be hot enough (at least 200°C/fan 180°C/gas mark 6) to rapidly turn the water in the butter layers into steam. If puff pastry is put into a cool oven, the butter will melt but there won't be enough steam power to prise apart the layers, leaving the pastry greasy and flat.

This is a reasonably dry dough, but that's necessary if the pastry layers are to be tough enough to encase the butter without tearing. Unfortunately, that dryness can make puff pastry a little difficult to roll out. You should find it simple enough for the first couple of turns, but later rolls might require a firmer hand. However, the added lemon juice provides a touch of acidity, relaxing the dough and making rolling easier. If your dough is particularly tricky to tease into shape, give it an extra 15 minutes resting time in the fridge before the next turn: this gives the gluten in the flour a chance to relax, for a more pliable dough.

Makes just over 1kg
500g plain flour, plus extra to dust
½ teaspoon salt
50g unsalted butter, firm but not
  fridge-cold, cubed

225ml cold water
1 tablespoon lemon juice

350g block of unsalted butter, chilled

1   Mix together the flour and salt in a large bowl, then rub in the cubes of butter
    using your fingertips until there are no visible pieces left. Add the water and
    lemon juice, using your hands to bring the mixture together into a rough dough.
    It ought to be combined, but it doesn't matter if it still looks slightly shaggy at
    this point — the important thing is not to overwork it, as too much mixing will
    tighten the dough, making it harder to roll out. Wrap the dough in cling film and
    refrigerate for at least 30 minutes.

2   Use a rolling pin to pound the 350g of butter between a couple of well-floured
    pieces of baking parchment, to a square around 20x20cm. Wrap this in baking
    parchment or cling film and return to the fridge to firm up again for 10 minutes
    or so while the dough finishes chilling.

3   Roll out the chilled dough to a rectangle around 50x30cm. Place the square of
    butter over one half of the dough, then fold the other half down to give a roughly
    square parcel of dough and butter. Take care to smooth out the dough to avoid
    sealing any air pockets inside. Use your rolling pin to press down the raw edges,
    sealing the butter inside. This is important, otherwise the butter risks seeping out
    during rolling or baking. Wrap the parcel in cling film and return to the fridge for
    a further 30-60 minutes, allowing the dough and butter to settle at roughly the
    same temperature.

4   Now for the first 'turn'. Unwrap the chilled dough and roll it to a rectangle twice
    as wide as it is long — around 60x30cm. Be gentle with the dough for this first roll:
    the butter is still a reasonably thick sheet and needs to be carefully teased out into
    a thinner layer. If you simply roll straight from one end of the dough to the other,
    you risk squeezing the butter along the dough and straight out of the other side.
    To avoid this, press lightly down with your rolling pin at intervals along the dough
    to flatten it slightly, then roll from the middle upwards, then from the middle
    downwards. Make sure that the work surface is lightly dusted with flour.
        Fold the left third over towards the centre and then the right third over that
    to give a squat rectangle, approximately 20x30cm. Now rotate this rectangle by
    90 degrees so that the folds now run from side to side rather than from top to
    bottom. You've just finished the first turn. Repeat for a second turn: roll to around
    60x30cm wide, fold into thirds, then rotate. Now wrap the dough in cling film and
    chill in the fridge for 30-45 minutes.

5   Do two more turns then chill the dough for a further 30-45 minutes. Give the
    dough a final two turns to bring the total up to six turns, then leave, wrapped, in
    the fridge for at least 1 hour. During these final turns you might find the dough
    more difficult to roll out: the more it is stretched, the tighter it becomes. Just be
    patient and don't get too hung up on rolling the dough to exactly 60x30cm each
    time. As long as you roll it to a reasonable size and fold neatly, it will work out fine.

If at any point during this process the dough begins to feel sticky, or the butter leaks out, return it to the fridge straight away to firm up. The trick is to keep the dough cool at all times. Granted, this isn't easy when you have to roll and handle the dough this much, but it is important. If your kitchen is particularly warm, you might even want to chill the dough for 20-30 minutes between every turn, rather than just every other turn.

6   The dough is now ready to use — a cool, silky smooth slab, faintly layered with butter. This recipe makes a lot of puff pastry: there seems little point making a small, single-use batch when it's so time-consuming. Save half of it for another project, either in the fridge for a couple of days or in the freezer for several weeks.

FIG & WALNUT ECCLES CAKES

I suppose that technically these aren't real Eccles cakes as there's not a currant in sight. Filled with sticky fig, walnut and rosewater, they feel more Middle Eastern than Mancunian. I like the delicate floral flavour of these, but do feel free to experiment with your own flavour combinations: perhaps dried apricots with grated marzipan, or diced apples and raisins, or even sweet mincemeat.

Makes 8-12
175g dried figs, finely chopped
1 teaspoon bicarbonate of soda
30g soft light brown sugar
1 teaspoon vanilla extract
Pinch of salt
Rosewater, to taste

30g walnuts, roughly chopped
½ quantity of puff pastry (see page 291)
   or 1 quantity of quick puff pastry
   (see page 251)
1 egg, beaten with a pinch of salt, to glaze

📷 p295

1   Preheat the oven to 200°C/fan 180°C/gas mark 6. Line a large baking tray with baking parchment.

2   Toss the chopped figs and bicarbonate of soda together in a large bowl, then add just enough boiling water to cover them. Leave to stand for 10-15 minutes, during which time the leathery dried figs will soften.

3   Once tender, drain the figs then combine them in a mixing bowl with the sugar, vanilla extract and salt. Add the rosewater a few drops at a time, to taste — it's strong stuff and can easily overpower. Stir in the walnuts. The mixture needs to be completely cool before the next step, so set it aside for a short while if necessary.

4   Roll out the prepared pastry thinly to a rectangle around 50x35cm. Use an 8-10cm round pastry cutter (or something approximately the same size) to stamp out 16-24 circles. If you need to re-roll the trimmings, layer them carefully on top of one another then roll again. Don't just gather the offcuts into a ball as you might for shortcrust pastry — it will ruin those layers of butter that you've so carefully created.

5   Puff pastry needs to be kept cold until the moment it enters the oven, so it's best

to move half of the circles to the fridge at this point — on a tray, covered loosely with cling film — until you're ready for them. Arrange the remaining circles on the prepared baking tray and prick them with a fork. Dollop a heaped teaspoon of the fig mixture onto the centre of each circle. The trick is to fill generously, without adding so much that you can't seal the parcel. Leave a 1.5cm border around the edge of each circle.

6   Retrieve the second half of the pastry circles from the fridge and drape one on top of each mound of filling. Firmly pinch the edges of the pastry bases and tops together to seal in the filling. Brush the tops of the Eccles cakes with the beaten egg then use a small knife to pierce two or three holes in each lid, to allow steam to escape.

7   Bake for 20-25 minutes in the preheated oven. The filling will be very hot immediately after baking so leave these to cool on a wire rack before tucking in.

MARMALADE ALMOND GALETTE

Traditionally, this would be a French *galette des rois* — an Epiphany treat made of two discs of crisp puff pastry and a fat dome of almond filling within. My version has an extra layer of marmalade inside to balance the sweetness of the almonds, while a couple of tablespoons of whisky give depth without leaving it tasting boozy.

Serves 8
150g unsalted butter, softened
100g soft light brown sugar
50g caster sugar
Zest of ½ orange
2 tablespoons whisky
2 large eggs

150g ground almonds
50g plain flour
Pinch of salt
½ quantity of puff pastry (see page 291)
5-6 tablespoons marmalade
1 large egg, lightly beaten with
    2 teaspoons water, to glaze

1   Preheat the oven to 200°C/fan 180°C/gas mark 6. Line a large baking tray with baking parchment.

2   Beat together the butter and sugars in a large mixing bowl until smooth and creamy. Add the orange zest, whisky (to taste) and eggs and mix. Don't worry if the mixture looks slightly curdled. Stir in the ground almonds, flour and salt, stirring until just combined. Set aside while you prepare the pastry.

3   Halve the prepared pastry, and roll one piece out on a lightly floured surface to a circle around 26cm in diameter, trimming with a sharp knife to neaten the shape. Lay this circle on the lined baking tray and spread with the marmalade, leaving a border of 2-3cm. Gently spoon the almond mixture on top, heaping it more towards the centre to give a dome shape. Paint the border lightly with egg wash. Roll the second half of the pastry to a slightly larger circle (28-29cm) and, using your rolling pin to help you lift it, lay it over the base and filling. Press down gently around the border to seal so that the filling doesn't leak as it bakes, but keep the edges of the layers exposed.

4   Use a pastry brush to glaze the top with egg wash. Take care not to let the egg run down the sealed edges of the pastry, otherwise it'll fuse the layers together as it cooks. You can decorate the top at this point if you want to: use a sharp knife to very gently score a pattern into the pastry. Press only lightly with the blade, otherwise you risk cutting right through the lid.

5   Bake in the preheated oven for 15 minutes before reducing the temperature to 180°C/fan 160°C/gas mark 4 and baking for a further 25–35 minutes. The galette is ready when the pastry is crisp and golden and the filling set.

Variation
For a sweeter galette, swap the marmalade for good-quality raspberry jam. You could even stud the almond mixture with pitted cherries for a fruity filling.

MILLEFEUILLE

Millefeuille translates as 'thousand layers', and although it sounds like a grand claim to make of a dessert, it's not nearly as hyperbolical as it sounds: each millefeuille slice has three sheets of caramelised pastry — each containing around 700 flaky layers — two tiers of custard and a dusting of icing sugar to top it all off.

The pastry sheets used in this dessert need to be weighed down as they bake. If puff pastry is allowed to rise freely, it can grow to six times its original thickness — such thick pastry would leave the millefeuille bloated and unwieldy. Baked under the weight of a baking tray, however, the pastry will still develop its characteristic layers, but in more elegant proportions.

These really aren't difficult to make, but they do involve a bit of juggling of equipment: you'll need to bake three pastry sheets, and each needs two baking trays, so unless you've got a lot of equipment and oven space, you might have to bake in batches. Just make sure you keep the pastry cool while rolling and cutting it, otherwise the butter will melt and you'll lose those thousand layers.

Makes 6 large millefeuille slices   p298
½ quantity of puff pastry (see page 291)
100g icing sugar
2 quantities of pastry cream
   (see page 312), well chilled

1   Preheat the oven to 200°C/fan 180°C/gas mark 6 and have a few large baking trays to hand.

2   Divide the prepared pastry into three equal pieces. Wrap two of the pieces of pastry in cling film and leave in the fridge. On a lightly floured surface, roll the remaining piece to a rectangle roughly 15x30cm. Sprinkle icing sugar generously over the top of the pastry and lightly rub it over the pastry to cover. Turn the pastry over, dust with more icing sugar and smooth over again. This icing sugar will caramelise as the pastry cooks, giving a slight sweetness and deep golden colour. Transfer the pastry to a baking tray lined with baking parchment, then drape another large square of baking parchment over the top of the pastry. Place

a second baking tray on top to weigh the pastry down. If you only have very lightweight trays, perch a couple of small ovenproof ramekins on top. Bake for 20 minutes, then remove the weights and the upper sheet of baking parchment and return to the oven for a further 5 minutes. Lift the pastry from the tray, peel off the bottom piece of parchment, and leave to cool on a wire rack. Repeat with the remaining two pieces of pastry, to leave three sheets of caramelised puff pastry.

3   The next step can be done in two ways. The first gives neat sides, with the custard flush to the edges of the pastry. The second is easier but less polished.

Method 1

Once the pastry sheets are cool, trim them slightly to around 12x25cm. They may have shrunk slightly in the oven already, so if there's not much to trim — don't worry. Spread half of the pastry cream over one of the sheets, using a palette knife or spatula to usher it right to the very edges. Place the second pastry sheet on top and spread the remaining pastry cream neatly over it. Now cut the final pastry sheet into a row of six rectangles, each around 12x4cm. Lay these rectangles on top of the pastry cream, aligning them neatly with the layers underneath. You should now have, from bottom to top, layers of pastry, custard, pastry, custard and the six small rectangles of pastry on top.

Use a very sharp knife to slice down cleanly through the pastry and custard layers giving six slices, using the pre-cut top pieces as a guide. (If you wait to cut the top layer of pastry once it's already perched on top of the custard, you might find that the custard gets squeezed out and layers slide apart.) If the custard is too soft, try freezing the whole thing for 10–15 minutes, then trying again.

Method 2

Trim the cooled pastry sheets to even rectangles, around 12x25cm each. Cut each of these into six smaller rectangles, approximately 12x4cm. You'll be left with 18 identical sheets of pastry. Use a piping bag with a wide nozzle (or a tablespoon and spatula) to divide the pastry cream between 12 of the pastry pieces. Perch six of these custard-laden slices on top of the other six, then top with the remaining sheets of pastry. You should be left with six pastries, slightly rough around the edges.

4   Dust the tops of the millefeuille slices with icing sugar, perhaps using a strip of baking parchment as a template to give a pattern. Serve straight away, as the pastry will soften if left sandwiching the pastry cream for too long.

BEFORE MIDNIGHT

I developed the next three recipes with midnight snacks and late-night feasts in mind. They taste all the better for being a little clandestine — eaten furtively under the duvet, or by lamplight. I'm not suggesting that you round off every day with an éclair, but there's no harm in indulging from time to time.

CHOUX PASTRY

This is a pastry that works under its own steam: without any help from either yeast or baking powder, it puffs to double or even triple its original size in the oven. The resulting pastries are light, crisp and almost hollow, and can then be filled with creams, custards, jams, ice cream, or even savoury fillings.

Choux pastry is the exception to just about every rule in pastry: it is mixed while hot, twice-cooked, and barely a thick paste when it enters the oven. The first period of cooking is done on the hob. There are many important processes happening at this stage — gluten is developed (helping the buns to stretch in the oven) but also partly broken down by the heat (stopping the pastry springing back again once puffed); meanwhile, the starch in the flour absorbs a great deal of water and forms a paste that will help to form a 'bubble' to trap the steam as the buns bake and expand.

The paste is then mixed with the eggs, piped into shapes and baked. Choux pastry relies solely on steam power for its rise, so it's important to start it off in a very hot oven: as the water in the dough evaporates, the steam produced forces the choux upwards and outwards. But until the outer surface of the pastry begins to set, the choux shapes remain incredibly fragile. Even a slight drop in temperature could cause the buns to collapse, which is why it's crucial not to open the oven door, even for a second, during the first 20 minutes of the cooking time.

As the buns continue to cook, the crusts set and the whole structure stabilises. But you shouldn't assume that the choux is ready the instant that it's golden brown: the buns will soften again once out of the oven, so if they're anything less than completely firm — almost brittle — when first baked, they'll collapse as they cool. If you plan to fill the choux buns with cream or custard, this is particularly important, as the pastry will soften in contact with the fillings.

ÉCLAIRS

You can tell a lot about a person from their reaction to a plate of éclairs. Some happy hedonists will reach straight for the fattest one and eat it gleefully with their fingers; others will politely take a small one and eat it, with curbed enthusiasm, with a knife and fork. The last group will insist that they are too full, or on a diet, or that they 'don't have a sweet tooth', only to tiptoe back to the kitchen table once everyone else has gone to bed, sit squarely down in front of the plate of éclairs and, guiltily, tuck in.

Makes 10-12
50g unsalted butter
80ml milk
80ml water
Pinch of salt
65g plain flour
2 large eggs, lightly beaten

For the filling:
200ml double cream

2 tablespoons icing sugar
150g raspberry jam

For the ganache:
150ml double cream
100g good-quality dark chocolate,
   finely chopped
1 tablespoon golden syrup

 p302

1   Preheat the oven to 220°C/fan 200°C/gas mark 7. Lightly grease a large baking tray
    (this will help to hold the baking parchment steady when you pipe on the choux)
    then smooth down a sheet of baking parchment.

2   In a small pan, combine the butter, milk, water and salt. Heat gently until the
    butter has melted and the liquid is scalding. Pour the flour in all at once and
    immediately start beating the mixture with a wooden spoon, keeping the pan on
    the heat. It will quickly thicken and begin to sizzle. Cook the paste for 2 minutes
    or so, stirring continuously.

3   Remove the pan from the heat and leave to cool for 5 minutes. Once slightly
    cooled, beat in the eggs a little at a time — if you add the egg mixture all in one
    go the mixture will form lumps. Once you've added around half of the egg, or
    the paste is slightly less stiff, switch to a wire whisk and gradually beat in the
    remaining egg. The mixture should be smooth, thick and glossy.

4   Prepare a piping bag with a 1cm metal nozzle, or just cut the tip of the bag to leave
    a 1cm-wide hole. Spoon the choux paste into the bag, taking care not to seal in
    any large air pockets. Don't overload the piping bag — you can pipe in two batches
    if necessary. Twist the top of the piping bag to seal it shut then, with the nozzle
    pressed close to the baking parchment, pipe 10-12 thick, 10cm-long lines of choux
    paste. Leave at least 3cm between each line, as they will expand when baked.

5   Bake in the preheated oven for 15 minutes then reduce the temperature to
    180°C/fan 160°C/gas mark 4 and bake for a further 15-20 minutes, or until the
    pastry is browned and crisp. It's crucial that you don't open the oven door, even
    for a second, during the first 20 minutes of the cooking time (see page 300). The
    cooked buns should be firm and crisp — almost overcooked — as they'll soften
    once filled with cream and jam.

6   As soon as the buns are out of the oven, use a serrated knife to split them in half.
    Leave their top and bottom halves cut-side-up on a wire rack to cool. Meanwhile,
    make the filling. Whisk the cream and icing sugar together in a large bowl until
    just thick. Don't over-whisk, otherwise the cream will separate as it's piped. Stir
    the jam through a sieve into a small bowl, to remove the seeds.

7   To prepare the ganache, heat the cream in a small pan until scalding. Place the
    finely chopped chocolate in large bowl and pour the hot cream slowly over it. Let

the mixture sit for a minute, then gently stir to combine. Add the golden syrup. The ganache should be smooth, glossy and loose enough to drip from a spoon.

8   Now assemble the éclairs. Fill a fresh piping bag with the cream mixture and pipe this onto the bottom halves of the cooled choux buns. Spoon or pipe the jam on top of the cream. Dip the tops of the buns in the ganache, or carefully spoon the ganache onto the buns — whichever way works best for you. Place the ganache-topped lids onto the filled buns and serve.

DILL & MUSTARD CHOUX BITES

These choux morsels are my snack of choice when the appeal of the usual film-night fodder — popcorn, crisps, takeaway pizza — wears thin. Serve with mustard-laced crème fraîche, to dip them in.

Makes 25 tiny bites
25g unsalted butter
40ml milk
40ml water
1 teaspoon Dijon mustard
Pinch of salt
30g plain flour
1 large egg, lightly beaten

Leaves from 2-3 fronds of dill, finely
   chopped

For the dip:
150ml crème fraîche
1-2 teaspoons Dijon mustard, to taste
Pinch of salt

1   Preheat the oven to 220°C/fan 200°C/gas mark 7. Lightly grease a large baking tray (this will help to hold the baking parchment steady when you pipe on the choux) then smooth down a sheet of baking parchment.

2   In a small pan, combine the butter, milk, water, mustard and salt. Heat gently until the butter has melted and the liquid is scalding. Pour the flour in all at once and beat continuously for 2 minutes, while the paste sizzles and thickens.

3   Turn off the heat and leave the choux paste to cool for a few minutes, then beat in the egg a little at a time, stirring vigorously between each addition. Once all the egg has been added and the mixture is smooth and glossy, add the chopped dill. Either pipe (using a piping bag or sturdy freezer bag with a 1cm-wide hole or nozzle) or spoon it into 25 very small blobs, each no bigger than a £2 coin. If the choux shapes have any peaks, pat these gently down with a wetted finger, otherwise they'll burn.

4   Bake in the preheated oven for 10 minutes before reducing the heat to 180°C/ fan 160°C/gas mark 4 and baking for a further 5-10 minutes, depending on how crispy you like them. They should be golden brown and firm to the touch. Once baked, make a small incision in each (to let the steam escape, so that they don't soften) and leave to cool on a wire rack while you stir together the crème fraîche, mustard and salt for the dip.

BAKLAVA

I stop short every time I pass the grand displays of baklava in the windows of the Turkish shops near my flat in north London. It's a glutton's dream: row upon row of tiny, honeyed pastries, dusted with jewel-green pistachio. These pastries are intensely sweet and buttery — over-indulge at your peril.

You can make filo pastry at home, but I wouldn't recommend it. It takes a lot of time, space and strenuous kneading to develop the dough and stretch it to such impossibly thin layers. The stuff you can find in the shops is a far easier option, and — unlike puff or Danish pastry — there's not much between homemade and shop-bought filo in terms of taste.

Makes 20-25 pieces
75g unsalted butter
150g filo pastry

For the filling:
200g pistachios
2 tablespoons caster sugar
Pinch of salt
1½ teaspoons vanilla extract
½-1 teaspoon rosewater
Zest of 1 lemon

For the syrup:
Juice of ½ lemon
3 tablespoons water
75g caster sugar
75g honey

20cm round loose-bottomed or spring-form cake tin

📷 p306

1   Preheat the oven to 200°C/fan 180°C/gas mark 6. In a small pan, melt the butter over a low heat then set it aside.

2   Prepare the filling: blitz the pistachios in a food processor or coffee grinder until finely ground, then mix most of the ground pistachios (saving a couple of tablespoons for later) with the sugar, salt, vanilla extract, rosewater and lemon zest. It won't look much at this point — just a nutty rubble — but once it's baked and doused in syrup it'll be very different.

3   Using the base of your tin as a guide, cut the filo sheets to 20cm circles. Brush the tin with some of the melted butter, then begin to layer the filo pastry in the bottom of the tin, brushing each layer with butter before adding the next. Keep the remaining sheets of filo under a damp tea towel until you're ready to use them, to prevent them drying out. Once you've stacked half of the sheets, spoon on the filling and press down lightly to form an even layer. Stack the remaining sheets of filo on top, brushing with butter as you go. Brush the top with butter, too. (I usually end up with 4-6 very thin layers either side of the baklava filling, but this will depend on the thickness and dimensions of the filo you use.)

4   Use a sharp knife to cut small diamond shapes, each piece no larger than 3x3cm (they're very rich), into the pastry parcel to make your baklava. It's important that you cut the pieces now rather than after baking, as cutting the crisp, baked pastry will just shatter it.

5 Bake in the preheated oven for 20–25 minutes until golden, preparing the syrup while you wait. Combine the lemon juice, water, sugar and honey in a small pan then simmer over a medium-low heat for a few minutes, or until syrupy. As soon as the baklava is baked, perch the tin over a roasting dish (to catch any syrup that might leak) and pour the syrup all over. It should soak down into the hot pastry and filling. Leave the baklava to absorb the syrup for a few minutes then, while it's still warm, unmould from the tin and prise the pieces apart. Sprinkle a little of the reserved ground pistachio on top of each slice. Finally — this might just be the only acceptable use for mini-muffin cases — place each piece of baklava in a paper case to serve.

Variation
For walnut baklava, swap the pistachios for walnuts, the lemon zest and juice for orange and the rosewater for orange blossom water.

EXTRAS

MILK

CUSTARD • PASTRY CREAM

VANILLA ICE CREAM

SUGAR

CARAMEL • TOFFEE SAUCE

MARZIPAN • BASIC WATER ICING

CHOCOLATE

SPREADABLE GANACHE

POURING GANACHE • CHOCOLATE SAUCE

FRUIT

JAM • LEMON CURD

Here are the unsung heroes of baking: curds, sauces, custards, ice creams, ganache and jam will bring your cakes, breads and pastries to life. A cheap jam or tub of ice cream will suffice when time is short, but if you want to give your baking the final flourish it really deserves, it pays to make your own.

MILK

CUSTARD

Instant custard is a godsend when time is short and the cupboard is bare — and I am fond of it — but everyone should have a recipe for real custard too. Until I ate my first egg custard, I had assumed that all custards were canary-yellow and thick enough to stand a spoon up in. The real thing is very different: rich, silky and smooth. It's in a league of its own.

Purists will insist that a true custard sauce should be thickened with egg yolks alone, but it will be far less likely to curdle if you swallow your pride and add a couple of teaspoons of cornflour. This stabilises the mixture and gives a slightly thicker consistency. You will still need to be gentle with the egg yolks, though, to avoid scrambling them. Add the scalding milk slowly to the egg yolks, and never the other way round. This step is called tempering. And once the ingredients are combined and thickening on the hob, keep your eye on the pan and don't stop stirring.

If you have vanilla pods, you can use these instead of the vanilla extract, heating them along with the milk and leaving to infuse for a while before you get started. For a richer custard, swap half of the milk for single cream.

Serves 2, as an accompaniment
200ml full-fat milk
2 large egg yolks

3 tablespoons caster sugar
2 teaspoons cornflour
1 teaspoon vanilla extract

1   Warm the milk in a small pan over a low heat. Whisk the yolks and sugar together in a mixing bowl for at least 2 minutes, until thick, smooth and paler in colour. Add the cornflour to the egg yolk mixture and whisk to combine.

2   Once the milk is scalding, pour it in a thin stream into the egg yolks, whisking continuously. Once combined, decant everything back into the pan and return to a low heat. Keep stirring the custard for 5-10 minutes. Follow a figure of eight pattern with your spoon or spatula across the base of the pan, to prevent the custard from sticking. It won't be long before the mixture begins to thicken: it will stop sloshing as you stir and instead move in shallower ripples; soon it will feel heavier and take on the consistency of double cream; eventually it will be thick enough to coat the back of the spoon. Don't let the mixture boil, though — keep the pan over a low heat and you should find that it thickens well before reaching boiling point.

3   As soon as the custard has thickened, take the pan off the heat, stir in the vanilla extract and serve straight away.

PASTRY CREAM

This is a very thick custard, made using extra cornflour for a smoother, firmer set. Thanks to the cornflour in this recipe, it's mercifully very difficult to accidentally curdle: as long as you stir continuously, you should have no problems. Use this in millefeuilles, custard doughnuts or as an alternative filling for the éclairs on page 300. Keep the custard covered once cooked, or it will form a thick skin.

As in the custard recipe on the previous page, you can use vanilla pods instead of the vanilla extract, if you want.

Makes about 300ml
300ml full-fat milk
3 large egg yolks

45g caster sugar
3 tablespoons cornflour
1½ teaspoons vanilla extract

1   Heat the milk in a pan over a low heat until scalding. Meanwhile, whisk the egg yolks with the sugar for 2 minutes in a large bowl, until thick and creamy, and then whisk in the cornflour. Once the milk is just shy of the boil, pour it into the yolks very slowly, whisking all the time. When all the milk has been added, pour the custard back into the pan and cook over a low heat, stirring continuously. Make sure that you cover every part of the bottom of the pan with your spoon, otherwise the custard will stick and catch.

2   As you heat the custard you'll notice it rapidly thickening. This is the work of the cornflour, whose starch molecules, when heated, disperse into the surrounding liquid and thicken it. After a few minutes, the mixture should be noticeably thicker. Once the first bubble breaks the surface, continue to stir it over the heat for one further minute. By now it'll be unctuously thick and heavy.

3   As soon as it's cooked, transfer the pastry cream to a clean, dry bowl, beat in the vanilla extract and cover with cling film. Lay the cling film across the surface of the custard itself, otherwise a thick skin will form. Leave to cool to room temperature, then refrigerate if not using straight away. As it cools, the pastry cream will continue to thicken, so don't be alarmed if it has solidified to a jelly-like block after a spell in the fridge — just beat it well before using, and stir it through a sieve if you want it perfectly smooth.

Variations
Add 30g softened unsalted butter just after the cream has finished cooking for a slightly richer custard. You can flavour pastry cream with spirits, too — a capful of rum or whisky works well.

VANILLA ICE CREAM

Once you've seen how easy it is to make your own ice cream, and tasted how much richer and smoother it is than the shop-bought varieties, you'll find it hard to return to those cheap 2-litre tubs of soft-scoop. You don't need an ice cream maker, either.

There are different ways of making ice cream, but the one that produces the best texture uses a simple custard base. Unlike the custard recipe on page 311, it's best not to use cornflour here, so the cooking process can be slightly more difficult. Fortunately, you only need the custard to be just thick enough to coat the back of a spoon, so as long as you keep the heat low and stir continuously, the mixture shouldn't become so hot that it separates and curdles.

Making good ice cream is all about minimising the formation of large ice crystals, which result in a crunchy consistency and slightly watery taste. The yolks in the custard help with this. Sugar and fat minimise crystallisation, too, but the only way to make a truly smooth ice cream is to churn it as it freezes. By regularly beating it, you break apart any large ice crystals and encourage smaller crystals to form instead. In an ice cream maker, this is no problem: it does the hard work for you, chilling and churning until the ice cream is very cold and smooth. Without an ice cream maker it's more effort but not nearly as hard as it's purported to be. You'll just need to beat the ice cream vigorously every 30-60 minutes until it's very thick.

I like to make this with vanilla pods (the speckling of tiny black vanilla seeds looks fantastic against the cream) but it's far from essential. Stir a couple of teaspoons of vanilla extract into the cooked custard if that's all you have.

Makes about 500ml, serving 4
1 vanilla pod
400ml full-fat milk
4 large egg yolks

75g caster sugar
150ml double cream

📷 p315

1   Split the vanilla pod along its length, scrape out the seeds with the point of a knife then put the seeds and pod into the milk in a medium pan. Place the pan over a low heat until the milk is scalding, then remove from the heat and leave to infuse for at least 30 minutes.

2   Once infused, pull the pod from the milk and return the pan to the heat until the milk is steaming. While it warms, whisk the egg yolks with the sugar in a large bowl until very creamy and thick — this will take 5 minutes or so. The air incorporated at this stage will help to give a softer set to the frozen ice cream. Pour the scalding milk slowly into the egg yolk mixture, whisking continuously, then tip the mixture back into the pan and return to a low heat.

3   Cook the custard very gently, stirring all the time, until it's just thick enough to translucently coat the back of the spoon. It's crucial not to overheat it, otherwise the eggs will overcook and the custard will separate. (It can help to have a sink of cold water ready while you do this: if the custard looks like it's on the verge of curdling, just dip the bottom of the pan in the water to cool the mixture and stop it cooking.) Once the custard has slightly thickened, turn off the heat, stir in the double cream, transfer to a large bowl and leave to cool. Once cool, transfer to the fridge to chill thoroughly.

4   Once the custard is completely chilled, pour it into an ice cream maker if you have one, and follow the manufacturer's instructions. Otherwise, decant it into a large, lidded tub (the shallower the better, as this will help the ice cream to freeze faster) and put it in the coldest compartment of your freezer. Remove the tub after 30 minutes and use a fork to beat the ice cream, paying special attention to the edges (which will freeze more quickly than the centre). Return to the fridge for a

further 30 minutes. Continue to beat the ice cream at regular intervals for 2–4 hours. Once it's very thick and slushy, you can leave it until frozen. There's no need to panic about stirring the ice cream precisely every half an hour — as long as you break up the crystals every hour or so, it will be fine.

5   When it comes to serving the ice cream, let it soften in the fridge for 15 minutes or so beforehand. Shop-bought ice creams are easy to scoop straight from the freezer thanks to the high proportion of air whipped into them. This ice cream isn't as airy, so will have a denser, creamier consistency: a small price to pay for a result that is 100% ice cream, not 50% ice cream, 50% air.

CLOTTED CREAM ICE CREAM

Vanilla ice cream is — apparently — plain ice cream, and we often include vanilla without even thinking. But this does a disservice not only to the vanilla (whose inimitable flavour is anything but 'plain') but also to the milk and cream that are at the ice cream's heart. Dairy is delicious, and it's not until it's showcased without its usual vanilla crutch that its flavour can really come to the fore. To make a version that celebrates the flavour of the best cream, leave the vanilla out of the above recipe, and replace the double cream with clotted cream.

RHUBARB RIPPLE ICE CREAM

Rhubarb and custard are made for one another. In this ice cream, the rhubarb is swirled through the vanilla ice cream in thick ripples.

Make a rhubarb compote by placing 200g of rhubarb, cut into 2cm chunks, in a pan with 3 tablespoons of caster sugar and heating for 10 minutes or so, until the rhubarb is soft but still blushing pink. Mash any large rhubarb chunks lightly under the back of a fork then leave to cool completely. Swirl it into the vanilla ice cream recipe above when the ice cream is very thick, but not yet fully frozen. Return to the freezer until set.

STEM GINGER ICE CREAM

Sour cream leaves this ice cream fresher and brighter than the usual double cream varieties. Don't scrimp on the ginger. Follow the vanilla ice cream recipe above, leaving out the vanilla and adding 300ml of sour cream to the cooked custard instead of the double cream. Stir in 100g of finely chopped stem ginger, then grate in 5cm of fresh ginger and the zest of one lemon. Cool and freeze as above.

SUGAR

CARAMEL

I have to admit that, even now, setting a pan of white sugar over a high heat feels like a game of Russian roulette. Some days, the sugar melts smoothly to a clear, deep golden caramel; other days — and with no discernible change in technique — I find myself standing over a cracked, crystallised failure: burnt in parts, set solid in others. Left none the wiser about exactly where it all went wrong, it's easy to fall into superstition ('it only works if I swirl the pan clockwise...') or disillusionment ('caramel just doesn't like me').

But although caramel is tricky, it isn't impossible. There are some factors that make caramel more likely to fail, and others that will put you on the path to success. The two most common problems are crystallisation (where the dissolved sugar forms back into crystals, giving a granular, crunchy texture) and burning. If you can avoid these pitfalls, you'll make a perfect caramel. Patience, care and a clear head are crucial — some of my worst caramel experiences happened when I was in a rush or a bad mood.

A NOTE ON SAFETY

I've broken down the process into manageable steps below, but before you get started:

— Usher small children out of the kitchen, and make sure that you can devote your full attention to the caramel.

— Have a sink of cold water ready to plunge the base of the pan into if the caramel looks like it may be on the brink of burning.

— It sounds obvious, but don't touch or taste the caramel until it's completely cool, although I appreciate that it's tempting when the smell of toffee begins to fill the kitchen. If you do, the hot caramel will stick to your skin and give you a very painful burn.

There are two ways to make caramel. The first, and the one described here, is the 'wet' method, which adds water to the pan along with the sugar. The second approach uses only sugar. The dry method burns far more easily, whereas the wet method is prone to crystallisation. And if the choice is between a crystallised mess and an acrid, burnt mess, I can't help feeling that failure with the wet method is the lesser of two evils.

This caramel hardens quickly as it cools, so make sure you know what you're going to do with it before you get started. Something similar is used in the Rye Apple Upside Down Cake on page 47, or you could add cream and butter for a softer set, as in the Toffee Sauce on page 319. Alternatively, dip toasted almonds or hazelnuts in the hot caramel to make caramelised nut clusters.

100g sugar
2 tablespoons water

📷 p317

1   Choose an appropriate pan: non-stick pans aren't suitable for caramel as they tend to encourage the sugar to crystallise. Make sure that the pan is wide enough to accommodate the sugar in a reasonably shallow layer (no thicker than 2cm) but not so wide that the sugar barely covers the base. The pan should be very clean, too — even just a little dirt could precipitate crystallisation.

2   Combine the sugar and water in the pan, stirring to ensure that no dry sugar crystals are left. Place the pan over a medium heat and stir very gently with a metal spoon just until the sugar has all dissolved. At that moment, stop stirring and keep the spoon well clear of the mixture for the rest of the cooking time: any agitation will encourage the sugar to regroup into crystals.

3   The syrup should now be clear and bubbling. The next 5 minutes or so are all about avoiding crystallisation. Keep the heat constant, don't even think about stirring and, if any small crystals form around the sides of the pan, use a small pastry brush dipped in hot water to brush them away. The crystals should dissolve upon contact with the brush, but any large clumps will need to be brushed upwards, away from the syrup.

4   After around 5 minutes, the syrup should be just beginning to take on a light golden colour. If it's colouring unevenly, very gently tilt the pan to swirl the mixture, but don't succumb to the temptation to stir it. Continue to let it bubble until it's a uniformly golden colour.

5   What happens over the next minute will seal the fate of your caramel. Take it off the heat too soon and it'll be blandly sweet, but leave it too long and it will blacken and turn. Keep a very close eye on it as it darkens to a golden brown, then to an amber colour. This is the perfect time to remove the pan from the heat — remember that the sugar will continue to cook for a short while longer, so it's better to stop cooking when the caramel is slightly too pale than too dark. If you take the caramel too far and it begins to smoke, immediately remove it from the hob and plunge the base of the pan in a basin of cold water (be careful of any spluttering or a rush of steam) to stop the caramel cooking further. If you're planning to mix this with cream and/or butter, or you like the slight bitterness of a dark caramel you can cook the mixture very slightly longer for a deeper flavour, but I find it's best to err on the side of caution.

TOFFEE SAUCE

This toffee sauce has a deep, caramelised flavour. It will thicken slightly as it cools, but you can easily bring it back to a pourable consistency by heating it gently over a low heat. Drizzle it over cakes, spoon it into doughnuts or use it for choux buns.

A little salt can make a big difference to toffees and caramels: use salted butter and an extra pinch of salt for a bold flavour in this sauce, or stick with unsalted butter for a simpler sweetness.

Makes about 150ml
100g caster sugar
2 tablespoons water

75ml double cream
1 tablespoon butter, softened
Pinch of salt (optional)

1   Make a caramel with the sugar and water, following the instructions for the caramel recipe opposite. Have the cream and butter measured and ready to add as soon as the caramel is cooked.

2   Once the caramel reaches a rich amber colour, turn off the heat and immediately whisk in the double cream. The mixture will bubble up as you add the cream, so keep the pan at arm's length and take care to avoid any sputters of the hot sauce. Once combined, stir in the butter and the salt, if using. Leave to cool slightly before serving, or let cool completely and refrigerate for up to a few days.

MARZIPAN

Homemade marzipan is incredibly easy to make. It's not quite as smooth or pliable as the lurid shop-bought stuff, so if you want to roll it thinly to cover a cake, you might be better off buying it ready-made. But for most purposes — studding cupcakes (see page 27), filling a stollen (see page 159) or just to nibble as it is — this marzipan is perfect. There's also a recipe for a pistachio version on page 159.

This recipe contains raw egg whites, so if you're concerned about eating unpasteurised eggs, it's worth buying a carton of the ready-pasteurised egg whites from the supermarket instead of using fresh egg. Once the marzipan is made, wrap it tightly in cling film; it will keep in the fridge for a week or so.

Makes about 450g
200g ground almonds
200g icing sugar

Pinch of salt
1 large egg white (40g)
1 teaspoon almond extract

1   Mix the ground almonds, icing sugar and salt in a large bowl. Beat the egg white and almond extract together in a small bowl then add this, a little at a time, to the almond mixture. Use a fork to mash the liquid into the dry ingredients as you go. It will seem far too dry at first, but as you continue the mixture will come together. Use only as much of the egg white mixture as is absolutely necessary to bind the almonds, otherwise the marzipan will become sticky and difficult to work with.

BASIC WATER ICING

I'm not keen on slathering a cake with buttercream — more often than not, it adds sweetness without subtlety, and leaves the whole thing excessively rich — but I'm not averse to a thin layer of frosty glaze or a messy zigzag of icing. It livens up a cake, pastry or biscuit without smothering the flavour. There's really no hard and fast formula for water icing: it's just icing sugar, water and any additional flavours, mixed to a consistency appropriate for the occasion. A thicker icing — almost paste-like — can be neatly piped over buns in bright white streaks; make a version with more liquid and it can be drizzled messily off a spoon or used as a shiny glaze.

Regardless of how thick or thin you want the icing to be, it's important to add the water very gradually. Add too much at once, and the sugar will clump and you'll have to sieve the mixture later. The first few drops of water should be enough to bring the icing sugar into a thick paste, and every drop thereafter is about fine-tuning the consistency. Be warned that water icing always seems thicker in the bowl than it will be when used: dilute too much and the icing will be too watery to even drizzle. The temperature of the thing you're icing will make a difference, too. Pour a thick icing onto a hot cake, and it will loosen and run off the sides, while the same icing will sit neatly on top of a cooled cake.

In terms of flavouring, this icing is very adaptable. Use lemon juice and zest in place of the water for a citrus version, add a teaspoon of vanilla extract to tone the sweetness, or stir in a little cocoa powder with the icing sugar. Using golden icing sugar gives a rounded, toffee flavour.

CHOCOLATE

GANACHE

This is just dark chocolate and cream, melded together to create a rich, glossy icing or glaze. It's very simple to make and really needs little instruction — as long as you chop the chocolate finely and avoid heating the ingredients too much once combined, it's difficult to get ganache wrong.

The ratio of chocolate to cream is quite flexible and will determine whether you're left with a thick, spreadable ganache or a pourable one. I've included two variants of the recipe below, the first suitable for filling or frosting cakes such as the Chocolate Fudge Cake on page 54, the second for a shiny glaze, like the one used on the Coffee Blackcurrant Opéra Cake on page 65.

Although it is possible to make white- and milk- chocolate ganaches, I wouldn't recommend it — the result is too sickly, and doesn't have the same thickness or glossy sheen as the dark version. Because dark chocolate and cream are the foundations of this recipe, they should be good-quality: no economy-brand chocolate or UHT cream.

I like ganache to be very dark and bittersweet, but you can add a couple of tablespoons of sugar to either of these recipes, dissolving it in the cream, if you prefer it a little sweeter.

SPREADABLE GANACHE

Makes enough to fill and cover one 20cm round sandwich cake
200g good-quality dark chocolate, finely chopped

200ml double cream

1   Place the chocolate in a large bowl. Gently heat the cream on the hob until almost boiling, then pour it over the chopped chocolate. Leave this to stand for a minute, then gently stir the mixture together until thick and smooth. If any stubborn chunks of un-melted chocolate remain, heat the ganache very slightly in its bowl, suspended over a pan of simmering water. Take care not to overheat it, though, or it'll lose its shine.

2   Let the ganache cool slightly to a spreadable consistency before using. Alternatively, refrigerate until firm, roll into smooth balls and toss in cocoa powder to make chocolate truffles.

POURING GANACHE

The addition of a little golden syrup helps to give this ganache a high-gloss finish.

Makes enough to glaze the top and
    sides of one 20cm round cake
150g good-quality dark chocolate,
    finely chopped

250ml double cream
1 tablespoon golden syrup

1   Follow the method on the previous page, stirring in the golden syrup once the chocolate and cream have been combined. If it's very liquid, leave to cool and thicken for a few moments. Otherwise, use straight away, pouring onto the top of the cake and letting it flow across the cake and down the sides. Use a spatula or palette knife to level it where necessary. For a very smooth finish, it helps to give the cake a thin coating of buttercream first. This 'crumb coat' will gloss over the uneven surface of the cake to ensure a perfectly level layer of ganache on top.

Variations
Add any of the following to the cream as you heat it in the pan to infuse the cream with their aromatics: a tablespoon of fennel seeds, a cinnamon stick, a vanilla pod, a dried red chilli or a couple of whole star anise. Strain them out before pouring the scalding cream over the chocolate. Whatever flavours you use, they need to be bold if they're to stand their ground against the robust dark chocolate.

CHOCOLATE SAUCE

Chocolate sauce is the difference between a good and a sublime ice cream sundae. It's not bad with bananas (see page 257), either.

This sauce works on exactly the same principle as the ganache recipes that precede it: chocolate is melted in scalding cream. The difference is that in this recipe, the high proportion of golden syrup keeps the sauce from setting and takes away ganache's grown-up, bitter edge.

Serves 4 generously, with ice cream
150ml double cream
100g good-quality dark chocolate,
    finely chopped

3 tablespoons golden syrup
Pinch of salt

1   Heat the cream in a small pan over a low heat until scalding, then pour it over the chopped chocolate in a large bowl. Stir the sauce until smooth and glossy, then mix in the golden syrup and salt.

2   If you're not serving this immediately, keep in the fridge for up to 3–4 days then reheat gently on the hob when you're ready.

FRUIT

JAM

I wish I could subscribe to the view of jam making as a cathartic exercise — homely and therapeutic — but in truth it's not very relaxing at all, standing over a pan of fiercely bubbling sugar and fruit. It's hot work, and you have to be very careful to avoid burns. But, fortunately, the results are worth it.

You can use more or less any fruit in jam: foraged blackberries or fistfuls of blackcurrants work particularly well, and tender stems of rhubarb will see you through the winter months. But you ought to be mindful of the pectin content of the fruit you choose. Pectin helps jam to set, and can be found in most fruits, although some contain far more than others. High-pectin fruits include blackberries, oranges, lemons, apples, plums, redcurrants and gooseberries, whereas strawberries, raspberries, cherries, rhubarb, blueberries and apricots have less.

To compensate for lower pectin levels, there are a few things you can do:

— Add a small amount of a high-pectin fruit to a low-pectin fruit jam. A chopped apple, for example, can help to set a batch of strawberry jam.

— Stir in the juice of half a lemon along with the fruit. The acidity will help to set the jam.

— Use a special jam sugar. This contains added pectin and acid, but you really shouldn't need it if you add a little high-pectin fruit and a spritz of lemon juice.

The amount of sugar to be used in the recipe below depends on the fruit you use: high-pectin fruits will need less, but low-pectin fruits should be cooked with an equal weight of sugar. If using plums, simmer them with 100ml of water for 30 minutes before adding the sugar and lemon juice.

Makes 2–3 250ml jars
400g fruit, stoned (if necessary) and
    roughly chopped
300–400g granulated sugar
Juice of ½ lemon

2–3 jam jars

📷 p323

1   Sterilise a few large jam jars: scrub well, then rinse with boiling water. Leave to dry upside-down on a wire rack while you make the jam. (If you have a dishwasher, you can use them straight from there.)

2   Combine the fruit, sugar and lemon juice in a large pan (not an aluminium one) and place over a low heat. Heat until the fruit begins to soften and release its juices, then let bubble for 10–15 minutes, stirring regularly.

3   The temperature at which jam sets — its 'setting point' — is 104°C, so if you have a sugar thermometer, hook this onto the side of the pan to monitor the temperature. You don't need one, though. I actually find the old-fashioned test more reliable: place a small plate or saucer in the fridge while the jam simmers, and after around 10 minutes spoon a small amount of jam onto the cold plate. Return it to the fridge for a minute or two then slowly push your finger through the layer of jam. If it wrinkles as you push it, it's ready.

4   Leave the jam to cool for 15 minutes once cooked — it'll settle during this time, and the fruit will be more evenly distributed. Pour into the sterilised jam jars and seal shut immediately. Leave to cool to room temperature. As long as the jars were properly cleaned and the jam brought up to setting point, the jam will keep for up to a year in a cool, dry place. Once opened, keep the jar in the fridge and use within 6 weeks.

Variations
Jam is versatile, so don't be afraid to combine different fruits and flavours. Add a vanilla pod to a pot of simmering rhubarb jam, or even a splash of rosewater to a strawberry one.

LEMON CURD

This curd has less butter and marginally less sugar than you might be used to. The result is a cleaner-tasting, brighter, zestier curd, and although it won't keep for quite as long as other versions, you should have no trouble using it up. If it's a little sharp for your taste just add more sugar. I've included quantities for an all-yolk version, too: this can be useful if you've made a meringue, mousse or sponge that has left you with a glut of spare yolks — the Lemon Meringue Roulade recipe on page 210, for example. Swap the lemons for limes or even passion fruit, as in the Passion Fruit Swiss Roll on page 64.

Makes one 250ml jar
Zest and juice of 2 large or 3 smaller
    lemons
1 large egg plus 1 yolk, *or* 4 large yolks
90g caster sugar

40g butter, cubed

1 jam jar, sterilised (see page 324)

📷 p325

1   Bring a few centimetres of water to a very gentle simmer in a small saucepan.
    Place the zest, lemon juice, egg and yolk (or just the 4 yolks, if using), sugar and
    butter together in a large heatproof bowl. Suspend the bowl over the saucepan,
    making sure that the base of the bowl isn't touching the water: this curd needs
    to cook slowly, using only the heat of the steam.

2   Keep a very close eye on the curd, stirring almost continuously. The mixture won't
    look promising at first, but before long the butter will melt, the sugar will dissolve
    and it'll start to thicken. It'll take 10-15 minutes for the curd to cook and it needs
    to be kept moving throughout this time. Patience is crucial. The curd is ready
    when it is viscous enough to coat the back of the spoon: it should leave a layer of
    yellow curd that will hold the track left by a finger swiped through it — not a thin,
    translucent film. It will thicken as it cools, however, so don't worry too much.

3   Remove the curd from the heat, decant into the jar and put a lid on immediately.
    Let cool to room temperature then store in the fridge for up to 4 weeks. If you're
    planning to use the curd within a few days, perhaps in a cake or dessert, then of
    course you needn't go to the trouble of jarring and sealing it — just keep in the
    fridge in any covered container.

ACKNOWLEDGEMENTS

To my parents, without whose patience, unfaltering support and cookbook collection this would never have been possible. Åsa, Caitlin and Tessa: thank you for being such understanding flatmates and caring friends. I'm sorry for making such a mess in the kitchen.

Thank you to Parisa and Poppy for believing in this book and for making it the best that it could be. I couldn't have hoped for kinder or more knowledgeable editors. To Nato and Anna — thanks for the wonderful photos, and the fun had along the way. Kate and Tim at Hyperkit, I'm so grateful to you for bringing these many disparate elements together and turning them into such a beautiful book. To Clare, Marion and Myra, for their sharp eyes and suggestions. Stuart, who had all those conversations I didn't have the nerve for. And, of course, Rukmini: I wouldn't have been able to do it without you. Thank you.

I cannot thank the rest of the Baker's Dozen enough for their reassurance, their guidance and their wealth of baking tips: Ali, Beca, Christine, Deborah, Frances, Glenn, Howard, Kimberley, Lucy, Mark, Rob and Toby. You are great friends to me — *Bake Off* would've been nothing without you. And thanks to everyone at Love Productions and on the *Bake Off* crew for giving me the opportunity to do this and for your help throughout. To Amanda Console in particular, who was there at the most difficult moments and stopped me from throwing in the towel.

Finally, to everyone who had to endure those early days of my terrible baking — this book is for you: Curtis, Rosa and Noah; Sheila and Violet, whose pride has spurred me on; everyone at Oasis in Lisbon — especially Jackson, my most dedicated taste-tester; Jess; the Philosophy common room regulars; Zoe at Bake-a-Boo, who made such exquisite cakes and let me read pastry books on the job; Ben — and his mum — for all the éclairs; and to everyone else whose company I so sorely missed while frantically writing this book. And last of all, to Adam — for always being there for me.

INDEX

Page numbers in *italics* indicate photographs.

Ruby Tandoh entered *Great British Bake Off* aged just twenty and in the first year of a Philosophy and Art History degree at UCL. She quickly impressed with her creative approach to ingredients and flavour taking precedence over decoration. Ruby is now a weekly food columnist in the *Guardian* and has written columns for British *Elle*. Raised in Southend, Essex, she lives — and bakes — in north London.

rubyandthekitchen.co.uk
@rubytandoh

Cover design by Hyperkit
Photography by Nato Welton

Chatto & Windus
Random House
20 Vauxhall Bridge Road
London SW1V 2SA
www.vintage-books.co.uk

✓ olive orange bread
~~saffron bun~~ (teacake variation)
  └ forget apricot
✓ almond cardamom buns
✓ blackberry ricotta c/cake
✓ ₿ saffron bun (lussekatter) dough, unorded

caramelised a
juniper
cola

glaze
↙ teacake w variation
f-d6
- pie
- strudel
- samosa

sesame pew choc

+ filling
q
~~joconde~~
~~garlic doughballs~~
~~fondants~~
~~freezbatcher~~

~~sticky toffee pudding~~
~~tiramisu cake~~
+ cherry spelt or (walnut)
~~biscotti~~
~~lussekatter~~
~~choc lime mudcake~~
~~turnovers~~
~~malt doughnuts~~
★ (pear streusel slice)

soda bread

7S suer.
120 wian